AF262869

Margaret Bondfield

Margaret Bondfield

The Life and Times of Britain's
First Female Cabinet Minister

Nan Sloane

BLOOMSBURY ACADEMIC
LONDON • NEW YORK • OXFORD • NEW DELHI • SYDNEY

BLOOMSBURY ACADEMIC
Bloomsbury Publishing Plc, 50 Bedford Square, London, WC1B 3DP, UK
Bloomsbury Publishing Inc, 1359 Broadway, New York, NY 10018, USA
Bloomsbury Publishing Ireland, 29 Earlsfort Terrace, Dublin 2, D02 AY28, Ireland

BLOOMSBURY, BLOOMSBURY ACADEMIC and the Diana logo are trademarks of
Bloomsbury Publishing Plc

First published in Great Britain 2026

A catalogue record for this book is available from the British Library.

Library of Congress Cataloging-in-Publication Data available.

ISBN: HB: 978-1-3505-1365-5
       ePDF: 978-1-3505-1367-9
       eBook: 978-1-3505-1366-2

Typeset by RefineCatch Limited, Bungay, Suffolk
Printed and bound in Great Britain

For product safety related questions contact productsafety@bloomsbury.com.

To find out more about our authors and books visit www.bloomsbury.com and
sign up for our newsletters.

Begin to live as you have it in you to live.

Margaret Bondfield
1898

Contents

16 I Had Not Stopped Growing 183

Epilogue: This Remarkable Woman 197

Illustrations

Images 1, 2, 3, 4, 5, 6, 8, 12, 13 and 14 are reproduced by kind permission of the Archives and Special Collections Library, Vassar College Libraries, Poughkeepsie, USA.

Image 7 is reproduced via Mary Evans Picture Library.

Image 9 is reproduced by kind permission of the National Portrait Gallery.

Image 10 from the Ramsay MacDonald papers is reproduced by permission of his granddaughter.

Images 11 (Hulton Deutsch) and 15 (Popperfoto) are reproduced via Getty Images.

Abbreviations

ASS	Adult Suffrage Society
AWTUL	American Women's Trade Union League
CWG	Cooperative Women's Guild
EFF	Election Fighting Fund
ILO	International Labour Organization
ILP	Independent Labour Party
IWSA	International Women's Suffrage Alliance
LRC	Labour Representation Committee
NEC	National Executive Committee
NFWW	National Federation of Women Workers
NUGMW	National Union of General and Municipal Workers
NUWSS	National Union of Women's Suffrage Societies
PLP	Parliamentary Labour Party
PSF	People's Suffrage Federation
RIC	Royal Irish Constabulary
SDF	Social Democratic Federation
TUC	Trades Union Congress
WFL	Women's Freedom League
WIC	Women's Industrial Council
WLL	Women's Labour League
WPPL	Women's Protective and Provident League
WSPU	Women's Social & Political Union
WTUL	(The British) Women's Trade Union League

Acknowledgements

I am greatly indebted to many people who have helped in the course of writing this book.

First, Atifa Jiwa and Nadine Staes-Polet at Bloomsbury for their patience, their support, and their understanding approach to deadlines. As always, producing a book is a team effort, and would not be possible without designers, proof-readers, publicists and many others. I am grateful to all of them for helping to bring my idea of Margaret Bondfield to life.

Dean Rogers at the Archives and Special Collections Library at Vassar College was endlessly patient with my many queries and requests both during and after my visit, and the Library has been generous with its permissions to use images in their keeping.

Staff at the Women's Library at the LSE and the National Archives at Kew were also both helpful and patient, as were staff at the People's History Museum in Manchester on my earlier visits.

Dr Paula Bartley very kindly shared her own research from Vassar Libraries, which was enormously helpful and made all the difference.

I am also very grateful to the journalist Ross Davies, whose decision to deposit his 1970s research at the Women's Library (now located in the LSE Special Collections) made sure that some really interesting and useful material was preserved, and this book would not be the same without his work and foresight.

Copyright material from the Ramsay MacDonald papers is reproduced by permission of his granddaughter.

Many people have, at one time or another, been generous with their time and expertise – there is not enough space to mention them all, but special thanks must go to Alison McGovern MP, Pam Cox MP, Lisa McGrady, Natasa Pantelic and Sue Dockett, as well as to Dianne Hill and others at Tunbridge Wells, Claire Richter and everyone at Chard Museum, and Sue Heward and the Margaret Bondfield Steering Group at Chard.

It would be remiss of me not thank everyone at Labour Women's Network for enduring my endless Margaret Bondfield chatter over the years and not rolling their eyes too much when I managed to shoehorn her into almost every conversation. But thanks also to those same magnificent women for all their continuing work to make sure that Margaret Bondfield's legacy persists in so many ways.

Finally, as always, to my family, from the oldest to the youngest, for putting up with me, indulging my endless Bondfield stories, and generally being supportive of my late-blooming writing career. It could not have happened without you!

Introduction: A Niche in History

Ever since photography began to play a part in politics, incoming governments have lined up in the Downing Street garden to be photographed. Until the end of the 1920s the resulting images all looked much the same – two or three rows of rather solemn men staring towards the camera and trying not to blink. But in 1929 something changed when a small, unobtrusive woman appeared on the back row. At the time she was instantly recognizable, yet as the years went by the public memory of her faded until, as she correctly predicted, 'the reports and pamphlets and newspapers that contain *(the record of my life will)* crumble, and ultimately very little of anything will be left – perhaps only my niche in history as the first woman Cabinet Minister!'[1]

The government of which Margaret Bondfield was a part was, perhaps, one of the most remarkable Britain has ever seen. When many of its members were born the chances of any of them getting into Parliament, let alone the Cabinet, were virtually nil. The Prime Minister, Ramsay MacDonald, was the illegitimate son of a farm-hand. The Chancellor of the Exchequer, Philip Snowden, was the son of a weaver and had started life as an insurance clerk. Many had begun their working lives as children, and several, including Bondfield, had distinguished careers as trade unionists behind them by the time they came into office. All of the 'great offices of state' – Prime Minister, Home Secretary, Foreign Secretary and Chancellor – were held by working-class men. None of them had had a university education. Margaret Bondfield is significant as the first female Cabinet Minister, but she was also part of a whole group of remarkable working-class people who rose to the political heights, in her case breaking many glass ceilings along the way.

Given that she was so well known in her day, it is frustrating for the would-be biographer to find how little Margaret Bondfield left behind in terms of private papers. This is not to say that there is nothing, for there is a large archive in the keeping of the Archives and Special Collections Library at Vassar College in the United States. This was deposited by the academic Helen Drusilla Lockwood, the closest friend of Bondfield's last years, who had intended to write something about Bondfield and to whom Bondfield had given several boxes of her papers and diaries. However, time, age, and other projects overtook Lockwood, and the papers languished more or less untouched until her death in 1971, when they passed into Vassar's possession.

The resulting collection is extensive, but it is nevertheless evident that a huge amount of material was destroyed, probably by Bondfield herself. Some of the remaining correspondence is in the form of type-written copies of letters she received, which begs the question of what happened to the originals. It is entirely possible that Bondfield kept them herself, and that they were thrown away when her house in Southborough in Kent was cleared after she moved into sheltered housing. Certainly she found dealing with her archive challenging; in 1949, a few years before her death, she wrote in her diary that 'Time races on and still I shrink from settling down to sort papers.'[2] It is quite possible that there is some cache of material somewhere waiting to be discovered. As is often the case, some destruction probably happened gradually over the years. Before 1930 she moved frequently from one set of rooms to another, few of which would have had the space for large amounts of paper. Later it may just have been inconvenient to keep having to take an increasing amount of paperwork with her whenever she moved. She kept most of her diaries, but key years are either missing or almost entirely blank. She kept letters of congratulation or commiseration, but not routine communications, and very little from anyone outside her immediate family to whom she was close. Some of the destruction seems to have happened after she finished writing her autobiography, which was published in December 1949. Gina Stace, who typed the manuscript up for her, told the journalist Ross Davies in the 1970s that:

> Writing did not come easily to her, and even more she hated handling papers. She had a wardrobe full of newspaper cuttings, which she tipped out onto a bed, and from these bits and pieces she tried to put a book together. As soon as she felt certain that the book was complete she started destroying her papers.[3]

Stace also said that: 'The papers she destroyed were for the most part personal letters from her contemporaries – Bernard Shaw and others,' adding, to the despair of later researchers, 'I don't think she would have destroyed anything of historic value.'[4]

Sadly, it is clear from the Vassar archive that that is exactly what she did. Some of the gaps in it are extensive, particularly in regard to her earlier life, and much of the archive is simply the material which went into her memoir. But there are other items of interest, too, and what was left out does sometimes say as much as what was included. There is still more work to be done on it, and the developing interest in telling working-class history through women as well as socialist and trade union men will hopefully lead to more interest in this resource.

Bondfield's autobiography, *A Life's Work*, is a huge, rambling tome, often difficult to read and sometimes inaccurate. Hunting her through it is undoubtedly a challenge. The organization of the book is confused, though the sheer scale of her activities, particularly in the early years, is so great that it is hardly surprising if she found herself unable to deal with the raw material effectively. When the publisher sent the first draft to the educationalist and author Margaret Cole for comment, she said that she 'thought it was much too long and too diffuse to command big sales'.[5] However, despite cuts being made, the result is still a jumble of stories, events and ideas arranged thematically rather than chronologically. It is also at times a tedious account which adds almost nothing to the reader's understanding. It is full of detail, but it jumps backwards and forwards in time, dealing with some events out of context and skipping lightly over various historic moments. There are large excerpts from diaries, most of which would have been better written up as narrative. There are extracts from reports and parliamentary submissions, almost none of which are particularly interesting and many of which can be found elsewhere. Questions that readers might want answered go disregarded, but questions that never occur are answered in full. The Labour government in which she served in a pivotal role has a chapter to itself but sheds very little light on what happened, and her time as a junior minister in the 1924 government is skated over relatively quickly. She has some interesting reflections on the many political heroes and villains she met, but overall studiously gives the impression of a dull, dutiful woman who plodded along and achieved high office more or less by accident and by being in the right place at the right time. This is not to say that she is not proud of her achievements, but she makes them sound very ordinary, even when she knows how extraordinary they were.

However, as so often with Margaret Bondfield, things are not always as they seem. Seeded through the book are clues about all kinds of aspects of her life, from the misery of much of her upbringing to the nature of her relationships, both personal and professional. While the hopeful biographer has to guard against seeing what she wishes to see rather than what is actually there, and while there has to be much caution not to over-interpret, the little tricks, obfuscations and misdirections become much easier to spot once their context is understood.

In the absence of large amounts of archive material there are three other principal sources to consider. The first is newspaper reports, journal and magazine articles and, in the later years, radio broadcasts, and of these there is no shortage. The biographical pieces about Bondfield are all pretty much the same, and in some cases it is clear that some passages in *A Life's Work* were lifted wholesale from already published material. But contemporaneous reports of meetings, elections, speeches, social events and conferences are invaluable, particularly when backed up by other evidence. In her day, Bondfield was highly newsworthy, and there was a huge amount of coverage of her activities. The second useful group are the recollections and archives of contemporaries – or at least, they would be if they were more plentiful. Unfortunately, very few of the women wrote their own memoirs or left archives unsanitized by well-meaning relatives. Some, like the trade unionist Mary Macarthur, died too young to write memoirs, while others, like Dorothy Elliott, who succeeded Bondfield as National Woman's Officer at the National Union of General and Municipal Workers (NUGMW), wrote them but did not publish. The journalist and MP Mary Agnes Hamilton wrote extensively about her contemporaries, and in 1924 published a biography of Bondfield. Given that Bondfield was still very much alive at this point, and had just been appointed to her first government job, not all of it can be taken at face value, but it is nevertheless an informative contribution. Male politicians and trade unionists sometimes mentioned her in their own memoirs but only infrequently; until relatively recently women politicians still found this to be the case, though the much larger numbers of women now in the most senior roles may change this for the future.

The third source is the archive of the journalist Ross Davies, who, in the 1970s, began work on a Bondfield biography. He managed to turn up some new material and he had *A Life's Work*, but both he and Bondfield's surviving relatives and friends were unaware of the Vassar deposit and he therefore could not find any significant archive of Bondfield papers. Many people who had been young during the second half of her long life were still alive, and he wrote to them to ask for their help and any recollections they might have. Their responses vary from enthusiastic helpfulness to friendly interest to curt coolness, but however useful and interesting their contributions they could not replace fuller archival material. Since he assumed that all her papers had been destroyed and that it would therefore be impossible to write anything that was more than a rehash of *A Life's Work* he gave up the unequal struggle and moved on to other projects. Luckily, however, he deposited the material he had been able to collect with the Fawcett Library, which subsequently became part of the Women's Library collection in the LSE's Special Collections, where it remains the largest single known collection of papers relating to Margaret Bondfield available in the UK. Meanwhile the archive at Vassar College was eventually catalogued and made available online, at which point more nuanced studies of Bondfield's life and work became possible.

One consequence of gaining access to the papers at Vassar is that it has been possible to develop some insight into Bondfield's personal life. When she died in 1953 the *Daily Mirror* said that: 'Like other shopgirls, Margaret Bondfield dreamed of a fairy prince as she served elastic and ribbons.'[6] In fact, so far as we know, she never dreamed of any such thing. She was very clear from the outset that marriage and a domestic life were not for her. As a result her sexuality has long been the subject of speculation, partly because there is no evidence of any romantic or sexual relationships with men, and partly because she herself never made any direct reference to it. The general disinclination to consider this aspect of her life, while understandable, is also unhelpful. In his 1987 book *Prudent Revolutionaries* the historian Brian Harrison accepts Beatrice Webb's view of the MP Susan Lawrence – and by implication also Bondfield – as belonging to the 'old order of irreproachable female celibates, which used to be an important caste in Victorian days and which has no votaries among the younger generation'.[7] The assumption that if a woman was not demonstrably sexually active with men she was probably not sexually active at all was always flawed, and seems even more so now, as does the idea, prevalent during Bondfield's lifetime, that lesbianism was not only shameful, but also a sign of abnormal or arrested development. As we shall see, her interactions with at least one woman in her life strongly suggest a lesbian relationship, and there may well have been others. To eliminate them from her story not only makes other aspects of it harder to understand but also does a disservice to the reality of her struggles. The level of concealment into which she was forced, for instance, may well have been a contributory factor to the mental ill health from which she suffered at various points throughout her life.

As always, the selection of what to include and what to omit has been difficult. Bondfield's circle of friends and acquaintances was enormous, and inevitably some have had to be left out. She knew everyone who was anyone in trade union, socialist, pacifist and feminist circles on both sides of the Atlantic as well as many political and religious leaders. She was an internationalist on principle as well as by inclination and had no difficulty combining patriotism with being a citizen of the world. The letters which survived the cull show someone with a gift for friendship who inspired affection in others. Her American journeys alone would make a study in themselves, as would her interactions with socialist and feminist peace movements in Europe and the United States. However, the dictates of space mean that many aspects of her life have had to be glanced at rather than examined in depth. The same is true of some well-known events which, if they did not impact on Bondfield's life directly, have only been alluded to or even omitted altogether, as have some of the campaigns and organizations in which she was involved. It is a measure of the sheer scale of her activities and interests that hard choices have had to be made, and an indication of how much else there still is to be written about her.

Margaret Bondfield was a woman who lived her life with courage, intelligence and a curiosity about people and places that never dimmed. She was the first woman to do and be so many things that she was almost forced to be different. There were no road maps for women in many of the jobs she did, nor templates for how women should behave. The idea that 'you can't be what you can't see', so prevalent now and so limiting to women's ambitions, was unknown to her. She was almost always the first, often alone, and rarely with any model in front of her other than the men who were already there. How she dealt with that, and how she more than survived the challenges, is the subject of this book.

Chapter 1

We Were Not Given to Tears

Margaret Grace Bondfield was born on Monday, 17 March 1873 in a thatched cottage at Furnham on the outskirts of the ancient Somerset town of Chard. A keen March wind was blowing intermittent rain against the windows, and although in the garden and fields surrounding it there were signs of the coming spring the temperature was only a few degrees above freezing. Beyond the cottage the wind ruffled the surface of a reservoir, and lying in the wooden tub that served as her cradle the baby could hear the trains as they puffed their way along the nearby railway line between Chard and Ilminster.

The household into which Margaret was born consisted of herself, her parents, and five of her nine older siblings. Her father worked as a foreman at a nearby lace factory and all the work of the house and the small-holding attached to it had been devolved to Margaret's mother. In this respect, William and Ann Bondfield were fairly typical of rural West-country working-class couples. They were not destitute, but they had no spare capacity, either. They relied on the income of the breadwinner husband, supplemented by whatever the wife could grow, make and sell. They came from large families deeply rooted in the county of their birth. They were non-conformist in their religion and politically radical. In his youth William had supported parliamentary reform and the abolition of the Corn Laws and had been involved in a famous Lace Workers' strike in 1842. Not having the vote did not deter Ann Bondfield from canvassing for Liberal candidates or pasting up their posters on the end wall of the house. As a result Margaret grew up with stories of protest and politics, and this generally radical environment almost certainly influenced the choices she herself would make in future years.

Margaret's paternal grandfather, John Bondfield, was a farmer whose colourful youth, believed to have involved smuggling, was also the stuff of family legend. He and his wife Grace had had ten children, of whom William Bondfield was the third. In the 1851 census John described himself as the 'Proprietor of houses and lands', and in 1871 his son William, who had probably used a small legacy to buy a property, described himself as a 'Lace Hand and Landowner'. The land in question consisted of a cottage with 'three fields . . . and the Orchard; a large garden for vegetables and fruit *(which)* surrounded the house . . . '[1] It sounds idyllic, and later a romantic mythology would be woven around Margaret Bondfield's 'poor but happy' rural origins, a myth which, as we shall see, bore only a tenuous connection to reality.

Having started work in a lace mill at the age of nine, William Bondfield was largely self-educated, but as a young man had attended classes run by a local radical clergyman, the Reverend John Gunn. Here he had picked up an interest in science, and particularly in the idea that one day it might be possible to build flying machines. He also had a lifelong passion for geology, which he loved so much that he once spent money destined for boots for the children on a new geological hammer.[2] Like many other working-class men at the time he prided himself on his erudition and passed a love of knowledge on to many of his children.

By the late 1840s William's active radicalism seems to have waned, and in early 1852, at the age of 38, he married 21-year-old Ann Taylor, the daughter of a dissenting minister. Ann's mother, Sarah Taylor, was a fiercely practical woman who delivered the parish babies, challenged local superstitions and 'strove for the cure of bodies as well as souls'.[3] William and Ann's first child, John Alexander, was born nine months later, and over the next twenty-five years Ann would go on to have another ten surviving children. At a time when there was no effective birth control this pattern was not unusual, and was, indeed, what the majority of women anticipated when they married. In addition to the near-constant round of pregnancy and breastfeeding Ann also, according to her daughter, 'made butter, washed clothes, cured the slaughtered pig, made jam, kept the house clean, made or altered our clothing, helped with the vegetable and fruit gardens, and kept two lovely flower borders . . . '[4] Inevitably, she must have been close to exhausted for much of the time. Both Margaret Bondfield and her early biographer, Mary Agnes Hamilton, present Ann as a model of what a good wife and mother should be – Hamilton says that she 'worked from morning to night, but never lost her spring or her good humour . . . She was the home-maker *par excellence* . . . '[5] According to this version of Margaret's upbringing Ann Bondfield was close to a saint. The family was active in the Congregational Church and Ann made sure that her brood attended. When she punished she did so swiftly and with the kind of rough justice that would make most twenty-first-century parents wince. She was also pragmatic, horrifyingly so to modern eyes. 'When one of the younger children developed measles she put the others to bed with it, that the thing might be cleared off at one go.'[6] As we shall see, this may have had far-reaching consequences for Margaret, who must have been one of those younger children.

In reality Ann Bondfield's life was much less relentlessly positive than her daughter was ever prepared to admit. The orchard, vegetable garden and hens may have supplied food, but there were a large number of mouths to feed and very little ready money coming in. Furnham Cottage (which was actually two small cottages knocked together) had no indoor plumbing and all the water had to be carried up from the well, often by the children before they went to school. Margaret was proud of the fact that, when old enough, she could 'carry two buckets, the handles over the iron hoop which came down to us from the first children'.[7] At the bottom of the garden there was a pump under which the children washed in cold water. An earth closet nearby provided the only toilet facilities. The cottage reeked of the paraffin used in the lamps, and cooking was done on a smoky range for which fuel had constantly to be found. The younger children usually wore clothes handed down from the older ones, and everything had to be mended and kept clean without the aid of machines. There were no servants, although when Margaret was born her mother's sister, Harriet Taylor, was living with them and presumably helped out. Aunt Harriet (usually referred to as Aunt Taylor) was profoundly deaf and as a result spent most of her life living with various relatives occupying a place somewhere between domestic helper and dependent.

Bondfield maintained that her mother never complained, but this seems an impossibly high standard of maternal martyrdom, and her own later eloquence about the hard lives endured by working-class women suggests that she herself knew as much. When explaining in her autobiography why she had remained single she observed that she had 'seen too much – too early – to have the least desire to join the pitiful scramble of my workmates *(to marry)*'.[8] This is often interpreted as a subtle reference to her sexuality, but in fact, and in context, means exactly what it says. Margaret Bondfield adored her mother, but for various reasons actually spent less than half of her childhood with her. She did, however, live with a variety of female relatives, and even as a young child she knew that a life of unremitting domesticity was not for her.

Like most large families, the Bondfield children separated into sub-groups by age. The three oldest – John, William and George – had already been launched into work before Margaret (called Meg in the family) was born. Their parents were very determined that none of their offspring should join their father in the lace factory, and none of them did. Before 1870 there was no state educational provision, so the children either attended free Methodist or Congregational Church schools, or money was found to send them to a cheap local dame school. As the boys turned 13 they were apprenticed to trades and began to earn their keep. The eldest girl, Sarah Anne (known as Annie) had been sent when very young to live with her Taylor grandparents some miles away at a village called Middle Lambrook. She was intended to become the family carer, but the other daughters, including Margaret, were destined for teaching, which was regarded as a respectable form of employment for bright working-class girls. Apprenticeships and teacher training required children to leave home in their teens, and as a result there was a steady churn of siblings departing, occasionally returning for visits and then inexplicably disappearing again. By the time Margaret was toddling round the kitchen only five of the children – Herbert, Allen, Ernest, Frank and Margaret herself – were still permanently at home. The three older boys were at school all day, and Frank and little Margaret would become inseparable playmates, forging a bond which would last all their lives.

When Margaret was four and a half years old the last member of the family, Catherine (known as Katie) was born. The baby was sickly and required a lot of care, and, given that Ann Bondfield was forty-seven years old, the birth may not have been easy. With four children still at home and an ailing baby in the house her work must have been cut out. Something had to give, and soon after Margaret's fifth birthday it was decided to send her to join her sister Annie in her grandmother's household at Middle Lambrook.

This practice of farming younger children out to helpful relatives was common at all levels of society. The children of wealthier parents might be sent to boarding schools, but in working-class families the rearing of children was regarded as a collective endeavour and children moved between homes as necessary. Margaret's older sister, Annie, had been part of her grandmother's household for over a decade, and Aunt Taylor had recently moved there from Furnham. Probably William and Ann thought that there would be enough familiarity in the house to make Margaret feel comfortable. They could not have been more wrong.

Middle Lambrook was (and still is) a pretty hamlet perched on a hillside and consisting of a honey-coloured manor house with a high wall and gates, a row of farm-workers' cottages, a small Congregational church and a Manse. Here Grandmother Taylor, Aunt Taylor, and Annie had set up a boarding school after Grandfather Taylor's death in 1877. As Margaret rather bitterly noted later 'These relations were all strangers to me.'[9] The move was the first serious blow of her young life, and it was hard to cope with. For over four years she had been the baby of the family, and now not only was she supplanted but, as it seemed to her, banished. She described Middle Lambrook as a 'new cold world' and so it must have been if, as is likely, she arrived there in winter. Both Aunt Taylor and Grandmother Taylor were deaf, and although Margaret loved her grandmother she was less sure about her aunt. The isolated little household seemed like another world to the confused five-year-old, and none of the people in it any kind of substitute for the mother she adored or her noisy brothers. It would be six years before she returned home on a permanent basis, and although there were visits in the intervening period, and perhaps even longer stays, particularly when she was ill, it was a terrible dislocation from which she never entirely recovered.

It might have been expected that the school would provide companions for her, but even this did not turn out particularly well. 'For the first time' she said, 'I was with other girls – with the adults all too busy to spare time for me. I much preferred my brothers' games and fun.'[10] She also said that she 'accepted this change of environment with interest' but since as an adult she tried to cultivate acceptance of what she could not change, hindsight may have had a part to play in this assessment. In fact, the overall impression which emerges from her account is one of real sadness and loss.

No letters home survive from this period, and there is no contemporary account of how she felt. However she did preserve a forlorn little letter from her sister Annie to the Bondfield parents. Writing in 1865 at the age of seven, in her best joined-up script and with an understandable lack of punctuation, Annie said:

> I am very anxious to know if you are coming down at Christmas and bring (*sic*) Hatty and Herby and Ally I want to see them so badly . . . I should like to see Papa and the boys but what would the pigs and the cattle do if you all left at once but I hope I shall see you all before long. We have all got colds. Now with love and kisses for all I remain your Affectionate Child.[11]

A few years later when the 1871 Census was taken Annie was still living in Middle Lambrook, and by the time Margaret arrived she was nineteen years old and helping with the school. Whether or not she remembered her own sense of exile and understood her sister's distress we do not know, but to Margaret she seemed like just another grown-up and hardly a sibling at all.

Bondfield's description of her time at Middle Lambrook is covered briefly in her autobiography and even more briefly elsewhere. Understandably it is rather confused, and the chronology not quite right. By the time she was writing she had outlived all her siblings and there was no one left with whom to check the details. It is clear, however, that something went seriously wrong. For one thing, she seems to have stopped speaking, or at any rate to have become very quiet, later describing herself as 'tongue-tied'. Exactly what happened will never be known, but at some point around the age of six she fell ill and lost her memory. There must also have been physical symptoms, since in one account she described it as 'an illness from which it was thought I could not recover'.[12] It is very possible that this illness was measles, some severe, if rare, complications of which can affect the memory, and which she might either have caught at Middle Lambrook or from one of her siblings. She may even have been sent home so that she could catch it from them when Ann put all the younger children into the same bed for that purpose.

She does not tell us if she was with her grandmother during this time or was nursed at home. She does not suggest what treatment she received, or whether or not she ever recalled anything about that period. What is certain, however, is that this was the first of a series of both mental and physical health problems which plagued her all her life to one degree or another. Perhaps, in this first case, the misery of being sent away from home was just too much, or perhaps there was another cause. It is impossible at this distance, and with no source other than Bondfield herself, to know.

There was, however, one traumatic event which may have affected her. At some point in the latter part of 1878 her twenty-four-year-old brother, William, came to stay. William had been apprenticed to a draper before Margaret was born and may later have gone to London, but in 1878 he fell ill and came home, or, at least, went to live with his grandmother, sisters and aunt, presumably so that Annie could nurse him. He was suffering from both tuberculosis and undiagnosed diabetes, and as his condition worsened the atmosphere in the house must have been both sad and deeply distressing. Despite the best of intentions, the needs of little Margaret cannot have been very high on anyone's list of priorities, and she must have been both lonely and frightened by the tragedy unfolding around her. She may have been sent home during the last few weeks before William's death in January 1879, but wherever she was she was surrounded by worried and grieving adults in highly stressful circumstances which she could not fully understand.

William was the first of the eleven siblings to die, yet neither in her autobiography nor in any other article or interview did Bondfield ever make any mention of him, not even giving any clue that one of her brothers might have died during this period. In her book, she lists all her siblings, their dates of birth and death, and their occupations and marriages.[13] William's year of death is wrongly given as 1887. She undoubtedly knew the right date; a hand-written note amongst her papers was clearly the basis for the list in the book and correctly has it as 1879.[14] The error also occurs in both drafts of *A Life's Work* and could therefore easily have been picked up at any stage.[15] Why it was not is puzzling, but both William's traumatic death and her own mysterious illness must have played a part in the child's developing outlook on life.

Once she had recovered Margaret was again sent away, this time to stay with her sister Harriet at Stembridge, another nearby village. Harriet (or Hattie) had left home to train as a teacher when Margaret was a baby, and Bondfield describes making her 'acquaintance' almost as though she was a stranger. At 21 Hattie was now a fully fledged schoolmistress with a little house of her own in which she took two of the daughters of the schoolmaster as boarders. Once more Margaret was the only child in a houseful of women much older than herself. Rather sadly, she remembered that there were few other children to play with, and her main recollection was that Hattie 'was good company and could sing well and was greatly in demand: I must have been a nuisance, as she had to take me with her, or leave me in the care of a neighbour.'[16]

At some point she returned home briefly, and she appears in the 1881 census as being with her parents at Furnham. Soon, however, she was once more on her travels, this time much further afield. Her oldest brother, John, had been living in Brighton and doing very well as a journalist. Grandmother Taylor had died, so Annie and Aunt Taylor had gone to join him, Annie in the role of housekeeper and Aunt Taylor to help. But it soon became clear that John was ill and in May 1881 tuberculosis claimed him as it had his younger brother. His father had gone to Brighton to be with him, and, while he was there, he, Annie and Aunt Taylor must have hatched their plan for Meg, which was that she would move to Brighton and attend a school where the education might be better than at the more rural schools in Chard. Despite all her problems she was obviously a clever child, and her parents may have thought that she needed something a little different. Attendance at school had just been made compulsory for children under the age of ten, but the new Board schools provided only the basics. Perhaps Brighton could offer Margaret new opportunities, and the new environment and sea air might help her through her obvious unhappiness.

Thus, at the age of eight, Margaret Bondfield was put onto a train by herself to travel to her fourth home. She had a label sewn onto her coat giving her name and her destination, and the train guard was to keep an eye on her. At the time this was not an unusual way for children to travel, and she may have enjoyed the adventure. After a long journey she eventually arrived safely in Brighton to be collected at the station and taken home to a narrow, white-fronted house in Victoria Street.

Unfortunately, this was yet another house full of anxiety and grief. Annie and Aunt Taylor were alone in a strange town with no male relative to support them and an urgent need to earn their own living. Aunt Taylor's deafness limited the options open to her, and neither she nor her niece had ever learned a trade or had to work outside the home. At just 22 Annie was suddenly responsible for the upkeep of all of them, and although some money for Margaret may have come from Chard Annie had to find the rest herself. She took in dressmaking jobs, taught music to children, painted greetings cards, and took on whatever little jobs would pay. Much later, Margaret understood the worry and uncertainty that hung over the household, but at the time she was protected from it as far as possible. What she was not protected from was the school to which she was sent, which she hated. She does not tell us why, but presumably her West Country accent, combined with her relatively poor education hitherto, did not help. After a year she was sent back to Chard.

Her life now entered a more settled period in that she remained with her parents until she was 14, but other factors meant that disruption of one kind or another continued. There were still five children at home, although her now teenaged brother Ernest turned out to be a bit of a bully and Allen seemed more like one of the grown-ups. She started to attend a small local school where, in addition to the basic subjects, she learned music and deportment. She particularly enjoyed music, learning a few simple pieces on the piano and accompanying her brothers' singing. Katie was a frail, rather fretful child who was frightened by her siblings' more boisterous games, but despite this Margaret began to develop a protective affection for her. She and Frank, however, were bemused by Katie's tendency to cry, making her 'a real puzzle. We were not given to tears. In all our partings I do not remember ever crying about leaving or coming back . . . In our world it wasn't done.'[17]

Any sense of security she may have felt did not last for very long. Since childhood, her father had worked at the same factory, rising to foreman and along the way inventing several new processes and patterns. Despite thinking of himself as an intelligent man, William appears to have been almost stunningly naïve when it came to his own interests. He did not ask for any payment for his designs, nor did he take any steps to register or patent his processes. He believed that he had a personal relationship of mutual respect with the owner and that, at some point, his contribution would be recognized. Instead, when the owner died, the factory was closed and all the workers, including William, were laid off with a week's wages. William had expected to be remembered in the old proprietor's will, but there was nothing. At 67 he was unlikely to find employment again, so he was faced with ruin. The family's earnings fell heavily overnight, and although there was a small income from the rent of some tumbledown little cottages William owned it was nowhere near enough to keep the family at the level they were used to. The food they grew ensured that they would not starve, but their financial situation was now dire, and the workhouse, the looming nightmare of every poor family, was a very real threat which haunted William for years.

In 1883 there was no unemployment benefit, no retirement age, and no pension for the vast majority of people. There was no child benefit and no support other than charity or the parish for anyone at risk of falling through the cracks into abject poverty. The workhouse was designed to deter people from failure to work and was punitive even when those entering it did so despite all their efforts to avoid it. Families were separated, wives and husbands were not allowed to see one another and while children were now sent to the local Board school to be educated they were also clearly marked out from the other children. Margaret well remembered the 'procession in grey cloaks, who marched up and down the main street twice a day'.[18]

Unsurprisingly, William became an anxious, depressed and angry presence in the house just as Margaret returned. At a point at which she should have been able to enjoy a new relationship with him he was withdrawn and distant, unable to understand or accept what had happened to him and constantly worried about what might happen next. The older children told her that when younger he had been 'a good companion', but to ten-year-old Margaret he was 'a stranger who punished with quotations *(from poetry)* and a slipper'.[19] Although she did her best to be a dutiful daughter, she could never feel the affection for him that she did for her mother.

However, by and large life was now more settled, and Margaret did not move again until after she had left school. Home in a large household with no servants or modern conveniences was hard work, and everyone had to pull their weight. Ann Bondfield had no truck with the common Victorian idea that daughters should dance attendance on their brothers, and both boys and girls were expected to take their turns with the many chores. This Margaret did, once getting into serious trouble for accidentally throwing a basinful of dirty washing-up water over her father. She weeded the vegetable garden, fed the chickens, collected the eggs, and did her share of the household chores. Efforts were made to teach her to knit, but she disliked it and on one occasion paid her pocket money to Georgina Vile, one of the workhouse girls, to finish some stockings for her. She later felt slightly ashamed of this, not because she had given Georgina the work, but because she pretended to have done it herself and thus won a prize. Cooking also came high on her list of things she was not inclined to do; by her own account she never cooked anything until the age of 75, and while this may be an exaggeration she certainly relied heavily on other people to feed her throughout her adult life.

Away from the cottage the children's education continued, though one immediate consequence of the disaster of William's unemployment was that they had to leave their private schools and go to the local Board school. This had been built as a consequence of the 1870 Education Act, and the education provided was intended to teach the basics as well as equip children for working life. However, the perception persisted that private schools were better, and none of the Bondfield brood had attended Chard Board School. Now there was no option, so off Frank, Margaret and little Katie went. When they got there Margaret was mortified to find that, far from being ahead of other children her age, she was actually quite a bit behind. The many moves and changes of school, combined with the year at the hated Brighton school and the months of illness before it, had seriously impacted her progress in everything except reading, and she had quite a struggle to catch up. Catch up she did, however, achieving the required standard and leaving school when she turned thirteen. As her parents had planned, she then embarked on the first stage of her future as an elementary teacher.

Prior to 1870 teachers had mainly trained by working as assistants, or pupil teachers, in schools. The 1880 Education Act, however, had required the establishment of local pupil-teacher centres which would provide what was effectively a form of secondary education combined with practical experience in nearby elementary schools. Once the pupil teacher turned 18 she could sit the Queen's Scholarship Examination; if she passed she could attend a residential training college, at the end of which she would be fully qualified. This was the path planned for Margaret, and the start to her working life was therefore employment as a 'monitor' or trainee teacher for the younger boys at the Board school she had just left. Her main job was to supervise 42 small boys in an over-crowded classroom described by the School Inspector as 'positively unwholesome' for the sum of just three shillings a week. After a year she was found to have done well in difficult circumstances, but she had already firmly decided that life as a teacher was not for her. In August 1887 she left the profession for good and without any shade of regret.

Throughout her life, Bondfield was to take sudden, apparently highly risky, decisions, some of which paid off and some of which did not. This rejection of teaching, which on the face of it would have been a natural occupation for her, was perhaps the first of these, an assertion of independence which would inform many of her future decisions. Even then she may have thought that there had to be more to life than anything a few years of teaching, followed by marriage, could offer. Her sister Hattie had married a civil service clerk and gone to live near London where she was already the mother of two children, and Margaret may well have baulked at accepting this as the pattern of her own future. At 14 she was probably as difficult to deal with as any other teenager, and her restlessness was made worse by the fact that her options were so limited. It is entirely possible, also, that she was again showing signs of illness or distress because eventually it was concluded that the best thing for her was a holiday. Accordingly, after months of kicking her heels at home, she was packed off again to her sister Annie and Aunt Taylor in Brighton, though presumably now without the label sewn into her coat. This time she took an active pleasure in the journey itself, a pleasure which would remain with her for the rest of her life. 'Always', she said, 'a journey alone opened the doors of adventure, a new experience, a wider horizon.'[20]

Since this visit was to be a holiday both she and her parents must have assumed that she would be back before Christmas. In fact, her absence would extend for more than five years, and she would never live in the West Country again.

Chapter 2
Eager, Attractive and Vividly Alive

Brighton in the late 1880s was, then as now, a major holiday destination. It had been steadily expanding since the early days of the century and by 1887 was able to attract visitors of all classes to its hotels and boarding houses. The arrival of the railways in the middle of the century created a boom in both day trippers and holiday-makers, particularly in the summer. Better-off families tended to avoid the high season but came and filled the more expensive hotels during the autumn months. There was some industry in the town, but also a racecourse, an art school, several theatres and an unusually large number of churches. West of Brighton the former fishing village of Hove had grown into a town in its own right with wide avenues, new residential estates and a spacious seafront. The revenue brought into both towns by the large temporary population supported a smaller permanent one which lived a life of its own away from the excitement of the holidaying crowds.

Annie Bondfield's life had improved somewhat since the desperate days in the wake of John's death. She and Aunt Taylor were still living together in the house on Victoria Street, but Annie was working as a dressmaker with a relatively secure income. The strained and fearful atmosphere of Margaret's earlier visit had gone, and Annie and Aunt Taylor were more settled. They had found their place in Brighton's Congregational community and Annie had become a prominent member of the Clifton Road church where she sang in the choir. The Congregational Church was non-hierarchical, and, amongst other things, accepted women in roles that were barred to them in other churches. It was possibly here that Margaret first heard a female voice speaking in public from a position of authority. The Congregational Church was at that time deep in a debate about the role of women, and it was by no means unknown for them to preach on Sundays. In later years Margaret herself would preach to the Clifton Road congregation, but as a bright, if awkward, teenager her mind must have been more on new friends and enjoying what Brighton had to offer.

The Clifton Road church was a social as well as a religious hub, and through it Annie had met a woman called Sarah Irving White who ran a baby linen shop in Hove. Mrs White's husband, Thomas, was thirty-six years her senior and suffered from dementia, so that Sarah was left to run the business on her own. She was doing well and was now looking for an apprentice who could be taught fine needlework. Annie thought the job might suit Margaret, to whom it seemed like the answer to a prayer. She 'eagerly grasped the opportunity of earning my living'[1] and in the autumn of 1887 she packed her bag again and moved into Mrs White's shop in Church Road.

In the 1880s an apprenticeship was still the main route through which young working-class people entered most trades. They could last anywhere between three and seven years and the employer was usually expected to provide board and lodging as well as training, basic pay, and some degree of care. Since it was unregulated the system was full of abuses and was wide open to being used as a source of cheap labour, and many apprentices found themselves out of work once they had to be paid an adult's wage. Nevertheless every year thousands of working-class boys and girls were indentured to every kind of trade, and when Margaret accepted Mrs White's offer there were over 300,000 apprentices around the country. Since retail was a major employer of women many of the girls were apprenticed in shops, and particularly in the drapery stores which were one of the mainstays of every high street.

Drapers' shops specialized in cloth, decorative trimmings, and haberdashery articles such as needles, pins and embroidery frames. Different drapers sold different combinations of items, with small drapers' shops tending to be crammed full of everything women accustomed to sewing at home and making their own clothes might want. Larger shops often had a number of departments, some of which sold clothes as well as curtains, domestic drapery and table linen. An assistant in a drapery shop had to have a wide knowledge of the products she was selling as well as the ability to advise customers so that they not only found what they wanted but also spent more than they had originally intended.

Mrs White's establishment was relatively small and most of the business was by mail order, so that Margaret did not have to spend the long hours on her feet that she would have had to do in other shops. Mrs White treated her staff well and Margaret seems to have felt, if not at home, at least safe. As a country girl she was very happy to find that, since Mrs White's adopted baby, Daisy, needed to be taken out for daily walks, she did not have to be confined indoors all day. Pushing the pram she could walk up and down the nearby Hove seafront observing holiday-makers and residents alike and breathing in the fresh air she otherwise missed. When not doing that she was taught fine needlework and embroidery. Mrs White bought plain baby linen in bulk, decorated it with delicate embroidery, and then sold it on to British families around the Empire and particularly in India. Margaret recalled spending hours 'at a window, around which a passion flower mysteriously bloomed, smocking lovely silks for babies' frocks'.[2]

Had she been able to complete her apprenticeship under Mrs White's tutelage her life might have been very different. However, Mr White's death in June 1889 resulted in new circumstances, not only changing her life but also causing her, in a very Victorian manner, to reflect more on death. The losses in her own family had been the occasions of real grief, but Mr White was an old man who had been ill for many years and even his wife regarded his passing as an occasion for calm acceptance rather than tears. As was customary, various people sat with the body until it was coffined, and fifteen-year-old Margaret took her turn. 'I remember' she wrote:

> . . . thinking about death as something we all must face and not make a fuss about. In that sunny room, amid beautiful flowers and scents, I was comforted to feel that this was not the end, but merely the beginning of a new kind of life.[3]

Once Mr White was decently buried his widow had to consider her future. Now that she no longer needed to work she decided to sell the business and move in with her widowed sister nearby so that together they could live off their legacies and bring up baby Daisy without financial worry. This meant that once more Margaret had to move on. She had not completed her apprenticeship, and, moreover, she had been working in a shop untypical of the industry. She had acquired excellent skills with her needle but did not really want to be a dressmaker or embroiderer. She needed another shop to take her on and found one in Hetherington's, a large drapery store on Western Road in Brighton. Here she stayed for the next five years.

Nothing in her life so far had prepared her for the shock of working in the 'ordinary quick turnover trade', and the sense of outrage and injustice that it engendered stayed with her and drove her later determination to change it. From being treated more or less as one of the family and allowed out for walks she found herself working ten-hour shifts before being locked up all night in a dormitory. What little control she had had over her life was now replaced by a regime of rules, controls and fines so petty that they sometimes seemed incomprehensible. The absence of either regulation or recognized trade unions in the retail industry meant that employers could impose any conditions they wished, and they did. Staff might be taken on at an agreed wage, but fines were then levied for every tiny infraction of the 'rules'. Shop assistants could be penalized for not approaching a customer who came in to browse, for not folding clothes correctly, for being late or just for sitting down. Long hours spent standing meant that both men and women, but particularly the women, developed joint and spinal problems, and the condition of their feet was an endless subject for discussion. For the women, this was made worse by the fact that they often had to wear thin, cheap shoes which looked fashionable but were very uncomfortable.

Since shopgirls had a reputation for moral laxity, they had to learn early how to fend off male customers and colleagues alike. Despite all this they were still required to be cheerful, welcoming and attractive at all times, and never on any account to show any sign of tiredness or discomfort.

Since shop assistants in England were regarded as servants they had to live on or near the shop premises in accommodation provided by their employer. This was known as the living-in system and was much hated by those who had to suffer it. Hetherington's accommodation was a cramped building on Stone Street behind the main shop. Here women and girls slept in shared rooms in a house with a lavatory but no bathroom and only very basic washing facilities. They were allocated a bed and a box in which to put their clothes and any other possessions. There was nowhere to hang up or iron long, heavy skirts, yet the women would be fined for untidy or crumpled clothing. There was almost no privacy. The room Margaret shared with three others was on the ground floor facing the street. On race nights men looking for sex sometimes banged on the windows and on one terrifying occasion forced them open and tried to climb in. Any sense of safety that she had had at Mrs White's evaporated, and she was now made acutely aware of what life was like for most young women of her age. At sixteen, she could do nothing about it, but every experience, every indignity, every moment of fear or apprehension was stored up for future use.

In the shop itself things were a little better. Throughout her time working in retail Bondfield rather enjoyed being in shops that sold good clothes. She was able to make her own outfits and enjoyed sewing much more than cooking or knitting. There were also opportunities to do more than just stand behind a counter all day. The underclothing department, to which she was initially allocated, had six tall windows which needed to be constantly filled and refilled so that she was able to learn the art of window dressing. She liked this, because it got her out of having to spend all her time standing at the counter. It was hard work and involved running up and down stairs from the stockroom carrying heavy boxes, but she was at least being trained properly by people who knew their business well. Once her apprenticeship ended she was taken on as a permanent assistant with the prospect of some kind of supervisory job if she worked hard. Her future seemed secure.

Other things, however, went less well. She did not have close friends amongst the other shop staff, and she had very little time off in which to have any kind of social life. On the subject of any kind of love life she is resolutely silent. Her long hours of work and the fact that she had to live in necessarily restricted her ability to meet new people, but she could go to Clifton Road church on Sundays and there she could see Annie and Aunt Taylor. She joined the choir, discovering she had a rich contralto voice. It was also almost certainly through the church that she met Louisa Martindale, a remarkable woman whose influence would reach through the rest of her life.

Mrs Martindale[4] was much the same age as Margaret's mother, but her life had been very different. As a feminist, she had ideas that seemed new and rather startling, but she was also profoundly religious, which chimed with Bondfield's own outlook. She had been living in Brighton for some years with her two teenage daughters, Hilda and Louisa. She was an active supporter of the Liberal Party, and although she did not try to recruit the young women she gathered around her she did offer a pattern of political activism which went beyond pasting posters onto house walls. She was a great founder and supporter of organizations of all kinds, including the British and Foreign Bible Society, the Cooperative Movement and the female suffrage campaign. She believed in solving problems rather than lamenting them, and when she concluded that governesses were an oppressed group of women who needed a space where they could meet she started inviting them to her house every other Saturday afternoon. Soon she was also inviting overworked and exploited shopgirls to visit her on Sundays, and it was only a matter of time before she came across Margaret Bondfield.

Hilda Martindale, who in later years would become one of the first women to reach senior rank in the Civil Service, was a couple of years younger than Margaret and remembered her as:

> an eager, attractive and vividly alive girl of sixteen . . . She was working in one of the large drapers' shops in Brighton and was not happy. She needed sympathy, and was ready to talk when she found that her hostess really wanted to listen. She told about 'living in' and all that it meant . . .[5]

Mrs Martindale listened to the girls' stories about their lives and she talked to them about things outside their experience. She lent them books and magazines and encouraged them to discuss what they read. She could even provide sex education to those who needed it. Like many other girls at the time Margaret Bondfield was completely ignorant of anything other than what she had gleaned from whispers and smutty giggling. The onset of menstruation before her move to Brighton had been a horrifying shock, but her mother had never said 'a word about its purpose in creation'. Louisa Martindale 'discovered my state of mind and set herself to weed out the unwholesome patch and plant instead a clean, sane knowledge, both biological and social, on this question'.[6]

The Sunday afternoon visits to the Martindale home in Stanford Road also offered Margaret a different version of motherhood from that she knew at home. Louisa Martindale was a widow with two young daughters, but unlike Ann Bondfield back in Chard her life was not one long grind of hard physical labour. The Martindale girls were able to continue their education for as long as necessary, with no need to earn a living. At 14 Hilda was still at school. Her older sister Louisa was attending Royal Holloway College in London laying the foundations for her future career as a pioneering surgeon.[7] Their mother could invite governesses and shopgirls to tea because she did not have to do all the work for it herself; she had a servant who, in 1891, was a young woman called Eliza Rolfe. Margaret could not have failed to understand the difference that class and money made, not only to day-to-day life but also to wider opportunities. Doors opened for the Martindale girls that were resolutely closed to her and Eliza Rolfe. Here was another set of experiences to be quietly stored away for future use.

Mrs Martindale made the young women who visited her feel both of value and valued, and most of them never forgot her. When she died in 1914 Margaret Bondfield wrote to Hilda that:

> Your mother is one of the great immortals who cannot die as long as memory lasts. She was a most vivid influence in my life, the first woman of broad culture I had met, she seemed to recognize me and make me recognize myself as a person of independent thought and action . . . I cannot bear to think of the difference it would have made to my life if that kind of influence had not reached me when it did.[8]

In 1894 Bondfield turned 21 and was finally in complete command of her own decisions. The more she thought about the ideas she encountered through Mrs Martindale, the more dissatisfied she had become with her life and the more critical of what she saw around her. 'I had reached,' she said:

> a stage of my spiritual pilgrimage which I must needs travel alone . . . I could no longer passively accept contemporary opinion on business morality, to which I applied the harsh judgements of the very young. The outward and visible sign of my protest was a sudden move to London.[9]

With what she described as several years of 'rigid economy' she had managed to save up the sum of £5,[10] which, out of an annual income of less than £15, was no mean feat. She could certainly expect it to tide her over while she found work and finding that work should not be too difficult. She was well qualified, young and strong, and pretty enough for the kind of shops who hired their assistants on that basis. She was not afraid of hard work and she was used to spending many hours on her feet. There was no reason why she should not be snapped up by a good ladies' outfitters in one of the better parts of London.

The retail industry in the capital had been growing and developing for several decades, and when Bondfield arrived most of the big department stores were already open. They were major employers of women, sometimes employing thousands, and even the smallest shops could afford cheap female staff. Shop owners often preferred them because, apart from anything else, they were easy to exploit. Women could be paid much less than men, and if they were living in as well the savings could be considerable. Middle-class married wives working for what was known as 'pin money' – that is, small amounts of money additional to the housekeeping given to them by their husbands – could be laid off easily with the ebbs and flows of trade. Working-class women who did not marry could go on to occupy more senior roles as floor walkers or buyers, or, in the larger stores, move into back-room or catering jobs. By the 1890s women were to be found in almost every area of the business except the most senior echelons of management, and there were good prospects for girls who were prepared to start at the bottom and work hard.

Bondfield began where she hoped to succeed, with the elegant West End shops selling beautiful clothes to women who could afford them. Unfortunately it soon transpired, first that she had unwisely chosen to arrive in London during the 'slack season', when trade was slow and demand for staff sluggish, and, second, that in any case she did not meet the basic requirements. These were not just fine needlework and good references but often also included height and a graceful, willowy figure, neither of which Bondfield possessed. 'We never engage anyone under five feet eight inches' one shop informed her, as they declined her application for work. Though slender and pretty Bondfield was only five feet tall. She tried every shop on Oxford Street, from department stores like the newly enlarged John Lewis to the smaller shops and boutiques. As she tramped doggedly through the dirt and traffic of the noisy streets or crowded onto the horse-drawn buses that took her across town to yet more hopeless possibilities her dreams began to recede. It was hard to find out where the most likely vacancies were, and it was a couple of weeks before she realized that the best information came from commercial travellers, who were constantly in and out of shops and generally knew what was going on. Another problem was that a great many other people were also looking for work, and sometimes even the rumour of a job was enough to cause long queues to form outside certain shops. Employers hiring new staff could take their pick of the applicants before putting up a notice saying 'No good waiting any longer – places filled.'[11]

As the weeks went by the precious £5 was spent, and there was no prospect of more coming in. There were no unemployment benefits and no safety nets; failure to find work would see her sinking inexorably through the cracks to the common lodging houses, whose dormitories made the accommodation provided for shop staff seem almost palatial, or to the workhouse. The continual disappointments began to grind her down, and she developed a rather better understanding of the terror that had haunted her father after the loss of his employment.

So bad did things become that had her landlady not taken pity on her and fed her she would have gone hungry for days on end. She learned, she said later, 'the bitterness of a hopeless search for work . . . Even today those first months in the great city searching for work carry the shadow of a nightmare.'[12] A different, less determined character might have given up and gone back to Brighton, or even to Chard, but Bondfield never gave anything up easily and she persisted until, after three long months, she got a job in the fancy goods department of a shop in Hammersmith. A few days into her first week she discovered that her desperation had led her unknowingly to accept a lower rate of pay than other women doing the same job. Despite the risks, she left at the end of the week, probably without a reference.[13] Soon after, however, she found a post in an outfitters shop on the Tottenham Court Road where she was paid £25 a year plus board and lodging; in cash terms this was considerably less than ten shillings a week and could be – and usually was – reduced by fines and deductions. But she had survived the worst, and although the conditions of shop work could rarely be said to be good, she was now earning more money than she had ever been paid before and even had a degree of job security.

Not knowing very much about London, she had initially imagined that working conditions would be better than they had been in Brighton. She was dismayed to find that they were, if anything, worse. The dormitory in which she now had to live was just as dismal as that at Hetherington's, and the rules even more petty and demeaning. Grown women and men could be fined for being out late without permission, for not keeping their beds and boxes neat, or for staying up after lights-out. Washing facilities were dismal, and baths unknown, leading to a mad dash to the public baths to get there before they closed on the one night of the week that they were open later than the shop. The women had to run 'at full speed for about half a mile. We could then . . . have exactly a quarter of an hour to undress, bath, and dress again before the attendant had to turn us out.'[14] In the shop itself they worked twelve-hour days six days a week, closing only on Sundays and Christmas Day. What had been irksome in Brighton now became increasingly galling in London, particularly since Bondfield's Sundays and the brief evenings after the shop had shut had begun to fill with absorbing new experiences and ideas.

Louisa Martindale and the Congregational Church in Brighton had provided their protégée with letters of introduction to the King's Weigh House church in Duke Street near Grosvenor Square. For someone adrift on her own in a strange city such letters were invaluable. Churches were able to offer much more than formalized expressions of worship. They existed as a network of connected communities, between which people could (usually) pass safely and within which they could find friendship, partners and social activity as well as a commonality of faith and approach to the world. A young and potentially vulnerable woman like Margaret Bondfield could be welcomed and drawn into a familiar religious and social life. All she had to do was turn up and hand over her letters of introduction.

On Sundays the shops were closed but the shop assistants were usually locked out of their dormitories during the day anyway. Some visited relatives or friends, and Bondfield may well have met up with her brother Frank, who was now working as a printer in London, but the main draw for her was the King's Weigh House. A brisk walk took her from Tottenham Court Road to Duke Street where she soon began to make new friends. She joined the choir and entered actively into the life of the church. She retained a strong Christian faith throughout her life, and the church was thus very attractive to her, but she was also always drawn to structured, rule-based organizations, and liked groups which could be navigated by a shared understanding of how things should work, and what to do about them if they did not. This was something she found in the church and, later, in the trade union and socialist movements, both of which drew on their members' experiences – good or bad – of religious organizations.

At some point, someone at the King's Weigh House suggested to her that she might be interested in a group called the Ideal Club. This was not connected to the church but met at 105 Tottenham Court Road and offered companionship, social activities and educational opportunities. There is very little surviving information about it, but there were many clubs and societies in London aimed at keeping working-class youths off the streets and out of trouble, and many young people cut adrift from their families belonged to them. The trade unionist P. C. Hoffman,[15] who was an apprentice shop assistant in the mid-1890s, joined one which catered for young (male) shopworkers. He described the Farringdon House Mutual Improvement Society which offered:

> debates, essays, chess and drafts tournaments, socials, etc., each week from November to April, finishing up with the annual dinner, when staff and firm met as if they had never seen one another before, and said nice things about one another which nobody really believed.[16]

What made the Ideal Club different from the general run of such clubs was that it was not connected to any church or employer, and that it was political. It had been set up by members of the Fabian Society, itself a relatively new group made up of liberals, early socialists and progressive thinkers. The Club's aim was to bring dislocated young people together to learn to think and to talk about how society should work as well as to break down class barriers and have some fun. In this it was certainly successful. Unlike the Farringdon club it had both male and female members, and it gave young women like Margaret Bondfield opportunities they would never have had anywhere else. There were talks and lectures to attend and new ideas to absorb. Through them she began to meet people she would never otherwise have come across, many of whom, including the young Ramsay MacDonald, the social thinkers and researchers Beatrice and Sidney Webb, and the Irish socialist playwright George Bernard Shaw, became lifelong friends and colleagues.

The Ideal Club, however, was not just about lectures, discussion and boldly progressive ideas. There were dances, expeditions and entertainments, all of which could be enjoyed in the company of both her brother Frank and her younger sister Katie, who, at the age of 17, had arrived to attend the Maria Gray College to finish her teacher training. The College had been opened in 1878 as one of the first such institutions for women and by 1894 was situated in Fitzroy Square just off the Tottenham Court Road. The quality of training it provided was very high, and once graduated Katie would be well qualified. In the meantime she could see her brother and sister, practise her piano playing at the home of supportive Fabians, and enjoy an interesting and educational social life.

Some of the progressive ideas Margaret Bondfield came across at the Ideal Club were transformative, including the discovery of rational dress. Like most other women she had hitherto unquestioningly worn the restrictive corsets of the Victorian age. In her working life, in particular, she would have been expected to conform. Corseting was seen as an issue of morality as well as fashion. Good women wore corsets; bad women rejected stifling Victorian social constrictions along with their stays. But many progressive women, as well as pioneering sportswomen, were advocating looser, more comfortable clothing which would cause less discomfort and fewer medical problems. Given the trade in which she worked Bondfield must have been aware of these ideas but she was unlikely to have met women who actually put them into practice. Now she did, and the simplicity and freedom of this unconventional and rather daring style must have come as a revelation. Much to the disapproval of her shopworker colleagues, Bondfield soon adopted it herself, later recalling that 'My room mates thought it was most improper of me to wear knickers instead of three layers of petticoats, and suspenders instead of corsets.'[17]

These early days were interesting and exciting, but they had a sense of marking time about them. Already, young as she was, Bondfield knew that there was more to life than the shop counter and the kind of genteel poverty to which shop assistants aspired. Whatever her dreams were then have gone unrecorded, but she was about to turn the most significant corner of her life and start out on the path that would take her towards all her future achievements.

Chapter 3
The Right Thing to Do

In the late summer of 1894,[1] when she had been in her job on the Tottenham Court Road for a few weeks, Bondfield did something which she later described as leading to 'another adventure of faith'.[2] The meals provided by her employer were often inadequate, and she estimated that she had to spend nearly a quarter of her cash wages to supplement them. On one particular day she bought 'a penn'orth of fish and a ha'porth of chips, that great standby of the very poor'.[3] Fish and chips came wrapped in newspaper, and as she walked round Fitzroy Square eating them her eye fell on a letter to the editor from James Macpherson, leader of the Shop Assistants' Union, a body with which she was almost certainly unfamiliar. He was 'urging shop assistants to join together to fight against the wretched conditions of employment'. Bondfield was astonished that such a thing was possible. 'I was working about sixty-five hours a week for between £15 and £25 per annum, living in. Here I felt was the right thing to do, and at once I joined up.'[4]

The trade union movement at this time – and for many years to come – was overwhelmingly male, with objectives that prioritized the male worker and the male wage. It had very few women members and very few unions allowed women to join. Most women working in shops were actively hostile to trade unions, at least in part because they saw them as the province of manual workers, amongst whom they did not count themselves. Bondfield, however, immediately found the idea of collective action appealing, and that night she wrote off to Macpherson for details of how to join.

The National Union of Shop Assistants, Warehousemen and Clerks – generally known as the Shop Assistants' Union – was founded in Manchester in 1891. Two years later it moved to London and by the time Bondfield joined it was being run from a small office in Chancery Lane. It was part of the new wave of trade unions which had developed following two famous strikes – those of the matchgirls in 1888 and the dockers a year later. The older unions catered mainly for skilled men, but the 'new' unions attracted manual and unskilled workers. A few even accepted women members, though they often made little effort either to recruit them or to represent their interests. Indeed, the received wisdom was that women were impossible to organize, partly because their working lives were episodic, and partly because their wages were often so low that they could not afford the subscriptions, but also because they were weak and unable to work together for any long-term goal.

Many trade unionists believed that women's presence in the workforce depressed male wages and made it harder to achieve their objective of the 'family wage' – that is, pay which would enable a man to maintain himself and his family at a reasonable standard of living without having to send either wife or children out to work. Since the weight of societal expectation was that women would leave paid work when they married much of the female workforce was either single, widowed or abandoned by husbands, and almost always paid less than men. But some married women had no option but to continue to work, and although some did so in shops and factories many others were concentrated in sweated industries where they were both very badly paid and, since they worked at home, next to impossible to reach or organize.

There had been a number of attempts to form women's trade unions, sometimes led by middle-class women who were very much resented by male working-class trade union leaders. When, in 1874, Emma Paterson[5] founded the Women's Protective and Provident League (WPPL), she did so because she saw that the problem was not women's willingness or otherwise to organize, but their ability to sustain and develop that organization in the face of so many challenges, including male opposition. Almost everything militated against women's trade unions, so that although they were often founded with much enthusiasm, they tended to fail quite quickly. The WPPL was an umbrella body which both set up new unions itself and provided support to fledgeling unions, helping them to organize, recruit, set up benefit funds for their members, and acquire negotiating skills. It provided a support network for trade union women, who might be few and far between and isolated in their trades. Moreover, it was a voice for women in the wider trade union movement, as well as on the national stage. Paterson and Edith Simcox (of the Shirt and Collarmakers' Union) were the first women delegates to the Trades Union Congress (TUC), with Simcox, in 1875, becoming the first woman to speak at Congress. Paterson worked hard, both to keep the WPPL going and to extend its membership and its influence. It fought a long, bitter and ultimately successful campaign for women factory inspectors which resulted in the first appointments of women to senior civil service jobs. When Paterson died in 1886 the WPPL could easily have died with her had it not been for two remarkable women who ensured its survival.

Emilia Dilke[6] and Clementina Black[7] would both later be considerable influences on Margaret Bondfield, at least in part because like her they were focused on action and the difference that action could make. Lady Dilke had been involved in one way or another with the WPPL since its inception. Clementina Black was a single middle-class woman in her thirties who had an acute mind, an eye for detail, and the ability to take an overview of complex situations and understand how they might be connected. When Emma Paterson died Black and Emilia Dilke grasped the ailing WPPL and brought it firmly into its next phase. They reformed its structure and funding model, set up a strike fund and appointed, in Annie Marland,[8] one of the first full-time female trade union organizers. In 1888 the WPPL became the Women's Trade Union League (WTUL) to reflect how it had gradually changed over the years. Clementina Black moved on to found the Women's Industrial Council (WIC) in 1894 to research and improve women's working conditions across as many industries as possible. Bondfield would soon become very familiar with both the WTUL and the WIC, but at the point at which she wrote off to James Macpherson she knew nothing about either of them. Quite what Macpherson thought when he opened her letter (which sadly does not survive) is unknown, but he must have replied positively. Once he had met Bondfield he quickly saw her worth – she was a little messianic, perhaps, in the manner of the young discovering a new thing, but she was also bright, keen, and very hard-working.

Macpherson was a forty-three-year-old shopworker from Glasgow who had been one of the moving spirits in the founding of the Shop Assistants' Union. Despite the fact that the industry employed many thousands of women, most of the union's members were men, and Macpherson understood that failure to organize the hitherto 'unorganizable' women and girls would undermine the union's ability to improve pay and conditions in the industry generally. He also knew that to do this he needed women organizers, and this is probably one reason why he welcomed Bondfield to the fold so quickly. But he also deserves credit for having done so in such a positive fashion; he did not lament the necessity of involving women as other trade union leaders did, but treated Bondfield throughout as an important part of the organization, providing her with training, mentorship and friendship and supporting her as she rose to prominence within the movement. Later, when she became the union's Assistant Secretary, Macpherson gave her 'equality of status'[9] and she became a family friend as well as a colleague, at one point lodging with Macpherson and his wife Elizabeth. This sustained support for a young woman making her way in an almost entirely male environment was a rare quality, and although there was certainly some self-interest in it Bondfield remained grateful for his open-minded welcome, without which her trade union career might never have taken off.

As soon as she herself had joined Bondfield tried to persuade her work colleagues to sign up too. They unanimously declined. Most shop owners detested trade unions in any form, and in some workplaces even the remotest contact with a union representative could result in instant dismissal. The shop at which she was working in 1894 did not take quite such a punitive stance, but it was still made clear to her that she should desist. Her next exploit was the idea of a women's branch, but this also failed. Her initial lack of success was a setback, but Bondfield remained keen. She talked to whoever would answer her questions and involved herself in whatever aspect of the union's work was open to her. Since she still had to work full-time to support herself her activities were necessarily limited, and the increase of pay and decrease of hours which she had hoped for did not materialize, but none of this deterred her. She regarded this early phase of her trade union career as one of the happiest, later recalling that 'My Union officers gave me all the work I could do in my scant leisure, and every kind of encouragement.'[10]

Everything else now took a back seat to the all-consuming excitement of this new life, and soon other opportunities opened up. She was asked to contribute monthly short stories to the union journal, *The Shop Assistant*, an invitation which she accepted with alacrity. To preserve her anonymity (and keep her safe from disciplinary action by her employers) she needed a pen name, and she chose Grace Dare, Grace being her middle name and Dare her great grandmother's maiden name. The family connection in her choice of last name was obvious but may also have reflected something of her view of herself. She had already acquired the habit of taking considerable risks, and there were many more to come. Indeed, the act of writing itself required courage, because there was no obvious time or place in which to do it. She was still working ten- or twelve-hour days and most of her spare time was taken up with union activities and the Ideal Club. The only answer was to break the rules of the dormitory in which she was compelled to live, and in which candles after lights-out were strictly forbidden. Bondfield rigged up a screen by the simple method of draping a towel over a chair and hiding behind it with a small 'halfpenny dip' candle which gave a light strong enough to write by but not so strong that it would be seen through the curtains or under the door. Had she been discovered she would have been heavily fined; a second offence would have resulted in dismissal. It is perhaps a measure of her work mates' tacit support that she did this for over a year without anyone ever reporting her.

What she wrote cannot be regarded as great literature, but it was appreciated by the audience for which it was intended. At first she produced little stories about shops and the people who worked in them, but soon she branched out into articles about interesting topics and exhortations to be more active in the union. As her confidence and reputation grew she became more authoritative. She wanted women, in particular, to join trade unions, but she also wanted them to understand that joining alone was not enough. 'Cease from your dreaming,' she commanded her fellow workers:

Begin to live as you have it in you to live. Do you fear that your efforts will be useless, that you will have no influence over others? Are you thinking that the work will go on better without you? Dismiss these thoughts and fears! You are necessary. You will find work to do. Paying your subscription is not enough. . . .when you rouse yourself and realise the grand possibilities now lying dormant within you, you will be filled with that spirit of enthusiasm and unselfishness, without which you cannot become a real trade unionist . . . Your heart will be full of love for humanity, you will recognise in the man or woman in the street your brother, your sister; and your life will be made beautiful by the love of comrades.[11]

At the Ideal Club there were relatively few trade unionists, but there was a great deal of political discussion in which everyone was encouraged to participate. As a working-class woman with no prospect of a vote politics had always seemed rather distant from her, but now she was surrounded by people for whom political ideas were immediate and important. The Club ran a role-play legislative chamber called the St Pancras Parliament in which Bondfield sat as the MP for Taunton. There was much discussion of changes to local government. The 1894 Local Government Act swept away the old church-based system of London vestries and brought in Borough Councils. George Bernard Shaw managed to get elected to the new St Pancras Council and persuaded them to build public lavatories for women, an innovation which made Club members very proud. Bondfield's work colleagues thought that it was 'not quite nice' to talk about public toilets, but 'in the Club we gloried in being pioneers. This was *our* Borough Council being progressive.'[12]

James Macpherson was a member of the Marxist Social Democratic Federation (SDF)[13] and for this reason if for no other Bondfield also joined. These were the days in which people thought it was perfectly reasonable to be a member of several different political organizations at the same time, so that both socialists and Liberals joined the Fabian Society, and socialists joined both the SDF (founded in 1881) and the newly formed Independent Labour Party (ILP). Margaret Bondfield joined them all. Eventually she became disillusioned with the SDF, mainly because of its advocacy of 'bloody class war', and turned her attention to the ILP and the Fabians, but like many others she may well have retained her nominal membership for some years.

In 1895 a general election gave her more food for political thought. The election was caused by the implosion of the Liberal government, and in the absence (as yet) of any unifying Labour Party, all the different parts of the Left stood their own candidates, with some cross-over between them. The socialist Keir Hardie,[14] though technically the leader of the Scottish Labour Party,[15] had stood in 1892 as an independent Labour candidate in London and been elected, subsequently horrifying the establishment press by turning up to take his seat wearing a red tie and a deerstalker hat. In 1892 the Liberal Party had stood aside to give Hardie a clear run. In 1895 they repeated the favour, though to much less effect.

The ILP formally stood candidates for the first time in 1895, but was already suffering from the difficulties that would, a few years later, lead to the formation of the Labour Representation Committee (LRC). The lack of trade union support, the hostility of some trade unionist MPs (who sat as Liberals and were known as Lib-Lab MPs), the fear of socialism and the perception that the ILP was just part of the endless grouping and regrouping of left-wing organizations, all contributed to its failure to get any of its 28 candidates elected. Keir Hardie, suffering from a combination of stronger opposition, neglect of the constituency (often in order to speak for other candidates around the country), and hostility over some of his stances in Parliament, lost his seat. No doubt Margaret Bondfield campaigned for him, getting her first taste of the excitement of an election and acquiring new skills. The result – a Conservative parliamentary majority of over 150 – was a bitter disappointment and showed Hardie and the young Ramsay MacDonald, who had stood in Southampton, that something more was needed than enthusiasm, aspiration, and a fervent belief in socialism and working-class organization.

At this time, socialism was regarded by its adherents almost as a religion. People spoke of being 'converted' to it and tried to live their daily lives by socialist principles. For young people feeling suffocated by the long Victorian age socialism seemed full of possibility, and there was much evangelical talk of new worlds and a future which would bring justice and equality to the exploited masses. For someone like Margaret Bondfield, instinctively drawn to faith, there was no inconsistency between this vision and that of Christianity; both aimed for something perfected and beautiful, and although some socialists rejected religion, many others saw how the two faiths could sit harmoniously together. In particular, the ILP and the Fabians were attractive to people who opposed war and political violence, views which Bondfield felt were compatible with her non-conformist outlook. As she became absorbed in and into all these new ideas and organizations, she had a profound sense of having come home, of having found 'her people' and her life's work. It was a sense she never lost.

Consequently she was very unpleasantly surprised to find that her church did not take quite the same view. After she became a member of the Shop Assistants' Union's Executive Committee she had to attend its monthly meetings. These were held on Sundays, since for most shop assistants and warehousemen these were the only days they had off. The committee members:

> often had to travel long distances on night trains, arriving early on Sunday morning, sitting for the transaction of business in a stuffy room, clouded with tobacco smoke, starting back again on Sunday night to be in time for business at 7.30 am on Monday; they were the pioneers, and to me they were heroes.[16]

She was therefore astonished to be summoned by the deacon of her church and told that her Sunday absences were unacceptable and that she must choose between the church and the union. She 'had not a moment's hesitation and chose the union'. She remained deeply committed to her faith, but no longer saw it as being necessarily attached to a church organization. It would be nearly twenty years before she rejoined the King's Weigh House, and then it would be with a much looser attachment to the Congregationalist loyalties of her youth.

The swiftness with which she made the decision between two things which mattered profoundly to her was characteristic. 'In trade union and political work,' she said:

> I have been spared the pain of indecision and have hardly ever felt the impulse to turn away from larger responsibilities . . . of course this illustrates my own limitations, of which I am very conscious. The valuable qualities of curiosity, criticism and introspection are almost entirely lacking . . .[17]

Both Bondfield's diaries and her life suggest that this last statement is more than a little disingenuous, since she periodically interrogated both her actions and her faith and sometimes endured self-doubt and even, occasionally, anguished self-loathing. But she was also right that she took important decisions rapidly, and that sometimes this played to her advantage and sometimes not. In the case of the choice between the church and the union she neither looked back nor regretted it. She felt that God had shown her two roads and was with her always on the one she had taken.

Neither in her autobiography nor anywhere else does Bondfield make any reference to her personal life during this time, other than to say that she had already decided that marriage was not going to be her escape route from shop work. It is hard to believe that as a young woman she had no close personal relationships – amorous or platonic, gay or straight – but this is the impression she gives and there is nowhere (so far discovered) a shred of evidence to disprove it. Decades later she described herself as:

> undisturbed by love affairs. . . . The very surroundings of shop life accentuated the desire of most shop girls to get married . . . I had no vocation for wifehood or motherhood, but an urge to serve the Union – an urge which developed into 'a sense of oneness with our kind'. I had the 'dear love of comrades . . . '[18]

This passage is often taken as a covert way of stating a sexual preference for women, and indeed it may well have been, but it also suggests a reference to her early struggles, to her over-burdened mother and her difficult, angry father. Both things may be true. She certainly admired, and was admired in turn, by both women and men, but, so far as we can know, she remained by her own choice a free agent, deeply committed to the new world she had found.

As her circle of friends and acquaintances widened, however, she began to see the deficiencies of her education with increasing clarity. The women with whom she worked during her long days had had similar educational experiences, and most would have left school even earlier than she had. The men she met through her trade union activities had also left school very young, with many working in factories or mines from the age of nine or ten. But the women and men she met through the Fabian Society, the ILP and the Ideal Club were different. They had often had access to much better educational opportunities, and even those who had not been to university had wide cultural knowledge and moved easily in a level of society in which education was taken for granted. Bondfield's schooling had provided her with basic skills, but had not gone beyond that, nor had it taught her how to think, how to analyse and evaluate information, or how to organize her thoughts. Many working-class trade unionists and socialists were autodidacts for whom night classes and extensive independent reading had to take the place of formal education. In her Brighton days Bondfield's mentor Louisa Martindale had given her books to read, but now she was surrounded by people who seemed to know a great deal more about almost everything than she did, and she threw herself into trying to make up the ground. She attended the Ideal Club's lectures and debates and read everything she could find about her new world. At SDF meetings she heard fiery speeches about capitalism, workers' rights and revolution. The Fabian Society offered much less certainty but some of the minds involved in it made the exploration of the uncertainties interesting and occasionally illuminating. Through the ILP she met other socialists who were interested in the potential of political activism in an evolutionary and democratic system as opposed to the SDF's revolution. There were many new cultural avenues to pursue – like her father she loved poetry, but there was also music and the theatre. All of these influences, together with new ideas about religion and the almost romantic thrill of the possibilities of life, crowded in on her in a vast jumble, and every minute she could spare from union work and earning a living she spent trying to broaden her intellectual and cultural horizons.

This drive led her to her next big opportunity. The tutor at a poetry evening class she was attending introduced her to the Women's Industrial Council who were looking for someone to go undercover to investigate abuses in shop work. Bondfield seemed the ideal person to do this. She was a genuine shop assistant, she was young and had no family commitments, and she was keen, intelligent and 'exceptionally level-headed'.[19] The WIC's plan was both interesting and exciting, but it would require a major sacrifice on Bondfield's part. She would have to give up her current job and get employment in a range of different shops. At some point she would either leave or be sacked, have a short break, and then move on to the next post. Her reports would eventually be forwarded to Vaughan Nash,[20] a well-known campaigning journalist who would write them up for publication in the *Daily Chronicle* once the investigation was complete. The ultimate aim would be to prod the government into providing some protective legislation for women (and men) who at present had none. It was an ambitious scheme with serious implications for Bondfield, who would, by the end of the two years the WIC envisaged the research taking, effectively have made herself unemployable in the trade for which she had trained. It was an act of boat burning of considerable courage for a young woman with no private means or resources to fall back on, and the women of the WIC were uneasily, if unrepentantly, aware of this. As Lilian Gilchrist Thompson, a member of the WIC's committee, later observed:

> This undertaking was in the highest degree self-sacrificing. . . . She was able to start in a high-class shop (but one of the worst, as we believed) and, as her references grew shorter, she descended the scale of the shopping world. She was thus ruining her future in her own profession for the sake of the well-being and safety of girls unknown to her. We undertook some financial responsibilities, but she insisted on limiting these severely.[21]

Bondfield herself later said that she undertook the investigation 'under a substantial guarantee', which may or may not relate to her later appointment as a union official. She knew exactly the risks she was running, however, though she did not regret them reflecting that: 'I enjoyed the spice of danger; this was my way out of the trap.'[22]

For the next two years she lived an episodic life in which periods of employment were interspersed with weeks in which she wrote up her notes, planned the next stages of the campaign and pursued her own trade union activities. Each target employer was chosen carefully to enable the worst aspects of the living-in system to be examined and exposed, but sometimes they had to wait for a vacancy to occur, and at others Bondfield was not successful in getting in. Despite this, she found work in every kind of drapery shop in every part of London, much preferring the shabby stores of the East End to the shiny plate glass establishments in Mayfair and Kensington. Although the hours were just as long, in the East End shops relations between shopper and shop assistant were:

> much more human. . . . I realized the self-denial which must precede the purchase of a new article of clothing. We could help to make five shillings go as far as possible in value. We would hear all about the joys and sorrows of the family and get glimpses of brave hearts under the most sordid exterior.[23]

In the fashionable shops, however, assistants were regarded as little more than servants with whom civility was unnecessary. West End ladies could be both 'charming as only cultured people can be charming' and 'rude as only cultured people can be rude'. To illustrate the point, Bondfield cited the incident of a woman who was extremely ill-tempered over the purchase of a pair of stockings. It was against the rules for the offended assistant to answer back in such circumstances, so Bondfield just stared at her with stony resentment. The woman went to the door but then turned back and 'with disarming frankness' effectively apologized. 'My astonishment' said Bondfield 'was not at her rudeness, but at her recognition of it.'[24]

Years later P. C. Hoffman wrote in his memoirs of his days as a shop assistant that the inquiry was: 'an undercover operation of the greatest importance to the future of shop life' and paid 'a heartfelt tribute to a piece of fine public-spirited work performed by a very noble woman'.[25] He also remembered the impact Vaughan Nash's articles had when, in April 1898, they were published in the *Daily Chronicle*. They came, he said 'as a bombshell to the drapery trade'. He and his fellow shop assistants looked forward eagerly to each new instalment and then started sending in letters about their own experiences so that the later parts of Nash's exposé were based on even more information than that gathered by Bondfield. Shop assistants across the country had the same reaction, and many people began to feel uneasy about the appalling regime to which so many young people were subjected. Within the union, Bondfield's reputation soared.

A soaring reputation, however, did not pay the rent, and since she could no longer work in the drapery trade – at least not in London – Bondfield had to decide what to do next. However, early in 1898 the Shop Assistants' Union received an anonymous donation which was coincidentally large enough to enable them to employ another member of staff to work with Macpherson. There had clearly been some discussion of this before Bondfield was offered the post, but the formalities still had to be gone through and in March 1898 *The Shop Assistant* duly announced that:

> The need for additional assistance at head office, and in the work of the organization having been discussed, the executive considered an offer made to the Union by well-wishers of the cause, in connection with the proposed appointment of Miss M E *(sic)* Bondfield (Grace Dare) as assistant secretary, with a view of enlisting the sympathies and active support of women workers in shops. It was unanimously decided to accept the offer, and our contributor, 'Grace Dare,' will commence her new duties at an early date. The Union has been fortunate in securing the services of Miss Bondfield, a lady who has had an extensive experience of shop life in London; is a good writer, an effective speaker, and full of enthusiasm for the movement.[26]

Margaret Bondfield now found herself in possession of a job, a couple of rooms to call her own, and a salary which seemed like riches. She was to be paid £2 a week, from which no fines or penalties would be deducted, and which she was free to spend or save as she chose. She was financially independent and doing a job which she loved and believed to be useful. For many women of all classes this was an unreachable and unrealistic ideal, yet Bondfield had managed to achieve it all by the age of just twenty-five. A new world was opening out before her.

Chapter 4

Organize and Educate!

In 1898 the Shops Assistants' Union membership stood at about 2,000, and the head office staff servicing them consisted, once Bondfield had joined it, of three people. As Secretary James Macpherson provided direction and leadership, Bondfield worked on recruitment and organization, and an office boy struggled with the filing and ran errands. The union's tiny premises were cramped and the meeting room at the back dark and stuffy. Macpherson and most of the men who came for meetings smoked, making the air so thick and heavy that Bondfield started smoking herself (she claimed) 'in self-defence'.

Soon after her appointment she set off on a series of journeys around the country to assess the union's level of grassroots organization, sending reports back for publication in *The Shop Assistant* under the heading 'Miss Bondfield on Tour'. In these pieces she reflected not only on the places she visited but also the people she met, the meetings she addressed and the different challenges each place presented. As usual, she found travel energizing and her reports are full of a sense of movement and a genuine interest in everything she encountered as well as enjoyment of the moment.

She began in South Wales, in the Rhondda Valley, where she found 'the president *(of the local Shop Assistants' branch)*, Vice-president, treasurer and secretary on the platform to meet me and I felt in the midst of friends in about three minutes!' She was delighted to find quite a big meeting to address and declared it 'exceedingly interesting; not only because of the really charming singing but also because two or three members made their maiden speeches!'[1]

In Pontypridd she was invited to address the Trades Council, and at the shopworkers' meeting a couple of days later was delighted to find that, very unusually, there were two other women speakers on the platform with her. From the Rhondda she went on to Cardiff, where she felt:

somewhat diffident in criticising the meeting. The first thing which impressed me was the curious antipathy the audience had to the first three front rows of chairs! I felt compelled to convince them that the chairs were perfectly harmless and when I found they trusted my judgement in this small matter, I gained courage to speak to them on other matters.[2]

In Merthyr Tydfil she was able to speak to 'a comparatively large audience with a good proportion of women' but was critical of the Merthyr branch committee, to whom she suggested that 'an agenda is not a difficult thing to prepare, and it adds considerably to the order and smoothness of a meeting'.[3] She found the iron-working town of Dowlais depressing, although she was encouraged by the branch's work to recruit young shop assistants and uplifted by their meeting, which included tea, dancing and games.

Moving north to Yorkshire, she encountered a large, well-organized branch in Bradford, where her meeting had been so well advertised that, when she arrived at the hall, she 'saw for the first time, *a crowd standing patiently waiting for the door to open!!!* Then I watched, from inside, the people pouring in steadily, until the great hall was lined from ceiling to floor.'[4] Over the ensuing years her reputation as a public speaker would grow exponentially, and she would often find crowds queuing to hear her, but perhaps none ever gave her quite the excitement and pride that this Yorkshire one did. Bradford had other qualities to recommend it, too. It had just appointed a female secretary, and there was a strong and active women's group.

In Hull she found a branch and committee less well organized but full of enthusiasm. She was very pleased to find that they intended to start a training school for speakers and hoped that women as well as men would be taught to 'cultivate the art of clear and lucid speaking'.[5] The public meetings were good, and the *Hull Daily Mail* published an interview with her under the headline 'A Lady Champion for Shop Assistants . . . Miss Bondfield Interviewed.' The *Mail* reported that her appearance on the platform at the meeting at St George's Hall:

> raised applause. Shop assistants admire pluck, and Miss Bondfield has plenty of it to go 'on tour' for the purpose of organising the forces. She made many points . . . and enlarged on them with a good deal of power, making severe comments about strength of character, independence and self-reliance.

In the Midlands she found the Potteries towns initially deeply depressing, asking 'Why O why must the people live and work amidst such wretchedness and stifling ugliness? . . . Not only vegetation, but human life; men, women and little children become poisoned and disfigured by the industry of "potting".'[6] She was more encouraged, however, by the union members, and by the shops and the shopworkers, who seemed familiar and oddly reassuring. She was impressed by the fact that the local branch had a 'Literature Department' and urged them to set about training up more public speakers. She spoke at a large public gathering at Hanley, met both employers and employees, and came away 'with regret, but with the firm conviction that I shall see it again someday, and that when I see it again I shall not find shops open needlessly at 9, 10 and 11 o'clock at night, because the assistants will then be in a position to refuse to submit to such an unnecessary lengthening of their day's labour'.[7]

Her tour took her five weeks in all, and at the end of it she felt that she returned:

> full of hope for my class! With my faith in the ultimate success of our work firmly established! And strong in the knowledge that in every district I have visited there are men and women who share this hope and faith, and whose watchword is 'Organize and Educate!'[8]

As she travelled around, however, she had done more than just assess the organizational strength of the branches she visited. Intentionally or not, she had laid the foundations of relationships and support which would give her a voice of her own in the Union as well as a base independent of other senior figures. Apart from anything else, she was a novelty to many of the people she met. There were very few female trade union leaders of any kind, never mind one who was young, working class and had come up through the industry. Her WIC investigation and the press coverage of it had made her a minor celebrity in trade union circles and some people came to her meetings just to have a look at her. Given that, in 1898, the prospect of working-class women voting or entering Parliament was still decades away it is unlikely that she harboured political ambitions at this stage, but the experience of building a base that had depth as well as breadth would not be wasted and would stand her in good stead in the future.

Touring the country meeting existing members was an exhilarating process, recruiting new ones much less so. She was expected to expand both the union's income and its influence by increasing the membership, a task which involved constant planning, risk and guile. She could not simply march into shops, distribute leaflets and invite the workers to join. Reflecting on the challenges she said that:

> I had to conquer my dislike of canvassing in shops for new members. I would perhaps have the names and shop address of a small group of potential members; calling during business hours was risky, as it might mean the sack for the assistant, so I tried to avoid the shopwalker, or anyone who looked managerial, until I had made contact. Perhaps an interview might be fixed up after the shop was closed, in a café, or even on the pavement, and then details would be settled about a place of meeting, the printing of bills, . . . I would go to a printer, wait for the leaflets, and then start the weary job of distributing them round the shop counters until I was ordered out.[9]

It was often unrewarding work, and there were days when nobody at all turned up to the meetings she called. When this happened in Brixton a well-known socialist and suffragist called Charlotte Despard[10] took pity on her, giving her tea, biscuits and sympathy. 'I loved her' said Bondfield, 'and cherished her friendship, unbroken till her death. I loved the way she dressed – her black lace scarf instead of a hat, and her tall, straight figure; when down at her cottage at Oxshott . . . weeding her garden at sunrise, she seemed to me a saint at prayer.'[11] Other encounters were less rewarding; one shop owner took one of her leaflets, tore it up and stamped on it and told her to go home and mend her stockings. She was outraged. '*My* stockings were always mended!'[12]

Despite the variable response, it was not long before her work began to show results. By 1900 the Union's membership had almost quadrupled and by 1908 it exceeded 20,000.[13] Gradually women members began to outnumber men, and the union increased its organizational capacity to look after them. More members meant more work, and at some point around the turn of the century, when the union's office moved to larger rooms at Gower Street in Bloomsbury, Macpherson and his family moved in also to live on the first floor. One of the attics was let to a Danish journalist and the other to Margaret Bondfield. From now on, whenever possible, she would live in close proximity to her work, and since over the next forty years her work would move and change so would she. Her home life would be peripatetic, passing from one part of London to another, never quite settling anywhere until after she retired. For many years she lived in bed-sitting rooms in shared houses, later graduating to rented flats. For long periods when on her various travels she lived in hotels and friends' houses, always packing up again and moving on. Like thousands of other single women of the period she understood all too well how the London housing market worked, and how little single women were assumed to need.

The third element of her union duties involved representing the Shop Assistants' Union at various inquiries, committees and national events. This was also valuable experience, enabling her to practise assembling, analysing and using information to support her case. The Union put her onto the Executive of the WTUL, where she met Emilia Dilke and Dilke's niece, Gertrude Tuckwell.[14] Lady Dilke was a strong believer in the power of working-class women to speak for themselves, an approach which chimed well with Bondfield and she grew to like and admire both women. Dilke's husband, Sir Charles, was a Liberal MP who tried to get legislation on both suffrage and industrial issues passed, and often spoke for women in a space which they could not access themselves.

Despite her busy new life, Bondfield also kept up with her political interests. The Ideal Club continued to provide her with both a social life and intellectual stimulation, and she was active in the ILP and, to a much lesser extent, the Fabian Society. Her friends were now drawn from the mix of people who inhabited left-wing Liberal, socialist or progressive organizations at the turn of the twentieth century and included working-class trade unionists, feminists and suffrage campaigners, middle-class researchers and thinkers and an assortment of journalists, teachers, organizers, campaigners and activists. Her next adventure, however, would propel her to much wider public notice and make her a minor national figure.

In September 1899 she was sent to the TUC Congress in Plymouth as the Shop Assistants' Union's sole delegate. There had never been very many women delegates at the TUC; in 1888 there had been just three, and little more than a decade later it was down to one, so that Bondfield found herself sitting alone, a female island in a sea of men. Accustomed as she was to being the only woman in the room on many occasions, she must have felt a little apprehensive. There were, it was true, women in the public gallery, including Lady Dilke, who every year held a lavish reception to lobby delegates about issues of concern to the WTUL. But only Bondfield was on the floor of Congress with a vote and, more to the point for her future career, a voice.

She arrived briefed to speak on a number of issues, including her own union's resolution on Sunday trading, but on the third day, before she had had the chance to say anything, she was asked to move the vote of thanks to the international speakers. One of these, an American, had said how odd it was that there were not more female delegates, and another had spoken about arrangements in Denmark, where there was only one union covering all trades. In no way intimidated by her audience, Bondfield got to her feet and, picking up on the American delegate's remarks, observed that she was: 'was amazed to find herself the only female delegate in attendance when there were so many toilers of her own sex. She hoped that such a thing would not happen at any future Congress.'

She further hoped that 'the delegates would go away with the feeling that they had done some practical work *(and)* had taken a step towards the realisation of their ideals' before concluding that Congress might do well to 'show that they were not above learning from even a little nation like Denmark by dropping pettifogging differences and grasping the real principles of trade unionism'. She sat down to 'loud applause' and the verbatim record of Congress, which never normally commented on the quality of speeches, noted that 'Miss Bondfield . . . surprised and delighted Congress with her stirring speech.'[15]

Later in the week she spoke in support of the resolution to set up the LRC, the body which, in 1906, would become the Labour Party, but it was the vote of thanks which brought her to the notice of trade unionists outside her own union. It even attracted national newspaper coverage, with the *Morning Leader* reporting 'Miss Bondfield's earnest, simple, and heartfelt home-thrusts', and describing her speech as:

> the feature of the day and the discovery of the day. Miss Bondfield is the only lady delegate. She is only a girl in years, and as she stood up among the

bronzed, hard-handed workmen her slight girlish figure, clad in a simple light grey frock, made her look even younger and more girlish than she is. But her voice, as clear as it was unostentatious, was heard distinctly in every part of the hall, and while she said what clearly she thought and felt, there was no trace either of nervousness or conceit. It was a striking picture this slip of a girl standing out and lecturing 300 or more men. . . . Congress listened listlessly at first, but soon discovered that the only lady delegate was a speaker of unexpected power and courage, and every head turned round towards the little grey figure and pale, smiling face at the bottom of the hall, and every voice and hand applauded her when she finished.[16]

This passage is worth quoting at length because this speech was the start of her reputation as a significant public speaker whose voice – at that time without artificial amplification – could fill the largest of halls and move both hearts and minds. Her rich contralto singing voice translated into an equally rich instrument for speech; one which, over time, she learned to use to great effect. She herself was never quite sure where this remarkable facility had come from. Like many Victorian children, she had sung and recited at Sunday School teas and Christmas parties, but the full possibilities of her voice had only developed once she became a trade unionist. 'I am often asked' she said:

how I learnt the art of public speaking. I didn't. I discovered it at a great meeting held at the Mile End People's Palace . . .. without warning, the chairman called upon me to move the vote of thanks . . . Afterwards I was told that I at once responded with a speech which brought down the house, but it was an automatic response, for I was literally stunned with stage fright. I hadn't the faintest recollection afterwards of what I had said.[17]

After that revelation she had started to train both her voice and her speaking skills so that by the time she arrived at Plymouth she understood her abilities better than most. She never lacked courage, and despite the challenges probably intended to use the occasion to make an impression as well as to speak for women in a space in which no woman's voice would otherwise be heard. But even she could not have anticipated the stir her impromptu speech caused, nor the long-term influence it would have on her career.

The TUC's resolution to found the LRC was followed up in February 1900 by a meeting in London which did just that. Bondfield was not present at it, but the Shop Assistants were one of the first unions to affiliate. Eight months later the country was plunged into a general election and although the LRC was not very well prepared it managed to stand 15 candidates including Keir Hardie who, together with the rail workers' leader Richard Bell, was elected. The election was dominated by the issue of the South African War (also known as the Boer War) which had broken out that year and anti-war candidates were not popular at a time of fervent patriotism. All of Margaret Bondfield's instincts – both political and religious – were against war in principle, and certainly she could not see how a conflict which served nothing but the imperialist interests of a rapacious capitalist government could or should be supported. She very much agreed with Ramsay MacDonald's assessment that 'Further extensions of Empire are only the grabbings of millionaires on the hunt.'[18] But in this she differed from many of her fellow trade unionists in industry, who were not only jingoistic, but also saw that their members would benefit from the increased work that war would bring.

One of the reasons for the Shop Assistants' Union's keenness to support the LRC was the belief that the only way of getting protection for its members was through changes in the law. They knew that, given the huge number of workplaces and the considerable difficulty both of organizing them and negotiating with a multiplicity of employers, it would be next to impossible to improve shopworkers' lot overall without legislation. Because shopworkers were regarded as a form of domestic staff they were usually specifically excluded from industrial legislation, and even where there were legal requirements the mechanisms for enforcing them were missing. One of the most notorious examples of this was the provision of chairs. Until the end of the nineteenth century most shop staff had to stand for the whole of their ten- or twelve-hour shifts. In 1899 shops were required by law to provide one chair for every three workers. But the Act did not specify that the workers should be able to use them, so that the presence of chairs (often actually sat on by customers) did very little to help. Similar problems had been encountered with the 1892 Act which theoretically restricted the working week to seventy-four hours, but for which there was no enforcement mechanism.

Experience of the various Truck Acts passed during the nineteenth century had demonstrated the success that a good parliamentary lobbying operation could achieve. The Truck Acts were designed principally to outlaw the truck system, which allowed employers to pay in kind rather than cash, a practice which, when expressed as tokens which could only be spent at the company's store, led to all kinds of problems, including unpayable debts and workers being unable to leave their jobs. The 1887 Truck Act had extended the protection to all manual workers, amongst whom shopworkers were included in terms of their wages, but not their board and lodging. In any case, shop owners could still circumvent the requirements without fear of prosecution, as Bondfield and many thousands of other shop assistants could testify. In 1896 the Union had managed to get some restrictions on the fines that employers were able to impose, though when Bondfield was carrying out her undercover work in that and the following year there was relatively little evidence of the new rules being implemented. The exclusion of board and lodging costs from the Truck Acts meant that employees were not entitled to demand cash wages instead of bad food and a bed in a dingy dormitory, and it was therefore extremely difficult to negotiate fair – and universally applied – wages or remuneration scales for shop work. Ultimately the Union thought living in should be abolished altogether, but as a staging post it wanted it covered by the Truck Acts, which would at least mean that there was a chance of regulating some of the worst abuses.

The Union also wanted to see the very long hours in the industry reduced and protected by law. Unfortunately, with the exception of a handful of men like Sir Charles Dilke there were very few MPs who had any real understanding of what shop work was like or the inclination to listen seriously to what working men and women had to say about their lives. Thus the Union had to keep up a steady stream of information, evidence to committees and inquiries and general lobbying and campaigning to keep their members' plight in the minds of legislators.

Between organizing, recruiting and campaigning Bondfield was kept very busy during these years, with hardly any time off and not much in the way of holidays. But she loved the job, regarding it as a vocation, and the knowledge that, despite the difficulties, people's lives would be better because of her work motivated her to still greater efforts. After the Plymouth TUC speech her stock in the wider movement rose, and by her late twenties she had become a senior and respected figure. Her speaking appearances were much anticipated, and she was sometimes treated almost like a visiting celebrity. Thus, when she arrived at Newcastle upon Tyne for the Union's conference in March 1902 she was met at the station by a new recruit whose job was to help with her bags and take her to her hotel. The twenty-one-year-old Mary Macarthur had already made a name for herself in Scotland, and was now about to burst onto the scene in England. Immediately and deeply attracted, Bondfield saw:

> a thin, white face and glowing eyes, and then I was enveloped by her ardent, young, hero-worshipping personality. She was gloriously young and self-confident. It was a dazzling experience for a humdrum official to find herself treated with the reverence due to an oracle by one whose brilliant gifts and vital energy were even then manifest.[19]

This sense of awe never left her. 'I was overcome', she later recalled: 'with the sense of a great event. Here was genius, allied to boundless enthusiasm and leadership of a high order, coming to build our little Union into a more effective instrument.'[20] In later years their roles would be reversed and Bondfield would work both with and for Macarthur, often finding herself left 'staggering along, gasping in the effort to keep in sight' in the wake of Macarthur's 'intuitive flights' and 'sudden dives' into 'the uncharted waters of life'.[21]

Macarthur was the daughter of a prosperous Ayr shopkeeper and had discovered trade unionism almost by accident. The conference at Newcastle was her first national event, and she made a considerable impression. For Bondfield, however, the impact was irresistible. At the end of the conference she cancelled all her engagements for the next week and travelled back to Scotland with her new friend. Here she stayed with Macarthur's parents for several days; what they thought of this sudden and unknown arrival can only be imagined. Nevertheless they seem to have welcomed her, and she and Macarthur laid the foundations of a relationship which would last until Mary's untimely death two decades later. At the end of the visit her host drove Bondfield to the station in his car, her first experience of a motor vehicle and one which she pronounced 'most exciting'.

For the time being Macarthur remained in Scotland, while Bondfield returned to London and her usual round of meetings, visits and recruitment projects. They met again in 1903 at the Shopworkers' Union conference in Manchester, and by June Macarthur had moved to London and was living with Bondfield in the little attic flat on Gower Street. When the Secretary of the WTUL, Mona Wilson, resigned her post, Dilke and Gertude Tuckwell, who had known that this was coming, had already been looking for a suitable replacement, and Dilke had even offered the job to Bondfield. Bondfield wanted to stay with the union, but recommended Mary Macarthur. When Dilke and Tuckwell interviewed her they encountered a young woman who was 'very silent but intensely attractive, with that air of subdued excitement which made one feel the air alive all round her and herself mentally holding out both hands to adventure, adventure which always came'.[22]

Emilia Dilke 'recognised her as Margaret Bondfield had done. This girl might make difficulties; in fact she did; but she would assuredly also make things hum; in fact she did.'[23] They appointed her immediately, and Macarthur continued to lodge with Bondfield for the next three years. Writing twenty years later Mary Agnes Hamilton said that Bondfield's 'association' with Mary Macarthur was 'the real romance of her life – and a very real romance'[24] but fails to define what, to her, the word 'romance' meant or included. Certainly, Edwardian women could – and did – engage in relationships which were intensely romantic without being sexual, and single women often lived together for all kinds of reasons. But equally certainly these relationships were often physical, too. It is now impossible to know what passed between Bondfield and Macarthur, but all the appearances are that Bondfield loved Macarthur profoundly but came to understand, as future events will show, that the core of her emotional life would lie elsewhere.

For the next few years these two women worked, together and separately, in the labour and trade union movement. Although they both worked with women and in organizations set up for them, neither saw women's separate organization as an end in itself or perceived the separation between the sexes as anything other than an interim measure. They had an acute sense of where power lay and knew that it was not with struggling women's groups on the margins of great movements. Unlike many of their contemporaries they knew from experience that simply allowing women into the room would not be sufficient to persuade men to share their privilege. If, in believing that once men saw the value of women's participation they would welcome them, they now seem naïve that is hardly surprising, Both wings of the female suffrage movement took the same view and thought that once women had the vote they would enter Parliament immediately in numbers. It was only as post-war realities began to bite that women's faith in their ability to change the system simply by being present wavered.

In 1903 the Shop Assistants' Union found itself faced with Lord Avebury's Early Closing Bill, a measure intended to help shopworkers but which many shop assistants themselves felt would only make matters worse. Lord Avebury had taken up the cause of shopworkers both in the House of Commons as an MP and in the House of Lords once he had been ennobled. In many ways his support was extremely helpful, but on the matter of early closing the Union thought he was fundamentally wrong. He believed that if shops were closed workers would not be working, and therefore focused on reducing trading hours and, in particular, introducing half-day (or early) closing on one day a week. The unions knew that this would not do anything to solve the problem, and that tasks such as stocktaking, cleaning and window dressing could and would be carried on whether the shops were open or not. Accordingly, they found themselves in the counter-intuitive position of resisting Avebury's Bill.

In June 1903 a mass meeting was held to protest. Although there were women on the platform, including Gertrude Tuckwell and Mona Wilson, Margaret Bondfield was the only woman advertised as speaking. Moreover, although James Macpherson, as the Union Secretary, was also on the platform he did not speak, and it was Bondfield who moved the resolution opposing the Bill. Both sides of the argument were represented on the platform, and she spoke with Lord Avebury himself sitting beside her, looking, according to Mary Macarthur's report in *The Shop Assistant*, 'visibly dejected'. Macarthur's account is obviously partisan, and her admiration for Bondfield clear, but even so her description of Bondfield's speech has resonance. Describing her, as so many others did, as 'a slim, girlish figure in white' – Bondfield was now thirty – she said that:

> With characteristic deftness of style Miss Bondfield moved the resolution. She seemed to take Avebury's Bill into both her hands and regard it in puzzled wonder. Calmly, she held it at arm's length for the inspection of the audience; deliberately she pulled it to pieces; deftly she tore each piece to shreds. One could almost hear it cracking! . . . Miss Bondfield concluded her speech with a really magnificent peroration, and . . . defiantly declared that, if . . . the Legislature would not offer anything better than Avebury's Bill, we would secure shorter hours without their aid. As the Assistant Secretary resumed her seat the tumult was deafening.[25]

The resolution was overwhelmingly passed by the 5,000 shopworkers attending, but the Union's opposition made no difference. The Early Closing Bill passed into law in 1904 and remained on the Statute Books until repealed in 1994. As the Union had predicted, it did not shorten working hours, and the fight for protection for retail staff has continued to this present day.

Chapter 5
Not Sex, But Class

When Margaret Bondfield addressed the Early Closing Bill demonstration her mother and her sister Hattie were listed in the press as forming part of the platform party supporting her. This suggests that her instinctively radical family were proud of her, but it also reflects a level of closeness to them which, apart from in the case of her brother Frank, she never really acknowledged, preferring to infer that she was relatively isolated from them. This was, at best, misleading, and in fact, as her diaries show, she saw both Hattie and Annie regularly over the years, eventually providing Annie with a home in her later years.

By 1903, however, the family was beginning to thin out. The first loss, in March 1901, was Bondfield's father, William. He had been suffering from dementia for several years, and she described his death as 'a happy release'.[1] Her relationship with him had never been easy, and she found it impossible to remember him with much affection. Her long absences from home as a child had made him a stranger, and by the time she returned he was ravaged by worry and rage. She knew that he had not always been as he had become, but also that the chasm could never be mended, later reflecting that she wished she could have 'known my father when he was in his prime. The older ones said he was a good companion, but by the time I was old enough to talk to him he had become very remote and he was haunted with the fear of the workhouse'.[2]

At the age of 70 Ann Bondfield was now alone for the first time in her life. At some point she had sold the cottage in Furnham and gone to live in Chard, where her daughter Annie and Aunt Taylor joined her. After William's death Frank Bondfield also moved back, setting up as a jobbing printer and remaining in the town for many years. In time he became a (Liberal) councillor and eventually, after marrying his second wife, moved to Bournemouth in the 1930s.

At the time of her father's death Bondfield's youngest sister, Katie, was working as a teacher in Dinan in France, where it was hoped that the milder climate would improve her health. In 1897 she had been diagnosed with tuberculosis, and despite the disease's very low survival rate Bondfield was determined to save her.

She took her to see Dr Jane Walker,[3] a pioneering physician who had introduced the new 'open air' treatment being developed in Germany. Walker recommended that Katie go to the sanatorium at Nordrach in the Black Forest, but this would be expensive and Bondfield had no money with which to pay for it. For perhaps the only time in her life she turned to her wealthy connections for help and 'in a demanding mood' asked Lilian Gilchrist Thompson of the WIC to cover the initial costs. Thompson immediately gave her the necessary funds and helped her to make the arrangements. Once there, Katie's condition improved considerably, and there seemed to be a real prospect of a cure. But back in London she grew worse again very quickly and spent time in sanatoriums in France and England, including at Dr Walker's own establishment at Nayland in Suffolk. All this continued to be paid for by Bondfield's friends and Katie's family, with Bondfield herself running up huge debts. Eventually Katie again made a recovery and moved to what was thought to be the cleaner air of southern France. Unfortunately, as so often with consumption, temporary progress had been mistaken for a cure. Katie grew rapidly worse but was desperate to earn enough to cover at least some of Margaret's debts and so did not tell her how bad things had become. At the end of the school term she finally did so and came home to die in August. She was aged just 24.

   Bondfield was devastated. Having done everything possible to save her sister she had still failed, and her grief was mixed with anger and guilt that she had not been able to protect her. Other members of the family had contributed to the costs of Katie's care, but Bondfield spoke and behaved as though Katie had been primarily her responsibility. This was the baby at whose birth she had been banished to Middle Lambrook all those years ago, yet she seems to have felt very little resentment towards her and her death clearly cut deep. 'You poor dear girl,' wrote Lilian Gilchrist Thompson in a letter of condolence:

> The meaning must be sought for in this life being only a part of a greater, bigger life, and each of us as only passing from one stage to another; otherwise there is no understanding. Looked at so everything gathers shape and meaning, and we are not just dropped into the world anyhow . . . It is impossible to think of her bright loving self as anything but alive and working, looking for good and loving.[4]

With Katie's loss Margaret Bondfield lost the immediate presence of all the siblings to whom she had been closest. Of her end of the family Katie was dead, Frank had returned home, and Ernest was soldiering in South Africa. 'I was,' she recorded: 'bereft indeed of all close family associations. I did not regard the older members of the family as "belonging" in the same sense as I regarded Katie, Frank and Ernest. From this time on I just lived for the Trade Union Movement. I concentrated on my job.'[5]

Once again, however, this was interrupted by a family loss. Having survived the Boer War, Ernest had stayed on in Cape Town, but he succumbed to rheumatic fever and died at the age of 35 many miles from home, not having seen his family for at least five years. Bondfield did not grieve for him as she had for Katie, but his death was still a blow. However, although she portrayed herself as being alone in London she was by no means as isolated from her family as she sometimes tried to suggest. Her older sister, Hattie, was now living with her husband and children in Woodford, near London. Mrs Bondfield seems to have moved for some years between living with Frank in Chard and Hattie in London, and in her later years may have lived for a time with Margaret. The fourth oldest brother, Herbert, was an officer in the Salvation Army and some years after Ernest's death moved to Walthamstow to become a restauranteur. Allen, the fifth brother was a journalist working for the *Financial Times*. Consequently there were always family members nearby if she needed them, and the evidence of Bondfield's appointments diaries and later letters suggests that she and Hattie, at least, remained close and saw one another often.

In 1906 Bondfield got her first taste of what electoral success was like. A change of Prime Minister from the Conservative Arthur Balfour to the Liberal Henry Campbell-Bannerman resulted in a snap election early in the year. James Macpherson stood as a candidate for the LRC in Gravesend, and Bondfield worked hard to support him. Her Shop Assistants' Union colleague, P. C. Hoffman, noted that she had a 'winsome manner' and that 'the local Labour men swear by her'.[6] Although Macpherson did not win, the election resulted in a breakthrough for the LRC, which won 29 seats, propelling both Ramsay MacDonald and the future Chancellor, Philip Snowden, into Parliament for the first time. Immediately, the LRC changed its name to the Labour Party, elected Keir Hardie as Chairman of the Parliamentary Labour Party (and thus its first *de facto* leader), and settled down to exploring ways of being both a disruptor and a possible future government. The Conservatives, who had won a landslide in 1900, now found themselves on the wrong end of one, losing more than half their seats to the tidal wave of Liberals, who, for the last time in their history, gained a significant majority in the House. The Labour breakthrough was regarded as shocking in some quarters, with a few perspicacious commentators ruminating that the new socialist party might, despite the landslide, spell the beginning of the end for the Liberals. This was certainly the view of MacDonald and Hardie, both of whom had grasped very early on that the route to government lay through the heart of the Liberal Party, and were now able to score a significant victory in the form of the Trades Disputes Act which amply demonstrated what could be achieved, even without governmental office.

This Act provided the solution for a problem which had been plaguing the trade unions since the start of the century. A localized rail strike in Taff Vale in South Wales had blown up into a major funding crisis for the whole movement, bringing challenges to even the smallest unions. In 1900 questions about the status of trade unions had resulted in the courts deciding that unions were, in legal terms, incorporated bodies and could therefore be sued by employers whose businesses were affected by industrial action. Since the state provided no sickness or unemployment benefits, most unions ran benefit funds themselves, and indeed membership of such funds was one of the main reasons for joining a union in the first place. However, very few unions held their benefit funds separately from their general accounts, and as a result both now became vulnerable to employers. Unions tried to get the courts to recognize the difference, but in July 1901 the House of Lords, then the highest court in the land, ruled that both funds could be taken into account for damages, and that a trade union's status as a corporate body made it 'suable in a Court of Law for injuries purposely done by its authority and procurement'.[7]

Having won this point, the Taff Vale Railway Company pressed home its advantage, sued the rail union and its leaders, and won. The damages awarded were enormous. Attempts to get the law changed failed and fuelled increasing affiliations to the LRC, particularly after the Conservative Prime Minister, Arthur Balfour, indicated very clearly in the House that the government had no intention of legislating on the subject. After the 1906 election, however, Labour found itself in the position of being able to exploit a division of opinion between the new Prime Minister, Henry Campbell-Bannerman, who inclined towards the union view of the matter, and the Home Secretary, Herbert Asquith, who did not. By dint of some clever political manoeuvring Labour was able to get its Trades Disputes Act through the middle, thus affirming in law the right to strike without being sued.

In the spring of that year Margaret Bondfield spent a holiday weekend at Charlotte Despard's cottage in Surrey. There she met someone who would play a significant role in the rest of her life. Marian Maud Adelaide Ward, known as Maud Ward, but during the early years of their relationship usually referred to by Bondfield simply as Ward, was just five days younger than Bondfield, having been born in Rowley Regis in Staffordshire in March 1873. Her father was the local vicar, and she was an unexpected child, born twelve years after the last of her four brothers and one sister. When she was twelve her father died, and her mother moved the family to Crosby in Lancashire. Her older sister, Agnes, was a painter and sculptor, but Maud had few artistic skills and spent most of her time helping her mother and trying to think of ways to get away. This she eventually achieved by going to London to take a two-year course at the National Training School of Cookery, subsequently developing a list of private clients including, perhaps rather incongruously, the SDF. They held a Wednesday lunch event with guest speakers and were prepared to pay well for a good meal. Already interested in both suffrage and socialism, Ward joined the SDF as well as the ILP. Through these she met Charlotte Despard, and through Charlotte Despard she met Margaret Bondfield.

Despite the fact that a handful of her later letters have been preserved, Maud Ward is an elusive figure. There are no known photographs of her, nor do physical descriptions of her survive in letters or other accounts. She was clearly a great influence on Bondfield's life, but Bondfield is guarded in her account of her in *A Life's Work*, and Ward herself left no known memoirs or papers. Nevertheless, despite the generally held idea that Mary Macarthur was the 'romance' of Bondfield's life, it is clear that the relationship with Ward was the most important in personal terms, and that, as Bondfield herself said, its influence ran through many later events.

Bondfield and Ward seem to have been immediately taken with one another and decided to go on holiday together. In mid-May they took the train to Cornwall and embarked on a tour of the West Country. Bondfield's account of this describes an idyllic time spent walking through spectacular countryside, lazing on beautiful beaches (although, even then, Bondfield spent some of the time writing minutes and correcting proofs) and riding to Porlock on the box seat of a horse-drawn mail coach. They climbed up and down precipitous cliffs, picnicked on narrow ledges and, on one memorable occasion, deliberately got cut off by the tide just to see what it was like. They walked miles every day over every kind of terrain, enjoying stormy weather as much as the hot sunshine. Bondfield, who had never really had the time for proper holidays before, was converted. 'This holiday . . . was a preparation for longer and more exciting walking holidays later on. I certainly learned at that stage that holidays formed an important factor in the art of living.'[8]

When they returned to London they continued to spend a considerable amount of time in one another's company, sharing a life of activism and public speaking for their various causes. They appeared on platforms together, sharing Ward's 'neat and exact' notes but basing quite different speeches on them. By 1908 they had moved into rooms in Ampthill Square in Camden, and although eventually they separated they remained close for the rest of Bondfield's life. 'Our friendship,' she wrote in 1947 'has lasted till this day – our partnership lasted many years.'[9]

The life Bondfield and Ward led brought them together in many organizations, one of which was the Adult Suffrage Society (ASS), a body which Margaret Bondfield had been instrumental in founding in 1906. For them, as for many other socialists and trade unionists, the most important dividing line in society was not sex but class, and they did not believe that the middle- and upper-class women who would be enfranchised if the mainstream female suffrage demand – the vote as it is, or may be, given to men – was met would do anything for working-class people afterwards. About 40 per cent of men could not vote before 1918, and there was some nervousness amongst middle-class people about what these (mostly working-class) men would do if they had equal rights with their employers and social 'betters'. Even people who were otherwise progressive baulked at the idea of universal suffrage, and on the Left there was a split between people who believed that limited female suffrage was the battering ram which would open up the rest of the system, and others who thought that the demand should be universal suffrage or nothing. Neither the ASS or its successor, the People's Suffrage Federation (PSF), ever had a mass membership, nor was it very successful in getting its case heard above the noise created by both the militant and the law-abiding female suffrage campaigns, but Bondfield, in particular, was profoundly committed to the enfranchisement, not just of some women, but of all adult women whatever their job, status or education.

This difference of approach partly explains why, even at this early stage, relations between Labour and trade union women such as Bondfield, Macarthur and Ward and the wider feminist movement were weak. Despite individuals often being friendly on a personal level, the different parts of the suffrage movement could be very hostile to one another, with one of the principal charges against the universal suffragists being that they were anti-women's rights or worse, mouthpieces of the patriarchy. But in fact Bondfield believed absolutely in the equality of women and men, and that women should have the same choices in life that men had. As early as 1898 she had laid this out in a Grace Dare article for *The Shop Assistant*. 'Am I,' she asked, rhetorically:

> doing the work I can do best? Or am I doing badly what some other would do well? Am I compelled by force of circumstances to do work for which I am unfitted? Is it force of circumstances or merely prejudice and conventionality which compels me to do the work I hate? These and similar questions are agitating the women of the world today. . . . But let us always remember that we cannot answer these questions for other women, but only for ourselves individually. Many married women find their highest happiness in waiting on their husbands . . . if she does her work well she is helping to build the nation. Other women have no aptitude for household work . . . they would sooner tackle a German grammar than a cookery-book recipe. These women are also helping to build up a nation. The injustice lies in the fact that the woman of the latter type is too frequently condemned to a domestic life through the economic pressure of our times . . .[10]

She concluded that the ideal couple would both be employed and would share domestic tasks equally, a vision which has still not been achieved.[11] In 1898 it was one which stirred up outrage, causing 'a storm of protests in the correspondence columns of *The Shop Assistant*'.[12] But Bondfield knew even then that anything less than equality could only be at the expense of her own class, and throughout her life her analysis of 'class before sex' persisted, though later in life it hardened into a rather unsympathetic inability to see that women were not able to compete on equal terms and needed specific provision. 'The question of the vote is a political question,' she said in a speech in 1907, 'and the real antagonisms are not those of sex but of class.'[13] Mary Agnes Hamilton suggested in 1924 that her 'emphasis on class was to disappear altogether later',[14] but there is no real evidence for this and it sounds more as though Hamilton was attempting to soften her friend's edges rather than reflect her enduring opinion.

One of the parliamentarians supporting universal suffrage, Sir Charles Dilke, himself spoke for many progressives when he observed that:

> The limited franchise, if it is ever carried, will be carried as a party Conservative measure intended to aid Conservative opinions and to rest the franchise upon an unassailable limited base, and it will be carried in that case against the counter-proposal of the suffrage of all grown men and women, made by those representing the advanced thought of the country.[15]

The Labour Party (or the LRC as it had been) had hitherto maintained a universalist approach, though this differed from the view of the ILP which supported the limited female suffrage case, though having done that they did very little to progress it. The first woman to speak at the LRC's Annual Conference was the redoubtable Isabella Ford,[16] who, as an ILP delegate, unsuccessfully raised the issue of female suffrage in 1904, and the question returned at regular intervals thereafter. Most trade unions, however, saw it very clearly as a class issue and were not prepared to support changes to the franchise that would continue to exclude the bulk of their members, and the impasse continued for years.

In 1906 Margaret Bondfield became the Chairman of the ASS, and in March, in the wake of the Liberal landslide, Sir Charles Dilke introduced a Franchise and Removal of Women's Disabilities Bill to the House of Commons. His proposal of a universal franchise measure was a regular event, and he was not deterred by the fact that it was always defeated. The first clause of the 1906 Bill read 'Every man and every woman of full age, whether married or single, shall be qualified to vote at Parliamentary or local elections who resides in the area for which the election is held and is duly registered . . . ', thus effectively removing all qualifications except age and residence. The female suffrage organizations invariably opposed Dilke's bills and were deeply suspicious of the 'adultist' argument, believing that persisting with it would delay the enfranchisement of any women at all, and that some women would always be better than none. They feared that the argument for universal suffrage was in fact an argument for manhood suffrage, which would be used by men to continue the oppression of women. Many middle- and upper-class women thought that the principle of equal criteria for the vote, which would involve acceptance of existing property qualifications, outweighed the need to widen the franchise so as to include the unpropertied working class. But they also maintained that, once enfranchised and elected, middle- and upper-class women would be able to look after the interests of their working-class sisters, and that they should be trusted to do so. For Bondfield, whose years behind the counter had taught her exactly how contemptuous of working-class women some middle-class women could be, this argument seemed nonsensical. Working women wanted higher wages and safer and more secure working conditions, and it was by no means clear that partial enfranchisement would in any way achieve this. Moreover, she was always resistant to the idea that working-class women could not speak for themselves and needed middle-class women to 'be their voice' and decide their best interests for them. All her life she worked with middle-class women, regarded many highly, and loved a few, but she was also insistent on working-class women's right to be heard as and for themselves.

The ILP's dilatoriness over the suffrage question had led Emmeline and Christabel Pankhurst, in 1903, to found the Women's Social and Political Union (WSPU) as a campaigning group for ILP women. By 1907 Christabel and her friend, Annie Kenny, had begun to use militant tactics, and both she and Emmeline resigned from the ILP. They then unilaterally abolished the WSPU's democratic structures and took control of it themselves, effectively setting up a command structure with themselves at the top. Given the guerilla campaign they intended to wage there was some logic in this, but for a number of Labour women it was a step too far and, led by Charlotte Despard and Teresa Billington-Greig, they left and formed the Women's Freedom League (WFL). They remained militant, but they renounced the violence which was increasingly becoming a feature of WSPU tactics.

One of the more popular ways in which differences of opinion on matters of public interest could be aired was through public debates, and these were not at all restricted to Parliament or the public schools and universities. Women and men of all classes debated the questions of the day – social, economic, political and religious – at large meetings which, at the end, voted on resolutions put to them. As with the debate on the Early Closing Bill in 1903, these events allowed protagonists to air their cases directly to the public rather than through the press and enabled audiences to expand their knowledge and understanding of the issues involved. Speakers were expected to turn in an entertaining, informative and (sometimes) impassioned performance, and debates were often headlined by well-known orators. In 1904 Isabella Ford (for the National Union of Women's Suffrage Societies (NUWSS)) and Margaret Bondfield had debated the suffrage question at a meeting organized by the Fulham ILP branch. They had originally wanted Sylvia Pankhurst[17] to argue in favour of the limited franchise, but she, then very young and describing herself as 'too modest to attempt to hold up our cause against so practised a speaker', had withdrawn in favour of the more experienced Ford. The debate was lively, and both sides claimed victory. Nearly thirty years later Pankhurst wrote in her memoir that:

Miss Bondfield appeared in pink, dark and dark-eyed, with a deep, throaty voice many found beautiful. She was very charming and vivacious, and eager to score all the points that her youth and prettiness would win for her against the plain, middle-aged woman, with red face and turban hat crushed down upon her straight hair.[18]

If the physical description of Bondfield is probably reasonably accurate, the use Pankhurst alleged her to have made of it seems somewhat improbable. Sylvia Pankhurst was always hostile to Bondfield, also suggesting that she 'deprecated votes for women as the hobby of disappointed old maids whom no one had wanted to marry', which again seems a very unlikely thing for Bondfield to have said if only because, at the age (in 1904) of 31 most people would then have regarded her as falling into the old maid category herself. But it also seems uncharacteristically spiteful; Bondfield knew and respected Isabella Ford, agreed with her on many issues, and was in any case not in the habit of using personal insults against people with whom she differed.

Despite the fact that it advocated votes for working-class men as well as women, the ASS attracted opposition from some high-profile Labour figures. Keir Hardie, in particular, was deeply unsympathetic, writing that 'It holds no meetings, issues no literature, carries on no agitation on behalf of Adult Suffrage. It is never heard of, save when it emerges to oppose the Women's Enfranchisement Bill.'[19] In fact, the ASS was as active as its limited funds and resources allowed it to be, and in Charles Dilke had an advocate in Parliament prepared to argue the case for universal suffrage as he did for shopworkers and others. His 1906 Bill went even further than votes for all adults and proposed that everyone, regardless of sex or marriage, should be able to stand for all levels of public office, including Parliament. This idea encountered much opposition, but Bondfield was entirely supportive of it. 'Having,' she said in an interview:

addressed a very large number of meetings all over the country on this subject during the last twelve months, I have come to the conclusion that the workers are tired of the existing electoral anomalies, and ready for a simple but comprehensive measure of adult suffrage for men and women.[20]

The Bill failed to get through, as all suffrage Bills did for one reason or another. The following year, in December 1907, the WFL and the ASS held a debate billed rather provocatively by the WFL as 'Sex Equality versus Adult Suffrage'. Teresa Billington-Greig spoke for the WFL and Bondfield for the ASS at a crowded and sometimes noisy event. The resolution to be debated proposed that the limited franchise demand was the 'speediest and most practical way to reach democracy'. Billington-Greig's view was that 'the gravest bar to real democracy, to true national self-government, exists in the sex disability, and that this should first of all be abolished'.[21] Bondfield, on the other hand, argued that although it was absolutely clear that women should be allowed to vote 'at the earliest opportunity' it was not at all clear that the granting of the limited franchise would achieve equality, if only because it was likely to exclude married women. She was infuriated by the suggestion that universal adult suffrage was a tactic used to block women's equality. 'Of course,' she said, 'you are all entitled to your own opinions, but as one who has worked strenuously for Adult Suffrage, I absolutely and emphatically deny that. I work for Adult Suffrage because I believe it is the quickest way to establish real sex-equality.' She told middle-class women that they should not:

> use the bulk of working-class opinion to enfranchise themselves. I have always said in my speeches and in my conversation that these women who believe in the 'same terms as men' Bill have a perfect right to go on working for that Bill, and I say good luck to them, and may they get it! But don't let them come and tell me that they are working for my class.

She also went on to point out that senior proponents of limited suffrage, including Millicent Fawcett, had 'definitely declared that the reason why they support the limited Bill is because they believe *it will be an effective barrier to the "dangerous demand for Adult Suffrage!"*'

The WFL's published report of the meeting enthusiastically attacked Bondfield personally on the grounds that her 'arguments were masculine arguments' and described her as 'only man's echo', observing that

> It is not surprising that in a country where women are trained from babyhood to mirror man's opinion, there should be found women to act as his mouthpiece. . . . We fail to see why it should be so very virtuous to fight against class-aggression and so very wicked to fight against sex-aggression. Those of us who hate any aggression are prepared to fight against both, thereby proving that we are more democratic than the red-tie Socialist, who can only imagine the existence of one kind of evil in this (to him) otherwise perfect world.[22]

Since most of the history of women's political activities during this period was written through the lens of the women's suffrage movement, this has been the charge against Bondfield ever since. Sylvia Pankhurst expressed the view that would persist for many decades when she said that:

> It is . . . a curious fact that the women who secured political office when the citizenship of women was achieved had none of them taken a prominent part in the struggle for the vote; the first woman Cabinet Minister having remained during the greater part of her public life uninterested in the question.[23]

The fact was that women like Bondfield and Macarthur, who worked principally in male-dominated organizations and whose primary focus was working-class women, saw the world differently from those whose experience had been gained mainly through women's groups and separatist organizations. The WFL's resolution was passed by 171 votes to 139, and, partly because of its identification with socialists, trade unionists, and the politics of class, the adult suffrage argument never gained the widespread support that the female suffrage campaign engaged. It would be no comfort that eventually Bondfield would be proved at least in part correct and that, in 1918, middle-class women over thirty would be enfranchised, leaving young and most working-class women to wait another ten years for full and equal citizenship rights.

Chapter 6
They Want to See Something Done

For Margaret Bondfield, as for many other socialists and trade unionists, the major issue of the day was not the vote, but poverty. The genteel poverty of the lower-middle classes was very different from the extreme deprivation suffered by millions in both industrial and rural areas; levels of hardship which blighted lives at every stage and from which people like Bondfield and many of her colleagues counted themselves lucky to have escaped. Attitudes to the relief of poverty broke down into various overlapping strands; there was the religious view that it would always be present and should be addressed through charity, the state view that poverty was the result of fecklessness and should be punished, and the social investigator perspective, which tried to understand the causes and effects of poverty and thus develop appropriate remedies. For socialists, the only cure for poverty was the overthrow of capitalism, the economic system by which they believed that the few enriched themselves at the expense of the many. In this scenario, poverty could never be 'cured' by either charity or vindictive Poor Laws, and though its effects could and should be mitigated by good practice and the repeal of punitive legislation, only fundamental economic change could remove it altogether. Christian socialists such as Keir Hardie and Margaret Bondfield saw no conflict between religious requirements to alleviate poverty and socialist aspirations to bring down capitalism and thought that the two dovetailed naturally together. For many socialist women, in particular, these obligations included doing whatever they could to help women escape exploitation and starvation wages.

One of these fights was against sweating, a system by which (mainly) women working at home were paid pittances to make clothes, hats and a wide range of consumer goods for both the cheap and the luxury markets. Much of this work was dangerous, not necessarily in terms of the work itself, but because raw materials had to be kept in the rooms in which workers and their children lived, ate and slept. Payment was by the piece, and the rates were often so low that parents had no option but to employ their children to help. Workers had to buy their own raw materials so that the cost of any accidents or spoilage was borne by them rather than the employers. Women working at home, often isolated and just about scraping a living, were frequently unaware that trade unions even existed, let alone that they might be able to help them.

Anti-sweating campaigns had been going on for decades, but although there had been some improvements the basic problems remained and something dramatic was needed to reinvigorate them. While in Berlin for an international conference in 1904 Macarthur and Bondfield had seen an exhibition about the evils of sweated labour and thought that the same thing might work in London. Together with other groups and individuals they organized a huge event at the Queen's Hall which showcased real workers carrying out their trades, staged lectures by prominent experts and attracted over 30,000 visitors. It did not change anything overnight, but it did make people uncomfortably aware of how consumer items were made, and of what the real price of the silk flowers decorating their hats might be.

In 1907 the new Liberal government set up a committee to look at the Truck Acts, which outlawed payment in kind for employees. After some negotiation, the Committee's scope was widened to include the living-in system, which, as we have seen, was not covered by the Acts. Margaret Bondfield and her colleague Philip Hoffman gave the Shop Assistants' Union's evidence in June 1907. They wanted a complete revolution in the way shop staff were managed and paid, and, in particular, they wanted the abolition of living in, of compulsory standard deductions for 'services' such as medical attention and boot-cleaning, which the employee might never use or receive, and of fines. They gave very detailed evidence of the scope and effects of the systems they opposed, particularly stressing the moral risks to young women of the living-in system, which was supposed to exist for their protection. '"I take it" inquired a member of the Committee, "that your contention is simply that the living-in system is no moral check?" "Exactly"' replied Bondfield '"and that everything that might conceivably happen to a girl in lodgings might equally happen to her living-in."'[1]

Some of the larger employers, such as Debenhams, Derry and Toms, and Gamages, gave evidence to the effect that they were also not in favour of the living-in system, and were in the process of dismantling it. But most employers either emphatically supported it or declined to give evidence at all. The Committee sat for almost three years, and when it finally reported it recommended a system of inspection for living-in premises. A minority report proposed its outright abolition. Clementina Black, reviewing the Report in the *Economic Journal* pointed out that since the Committee had never laid down any first principles its conclusions were inevitably fudged. 'The notion,' she said:

> that an employer has a quasi-royal or quasi-paternal right to guide and regulate the lives of employees out of working hours is one that ought . . . to

be strenuously resisted. . . . the mere fact of paying B. to do certain work does not entitle A. to regulate B.'s private life and expenditure.[2]

Despite the Report's failure to support abolition , however, Bondfield hoped that when it was debated by the House of Commons supportive MPs would 'impress upon that House the primary right of every citizen to spend his money and his leisure untrammelled by the dictation of any lesser authority'. They did, but it made little difference. 'And that was that,' said Hoffman rather bitterly of the Report, 'for nothing was ever done about it. . . . But although no government did anything, shopworkers did. They rebelled and did what the committee had not the will to do. They ended it.'[3] They had to wait until after the First World War, however, when it was gradually, as Hoffman said, starved out by employers simply ceasing to enforce it rather than the unions being able to celebrate a definite point of victory.

The campaign against living in continued throughout the period of the inquiry, and in February 1908 a play called *Diana of Dobsons* enjoyed both critical and popular success on the London stage. The central character, Diana, was a shopworker, and Bondfield was employed as an adviser to help with the set showing the shop dormitory. She had great fun making sure that 'it was the real thing, with boxes under the bed, clothes hanging up on hooks, the general dinginess, and a reproduction of the actual furniture'.[4] She served in a similar role to two other productions, one about sweated industries and one about sexual equality, and remained deeply interested in the theatre for many years.

In June that year Margaret Bondfield took one of her apparently sudden decisions. She resigned from her post with the Shop Assistants' Union and announced her intention of becoming a speaker and lecturer for the ILP and other socialist and women's organizations. Her letter to the Union's Executive was short and to the point; she had completed ten years in their service, she had 'come to the conclusion that a change of work is not only desirable but inevitable', and her decision was final.[5] As soon as the letter was sent she and Ward went on holiday to Switzerland, partly because Bondfield felt 'drained of vitality', but also so that there was no possibility of her being talked out of her intention before it became public. The decision was, she said 'like a grief and a deliverance . . . '.[6] This was probably true, but it was by no means the whole story.

By and large Bondfield's explanation of events has been taken at face value. Hamilton went no further in her 1924 version than to say that although 'There were immediate and disillusioning circumstances . . . She left because she felt the call of a wider sphere.'[7] She did not elucidate what those circumstances might have been, but contemporaneous accounts, and, in particular, that of Mary Macarthur, shed a little more light on why Bondfield would turn her back on a secure income, a job she loved, and status within the movement she believed in in order to adopt the life of an itinerant lecturer.

Whatever she later suggested, the decision actually came at the end of an unhappy time in which the Union was embroiled in a series of internal wranglings and rows. The last straw seems to have been complaints about an increase in Bondfield's salary, which had risen over the years from £2 to £3 per week, but from Macarthur's furious defence of her friend in *The Shop Assistant* the problems seem to have been ongoing for at least a year. 'She has ungrudgingly devoted the best years of her life to the service of the shop assistants,' she wrote, 'She has not looked for reward or gratitude, and it is as well, for neither has been forthcoming from the members of the Shop Assistants' Union.'[8] This evoked a furious response from Ben Wilson, a member in Bradford, who said that 'Miss Bondfield . . . possesses the esteem of our membership to an unusual degree.'[9] Macarthur replied to give chapter and verse.

I have not seen Miss Bondfield since her resignation was announced. But the resignation did not surprise me. . . . I am only surprised that it has not come sooner. Even a woman who was not highly-strung and sensitive – and it is part of Miss Bondfield's strength that she is both – must have been deeply wounded again and again by the 'unusual' evidences of 'esteem' which some of my fellow members have thought fit to exhibit.

She waxed eloquent too on the treatment meted out to union officials as a whole.

Trade union officials have at best a thankless task. The officials of the Shop Assistants' Union have had, it seems to me, an impossible task. In other Unions the paid officials are the leaders, and rightly so, for they are the best men and the best women. In our Union . . . Their counsels are not sought. At our annual conferences their voices are either not heard, or are heard on sufferance.

Her most damning allegation was that Bondfield had been deliberately blocked from an achievement which could and should have been hers.

A year ago the Trade Union world would have delighted to honour Miss Bondfield by electing her to the highest position it can offer. She would have won easily a place on the Trade Union Congress Parliamentary Committee but the 'unusual esteem' . . . refused to qualify her by sending her as a delegate to the Congress. Miss Bondfield's ability is great, but more attention is paid by some of our members to a paltry increase in her salary.[10]

Macarthur's view on this was almost certainly correct and is borne out by the facts of what happened at the TUC in 1907.[11] In that year the Parliamentary Committee – effectively the TUC's National Executive – had brought in a new structure intended to enable the smaller unions to win places without having to compete directly with the big industrial bodies which, given the use of the block vote system,[12] would always dominate. The Committee was expanded from 12 to 16 members, and elections were held in sections, with the main industries grouped together leaving a large Miscellaneous section for everyone else, including the Shop Assistants. In 1906 Bondfield had stood for the Parliamentary Committee under the old, open system, and come third in the list of those not elected. Under the new system she would not have had to compete against the major manual unions and would have been able to draw support from a wide range of the smaller bodies whose votes would not have been pledged elsewhere. As a well-known and generally liked figure with an existing national reputation, she would almost certainly have been elected as the first (and only) woman at the highest level of trade union organization. It is thus all too understandable if she was outraged at being blocked by internal politics, not to mention the kind of sexism that she always wanted to believe did not exist in the movement she loved, but which undeniably did.

This experience taught Bondfield a hard lesson about the difficulties of working in mixed-sex organizations. She was committed to the idea that men and women must be equal and believed that this could not be achieved if women had their campaigning and political lives solely in single-sex organizations. When she came into the union there had been a sense of teamwork amongst the tiny group of union staff, and Macpherson had treated her (she thought) as an equal. But the fact was that there were then no male organizers to compete with her and, inevitably, as the Union grew, so too did male resentment of her position, her salary and, most of all, her power. The idea that she, rather than they, should represent both male and female shopworkers on trade unionism's most senior body was a step too far. In 1908 James Seddon, then President of the Shop Assistants' Union who had been elected to Parliament in 1906, took the coveted place.[13] The sense of rejection must have stung, and all the more so since the huge increase in the Union's membership had been the result of a decade of hard work on her part. When her employment ended on 1 September Macpherson ensured that there was a reception for her and that she was presented with gifts to mark the occasion. Her friend Margaret Llewelyn Davies[14] of the Cooperative Women's Guild wrote that: 'No workers in any movement ever had a colleague who was more single-minded, generous, and loyal. She is in many ways the type of what all Labour women should be – unflinchingly staunch to her cause, fair to her opponents, radiating goodwill to all.'[15] Walter Thompson, the Union President, said that 'For ten years of her life she gave unstinted service and all the best that was in her on behalf of her class. All these brilliant gifts with which she is endowed were generously placed at their disposal, and it is impossible to exaggerate all that Miss Bondfield has been and done for our Union.'[16]

That all this was true did nothing to improve matters, and Bondfield never worked for the Shop Assistants' Union again, though she continued to campaign on many of the issues affecting shopworkers. For the next few years, she would be on her own.

In the period between handing in her notice and actually leaving, Bondfield had given some thought to how she and Ward were to earn their living. Though still interested in cooking and food generally, Ward wanted a more political life, and neither was the sort of woman who could sit still for long. However, both were excellent public speakers – in Bondfield's case gifted – and there was already a strong socialist tradition of women being paid to take the movement's message around the country. The ILP, in particular, employed both male and female speakers to put the socialist case, and most women's organizations had lists of women who could be called upon to appear at debates, lectures and on various protest platforms. Some women, like Emmeline Pankhurst, Isabella Ford and Margaret Bondfield, were regarded as amongst the best orators in the country, and people would attend events just to hear them. Life as an itinerant speaker was precarious and payment was by the meeting, often from the collection made at the end, so that a poorly attended meeting would result in a low fee. But good speakers were always in demand, and the ILP's paper, the *Labour Leader*, reporting her departure from the Shop Assistants' Union, remarked that 'her advent as a lecturer on Socialist and Labour platforms will be warmly welcomed'.[17]

The ILP alone, however, would not be enough to keep her going, and she also worked with the WTUL and the WIC. The WIC was working on a large research project on the vexed question of married women and work and was sending researchers out across the country to examine the situation in a variety of industries. In 1909 Bondfield, who had good connections in Yorkshire, went to Leeds and Bradford to inquire into the woollen textiles industries. In some respects what she found was exactly what might have been expected. People were divided over whether or not married women should work, the women themselves were severely underpaid, and the conditions in which they were employed were often dreadful. Some places and occupations were actively dangerous, and fatalities were not unknown. Religious and charitable organizations generally thought that working mothers led to delinquent and neglected children and wanted legislation to remove married women from the workforce. As usual, there were women who supplemented their meagre incomes with prostitution; in Bondfield's experience this happened in shop work, too, and she was not surprised to find it in other industries. What she had not come across before in quite such an endemic way was what was happening to women at home, and the general level of ignorance that seemed to prevail. A woman running a hostel for pregnant girls told her that:

Many street girls smoked and thought it would act as a preventative to contraception. Others used other and more dangerous methods to procure abortion. Sometimes girls were told they must go out with as many different men as possible to avoid conception.[18]

Leeds and Bradford had quite different approaches to prostitution; in the former women could work in brothels where they could make enough money not to have to work at anything else as well. In Bradford, however, the police had closed down all the brothels, thus forcing the women onto the streets, where they could be prosecuted if they had no other means of support. Many therefore also worked in mills 'as a blind'. 'It was', said Bondfield, 'an open question as to whether the dispersal of prostitutes made for a better standard of morality.'[19]

It was not just on the streets that women were at risk, however. The lack of adequate and affordable housing meant that whole families lived in one room and slept in one bed. As a result incest was not uncommon, and Bondfield's contact knew of 'a number of cases of sisters bearing children to brothers, and daughters to fathers. . . . One family consisted of a mother with two girls, a boy of nineteen and a boy of twelve, all lying in the same bed. Both girls had children to brothers. . . .' The conditions in which such families lived were shocking, and the consequences even more so, so that for many people housing policy was as much a moral issue as anything else.

The WIC's married women's work inquiry soon became mired in disputes as to how to report and present the evidence the researchers had collected, and Bondfield's straightforward account of the plight of the working women of Leeds and Bradford may have formed an element of that disagreement. In 1910 this, combined with proposals to change the WIC's structure, came to a head and Bondfield, together with most of the other Labour women, resigned from the Executive. The report was not published until 1915,[20] by which time all reference to prostitution, incest or the abuse of young women and girls had vanished. Thirty years later this obviously still annoyed Bondfield; her autobiography includes several pages outlining her findings, at the end of which she quotes one of the first female Factory Inspectors, Dame Adelaide Anderson, who noted that: 'Ultimately, when due care has been secured for the poorest child-bearing woman, the tale of their past suffering and neglect will seem a terrible and incredible thing.'[21]

If relations with the WIC became strained, those with the WTUL continued to be cordial and Bondfield spoke at their events as well as on Fabian Society and ILP platforms. But the two groups into which she put most time and effort were the National Federation of Women Workers (NFWW) and the Women's Labour League (WLL), both of which had been founded in 1906, and both of which were to give her work, comradeship and, in the case of the WLL, problems for a number of years to come.

The WLL had been set up by Margaret MacDonald and others to give women both a role in the new Labour Party and a political home. MacDonald was the wife of the Party Secretary, Ramsay MacDonald, but she was also a significant woman in her own right. She was a gifted statistician and was one of the first women to join the Royal Statistical Society. She came from an affluent background and had used her resources to enable the fledgeling LRC to get off the ground when, in its first few years, affiliations and funding had been slow to come in. Bondfield first met her through the WIC, in which MacDonald had been involved since its inception. Bondfield, then still young and judgemental, had viewed this new acquaintance with deep suspicion, later recalling that: 'she seemed just a wealthy young woman who was interested in studying my class' and she was not at all pleased to hear of the forthcoming marriage to Ramsay MacDonald, widely regarded as the rising star of the labour movement. However, the 'stiff congratulations' she offered:

> revealed to this intuitive woman my disapproval of his choice; and with the utmost good nature and tact she began to talk of her views of life and its responsibilities, and to make it quite clear that she would not try to take J.R. away from us . . .[22]

Margaret MacDonald soon became a firm friend, and one whom Bondfield both admired and loved. She did not, however, love meetings held in the (more or less) organized chaos of the MacDonald home, where children roamed about barefooted and assorted child-related debris had to be cleared from tables before work could start. 'Come back to my rooms,' she suggested on one occasion, 'then I can be sure of getting your attention. What with babies, telephones and callers, etc. that is impossible at your home.'[23]

In 1900 it did not occur to the founders of the LRC to allow for individual membership, and thus unless women could get to the party's conference as delegates from the ILP or a trade union there was not much female involvement in the party's development. Very few women attended or spoke at the Labour Party's Annual conference and there were no women on the National Executive Committee (NEC). Margaret MacDonald wanted to rectify this by establishing women as organizers and campaigners parallel to the party but independent of it. Despite various challenges the WLL got off the ground quite successfully, and Bondfield was elected to its Executive in 1909. Much as she wanted women to be involved in politics, however, she found the Committee atmosphere trying at times. There seemed to be a lot of discussion without much clarity about outcomes, whereas, elsewhere, there was less time for deliberation. Speaking of a meeting in the East End of London, for instance, she remarked; 'That is what I like so much about meetings of working women – they're no great talkers; *they want to see something done* . . . To the poorest of homes the love of comrades brings some joy . . . '[24]

This was a view shared by Mary Macarthur who put it into practice by founding a new trade union for women in low-paid trades. After two years working for the WTUL she had come to the view that the problem was not that women were incapable of organization but that they did not know how to go about it. Women workers had a tendency to walk out on sudden strikes because they had no machinery for negotiation and did not know how to go about developing one. Macarthur understood that workers generally had a better chance of getting what they wanted if they negotiated. Although she fully believed in strike action as a necessary tool of the struggle, she did not think that it should be used indiscriminately, or as the first rather than the last resort. The NFWW was very quickly successful, growing, at its peak, to exceed the size of many smaller unions and achieving status and voice well above its size. Over the coming years it employed a number of organizing staff, three of whom, as we shall see, went on to become Labour's first female MPs.

The 1906 Liberal government came in with a reforming agenda and the belief that something could and should be done about poverty. In April 1909 the Chancellor of the Exchequer, David Lloyd George, introduced what became known as the 'People's Budget' into the House of Commons. Although not entirely as radical as it is sometimes presented as having been, it was still an innovative attempt to use taxation to drive and fund social change. Death duties were to be increased and both land and higher incomes were to be taxed. These proposals were seen as direct attacks on the fabric of society and were fiercely resisted. There was to be a state insurance system for workers, including, controversially, domestic servants. Employers were outraged. Sylvia Pankhurst rather sardonically reported that 'all the conflicting catch cries of the factions opposing the Bill were heard on suffrage platforms'[25] as middle-class and aristocratic women fought the plans to provide welfare for the working-class women who made their activism possible, thus inadvertently entirely justifying Bondfield's belief that they would do nothing for working women once they had power. Lloyd George and the Liberals, however, regarded the budget with almost messianic enthusiasm, with Lloyd George admitting that: 'This is a war Budget. It is for raising money to wage implacable warfare against poverty and squalidness.'[26]

Since the House of Lords refused to pass the Budget the ensuing constitutional impasse made a general election inevitable. In late 1909, however, as this was becoming clear, the House of Lords made a decision which would have an immediate and damaging effect on Labour's election campaign. Trade unions affiliated to the party raised money for it by collecting a compulsory donation – known as a levy – from their members. One of the Railwaymen's Union branch secretaries, a man called Walter Osborne, objected to this since he was opposed to socialism and did not see why he should be forced to fund it. His case went to the House of Lords, who ruled that the levy was unlawful and must cease. This judgement applied to all unions, not just the one involved in the case, so that at a stroke the party's main source of funding was removed just as an election loomed.[27] There was also very little time in which to prepare for it; what became known as the Osborne judgement was delivered on 21 December and the election was set for January. Despite this, Labour still managed to field 78 candidates across the country with every prospect of improving on their 1906 tally of 29.

For Bondfield, the main focus of campaigning was Woolwich, where she had recently been elected as a Town Councillor. Unfortunately, Will Crooks, the Labour MP, was in Australia when the election was called and could not possibly get back for the campaign. The electoral fort had to be held by the local party until he could arrive. The parliamentary agent, Mr Barefoot, asked Bondfield if she could '"play candidate", which meant being prepared to make the principal speech, and answer questions, on behalf on the candidate, on the Party programme, etc.'.[28] She was not the only person asked to do this, but she was the only woman, and she took the job up with enthusiasm. The Labour manifesto for this election was fairly straightforward – 'Down with privilege. Up with the people' it urged, advocating the abolition of the hated Poor Law, and the introduction of a legal right to work, universal suffrage and land reform. This was not a difficult programme to advocate, and Bondfield did so well. She also spoke for other London candidates, including George Lansbury in nearby Bow and Bromley. The outcome of the election proved disastrous for the Liberals, who lost over a hundred seats and found themselves having to deal with a hung parliament. Labour did well, increasing their seats to 40, though Crooks, who just about got back for polling day, lost his seat in Woolwich. Bondfield 'felt terribly the loss of the seat, and indignant at the tactics of the Tories in declaring that Will had been wasting the taxpayers' money in riotous living abroad instead of doing his duty at home'.[29]

On 8 February, Bondfield's mother died at the age of 80. In recent years she had been living in London with her daughter Harriet at Woodford, though towards the end she may also have stayed with Bondfield and Ward. Bondfield's relationship with her mother had been less complicated than that with her father, and Ann had lived long enough to see and appreciate some of her daughter's success, but Bondfield still felt the loss keenly. She never forgot the struggles her mother had had to keep her children fed and clothed, and she took the memory of them with her into her campaigning. Ann Bondfield's remains were taken back to Chard and buried in the family grave 'amid many signs of esteem and regret'.[30]

Hard on the heels of this sadness, however, came an opportunity which gave Bondfield her first taste of being a candidate. Following her election to Woolwich Town Council she stood, in March 1910, for the London County Council. She was one of the first women to do so following the passing of the 1907 Qualification of Women Act which allowed women to stand for and vote in elections for County and Borough Councils, and although she was not elected she was generally agreed to have run an excellent campaign, coming ahead of the Liberal and gaining almost 7,000 votes. Some local members had initially queried whether or not her health would be up to what was going to be a ferocious campaign, but in the event her agent, the formidable William Barefoot, called her a 'magnificent' candidate, writing to her that:

> The sustained energy with which you met the strain of the fiercely-fought election was a marked feature of that strenuous time, and the magnificent audiences you addressed are a testimony to your eloquence . . . We could not have had a better candidate.[31]

Elsewhere in London two women were elected, one of whom was the Conservative (Municipal Reform) Susan Lawrence in Marylebone. By 1912, influenced by Beatrice and Sidney Webb as well as Mary Macarthur, whom she met during a cleaners' strike at County Hall, Lawrence defected to Labour where she remained for the rest of her life, ultimately becoming an MP and the first female Chair of the Party. Bondfield's time in local government was relatively short, and it was never where her heart was, but she greatly enjoyed the campaigns, if only because they played to her strengths of public speaking and connecting with ordinary people. Election campaigns were generally much shorter then than now, and the pressurized whirlwind of speeches and meetings suited her. All of her future agents would agree with Barefoot's assessment, and in some respects she was never better than during an election when the need to do anything other than win could be allowed to fall away for two or three weeks.

Soon after this, at the WLL's conference in Portsmouth, she met a wealthy American suffragist called Elizabeth Glendower Evans, who, impressed with her oratorical skills, invited her to undertake a lecture tour in the eastern United States. This was far too good an opportunity to miss, and that July, with much excitement and apprehension, Bondfield and Ward set sail for New York.

Chapter 7
Bread and Roses

Although Ward and Bondfield had crossed the Channel before, they had never undertaken a long sea voyage, and the first thing Bondfield learned was that she was an indifferent sailor. For the first few days she was very sick indeed and had to be looked after by Ward who, she recorded, had 'been wonderful, all things considering – just a little squeamish at times'.[1] Not having very much money they were travelling as second-class passengers accommodated in an inside cabin which only made her sickness worse. Apart from this, however, she discovered that she loved everything about transatlantic travel, including the random mix of people it threw together and the new friends it was possible to make. This enjoyment would last for the rest of her life through many voyages, with this first one remaining almost magical for her.

The ship's landing was delayed by fog and Bondfield described the last night on board as 'a perfect orgy, many getting quite tipsy, both men and women'. When they disembarked they had to go through a rather alarming immigration process before travelling by train from New York to Boston, where they met up again with Mrs Glendower Evans and embarked on a series of speaking engagements for the Boston Suffrage Society. In Britain, the tension between sex and class had largely kept Bondfield off female suffrage platforms, thus allowing opponents of universal suffrage to paint her as a male mouthpiece opposed to women's enfranchisement. In America, however, the situation was very different. Something approximating white manhood suffrage already existed, at least in theory, in most states. Black men's right to vote had technically been established by the Fifteenth Amendment, but in reality very few were able to use it. Crucially for the women's campaign, most states had long since abolished property qualifications, so that the female suffrage demand included working-class women without the need for the divisive debate going on in Britain. This was a revelation to Bondfield, who immediately felt liberated and found herself able to speak proudly on suffrage platforms she would have been excluded from at home.

The time in between speaking engagements was spent sightseeing and meeting new people. On 2 August they started their tour of a string of cities and towns, including Concord, where they visited the homes of poets and novelists and walked round the graveyard at Sleepy Hollow. Bondfield admired the décor of the houses; 'Polished floors and Persian rugs – no stuffy carpets in New England houses.' They ate in the Cafeteria and the Laboratory Kitchen, both projects providing cheap food in clean, healthy surroundings. The round of meetings and sightseeing continued wherever they were, with most of the collections at the meetings bringing in more money than they could usually expect in England. Since this was what funded their living and travel expenses, they were always a matter of keen interest. 'Altogether on Saturday,' Bondfield wrote of one day, 'our collections came to 14 dollars. We like American crowds.' By the end of their first fortnight in America they were happy with how things had been going, 'with only an occasional ruffling of tempers under great stress'.

One such ruffling came at Flitchburg, which Bondfield described as 'a horrid town for food. Dirty restaurants. Typhoid raging.' She was delayed arriving at the evening meeting and did not get there until half an hour after it had started, when she found:

> Ward and the others quite exhausted. Ward had spoken four times already that day and was speaking when I arrived to relieve her. At home I got the full blast of Ward's reaction to the day's hard labour and disappointments.

Flitchburg's food may have been dismal, but it also had Hastings Hall, a residence for women the like of which Bondfield had never come across in England. It had:

> Comfortable bedrooms with deep hanging closets and shelves. Comfortable chairs and beds. Lovely bathrooms and ample supply of very hot water. Quiet corridors, spacious common rooms, great easy chairs. . . . No irritating rules, religious texts or anything objectionable.

Early in September Ward went down to Atlanta to meet Mrs Glendower Evans' friend, Fanneal Harrison, who had invited them to stay with her. Bondfield was left alone in Boston, though the plan was for her to follow Ward a week later. On 5 September – Labour Day – there was a large parade through the city, only slightly marred by heavy rain in the latter stages. A few days later Bondfield started her journey south to meet Ward in Georgia. At Washington she found that there had been a mix-up with her booking and the sleeper train she had been due to travel on had no room for her. She had no idea of where to go or how to resolve the problem and simply stood weeping with exhausted frustration. A 'compassionate train conductor patted me on the shoulder and said "We will take care of you, Don't cry."' He was as good as his word, finding her a berth which 'seemed like heaven' until she found that it was a top berth which she could scramble into, but had to summon the porter to help her out of.

Bondfield and Ward met up again at Tallulah Falls north of Atlanta where they were to have a break with friends amidst the beautiful scenery of the area. Ward thought Bondfield looked 'terribly tired' and Bondfield herself admitted that she needed rest. The campaign in New England had been 'far more strenuous than we expected it to be', and she was 'not really sorry to have a complete rest'. Ward got hay fever, Fanneal Harrison had a cold and was bitten by insects, and Bondfield's bed turned out to be infested by a nest of chiggers, none of which sounds particularly restful, but there were beautiful walks to be had and interesting new people to meet and overall it was enjoyable. After a week they went to Harrison's home at Fernbank, and then on to Knoxville, where their speaking engagements were to start again.

Knoxville was a very different proposition from Boston and New England. In the north their meetings had received support from men as well as women, even when the topic was female suffrage, but in Knoxville the idea that a woman:

> may make as great an intellectual demand on an audience as a man seems to come as a surprise. The attitude of the men towards women here seems to be that they are hopelessly silly, of course, but that they must be petted and humoured, and it is necessary to keep on the right side of them. The way to do this is to patronise them if they want to do public service, and to flatter their vanity.

Relentlessly, the round of meetings and speaking engagements continued, so that by the end of September Bondfield was feeling strained and exhausted. Ward, keeping an anxious eye on her, was relieved that her address to senior women students at Athens Normal College went well and 'seemed to think that this showed recovery'. In early October they went to the Conservation Conference in Atlanta. This was an event to discuss various aspects of what would now be called environmental policy and attracted high-profile speakers, including Theodore Roosevelt, whose second term of office as President of the United States had finished the year before. Bondfield cast her professional oratorical eye over him and pronounced him:

> so much more dignified and careful in language than we had expected. He combines the statesman and propagandist orator very effectively. . . . He seems able to interpret the best that is in the American people to themselves, and hold up the things that they would like to have and to make them want to get them.

On 10 October Bondfield and Ward left Georgia for Chicago, a city which Bondfield described as 'ugly, and the slums terrifying'. But Chicago was also a city of great progressive innovation, with women at the forefront of projects to improve social and industrial conditions. One of the centres for this was Hull House, where Bondfield and Ward stayed during their Chicago visit, and which Jane Addams and Ellen Gates Starr had set up after a visit to London. The settlement movement, of which Hull House was a part, had begun in 1884 with Toynbee Hall in Whitechapel, and stemmed from the idea that the better-off members of society had a duty to help the poor, and that this could be met, at least in part, by living amongst them and providing both practical and educational support. Making the classes better acquainted with one another would, it was thought, contribute to the general improvement of society and reduce misunderstanding and hostility. Hull House was founded in 1889 but, unlike Toynbee Hall, was run by women for women, and, in particular, for working-class women who had recently arrived from Europe. Addams herself lived there with her partner Mary Rozet Smith and it had become a great centre for women's activism. Addams was also involved in industrial campaigns advocating an eight-hour day, the removal of children from sweated industries, and the provision of good education for working people. Bondfield was hugely impressed by her; 'She was,' she said, 'carrying on a long battle against privilege and graft, so prevalent in local administration.'

Chicago itself was both shocking and exhilarating. There was an active branch of the American Women's Trade Union League (AWTUL) which was a much more proactive body than its namesake in London and through which Bondfield met many of the leading female trade unionists of the day. When she and Ward arrived Chicago was gripped by a garment workers' strike over pay and conditions; this involved over 40,000 operatives, many of them women. Bondfield was fascinated to find that they needed seven separate committee rooms to accommodate the different languages spoken by the strikers, but she was also shocked to see both sides carrying and using firearms. She did not think that the Second Amendment was an adequate excuse for this, commenting that it was 'evidence of the slow emergence from pioneer days'. Some strike meetings were held at Hull House, where Addams, in the teeth of much external opposition, insisted on giving the strikers practical support. Again, Bondfield was filled with admiration, noting that although she had 'no doubt Hull House finances lost as a consequence, . . . she (*Addams*) won a place in the hearts of the workers'.

Soon the steady churn of travel and meetings was resumed, with visits to Milwaukee and Madison and speeches and meetings at universities. It was almost unimaginable that British universities would invite a working-class woman to address them about anything, and some of the disparities between the British and American attitudes to both education and work were a revelation. One professor introduced them to the waiter who brought their soup at lunch, calling him 'my most brilliant student. . . . It seemed to us astonishing that such a gifted youth should not be in the least embarrassed by his position as a waiter. I wondered what sort of attitude one would find for a similar case, say in Eton or Harrow. Here his fellow students were proud of him.'

At Madison they also met Caroline Hunt, an expert on food and home economics who had been a professor at the University of Wisconsin and now worked for the government producing guidance and advice for women and the agricultural industry alike. What marked Hunt out from many others, however, was her commitment to racial equality. Throughout her various American visits, Bondfield was both fascinated and repelled by the American approach to race, particularly in the south. Hunt, said Bondfield, 'felt particularly strongly about racial discrimination, and was particularly glad to welcome some of the negroes *(sic)* as friends, even to the point of shocking some of her other friends with white skins'. Throughout the tour Bondfield met and listened to as many Black women as she could and, while recognizing that such conversations gave her only a fleeting and superficial understanding, she tried to learn about and recognize Black women's lives, particularly when, as in Chicago, they were trade unionists and involved in industrial action. Many white American attitudes to race struck her as both irreligious and unjust, and within the limited range of her understanding and experience she tried to demonstrate what would now be called allyship.

Towards the end of October they began to prepare for their voyage home, but first there was more sightseeing to do. They visited Niagara Falls, from there going on to Philadelphia and Washington DC, where their hosts took them on the usual tourist trail, including a visit to the State Rooms in the White House. At the beginning of November they took the train back to New York, staying at the Henry Street Settlement and meeting the women of the AWTUL, including Rose Schneiderman, another inspirational woman to whom Bondfield became close. Schneiderman was a trade unionist, feminist and suffragist whose focus was organization and action, which alone was enough to make her attractive. Later she was credited with being the originator of the phrase 'bread and roses' when in 1912 she told an audience of middle-class women that 'You have nothing that the humblest worker has not a right to have also. The worker must have bread, but she must have roses, too.'[2]

In New York Bondfield was able to increase her understanding of 'the race question' when she was introduced to Professor W. E. B. du Bois, who, in 1909, had been one of the founders of the National Association for the Advancement of Colored People. Ward, who had recently read a well-known book on the subject of race, went round asking lots of questions, but Bondfield was more interested in listening to what people wanted to tell her. The First Universal Races Conference was to be held in London the following year, and Bondfield and Ward were invited to a reception for the Black delegates who would be going. Here she found a highly educated group of people who often had a very different outlook from the poor communities of northern industrial cities and the rural small-town south.

On 5 November, having returned to Philadelphia, they embarked on the SS *Haverford* for what turned out to be a stormy voyage back to London, which they reached ten days later. This long American visit was one of the most influential experiences of Bondfield's life, opening her mind to new ideas and introducing her to new people in environments she could never have been part of in Britain. Despite its quirks, downsides and challenges, the United States seemed to offer a level of personal freedom that even London, for all its cosmopolitan airs, could not quite match. The class system, too, though definitely present, seemed weaker than at home, and although wealth and privilege still conferred opportunities not open to the poor, the divisions (except in the case of race) seemed much less entrenched. Over the years America would draw her back again and again and many of the women she met would become close and loving friends over many decades.

Bondfield and Ward arrived back in London to a political situation which had heated up considerably and within weeks they found themselves campaigning in the second of the two 1910 general elections. The House of Lords had, reluctantly, passed the People's Budget in April, but this had only partially resolved the problem. The Irish Parliamentary Party held 71 of the 103 Irish seats and was crucial to the survival of the government. Its leader, John Redmond, had made it clear that continued support was contingent upon the introduction of an Irish Home Rule Bill, which both he and the Liberal Prime Minister, H. H. Asquith, knew would be staunchly resisted by both Conservatives and the House of Lords. On the other hand, there was now a consensus that the unelected Lords should not have the power to block government measures which had been included in a manifesto, or which were 'money bills', and the government proposed to legislate to achieve this.

Meanwhile Asquith also had problems on the suffrage front. Before the election in January the Women's Liberal Federation had managed to persuade him to allow a free vote on female suffrage if it was attached to another constitutional reform bill and not introduced as a separate, free-standing, measure. This seemed quite reasonable when Asquith had a large majority, but the disappearance of that majority in January inevitably made the situation more complicated. The Irish Parliamentary Party did not support female suffrage, and Redmond was very clear that if Home Rule succeeded Irish women would not be given the vote. Even if the Labour members had been united on the issue there would not have been enough of them to get the measure through, and in any case they were not united since universal adult suffrage remained party policy while individual members like George Lansbury supported limited female suffrage. Asquith now agreed to give parliamentary time to a limited bill, and a cross-party Conciliation Committee was established to draw one up. The First Conciliation Bill, introduced in the late spring of 1910, proposed to enfranchise over a million unmarried propertied women and passed its first and second readings with relative ease, but then Asquith announced that no more parliamentary time would be allocated, and the Bill fell.

All this had happened while Bondfield was in the United States, so that she and Ward were reliant for news on out-of-date newspapers which they went to public libraries to read. By the time she arrived back in England, however, matters were coming to a head, and whatever reservations she might have had about the more extreme tactics of the WSPU, she was horrified by what unfolded next. On 18 November, when Asquith announced that there would be an election in December, a large delegation of women attempted to enter Parliament to lobby MPs for the vote. They were prevented from doing so by police, who had come prepared for violence, and who assaulted the women both physically and sexually and arrested over 100. Photographs of prone women with male police and civilians looming over them were on the front pages of the newspapers, though most of the coverage was hostile to the women. The date went down in suffrage history as Black Friday and the victims were hailed as heroines. The WSPU became even more militant in its tactics, and although Asquith promised that a female suffrage amendment to a proposed bill to enfranchise more men would be tacitly supported, trust had completely broken down. The WSPU ran a campaign of extensive window-smashing, and ministers and their properties were attacked. The whole issue was mired in suspicion and bad feeling, and the election of December 1910, called to secure support for the Parliament Bill, did nothing to resolve it.

By now the Osborne judgement had begun to bite, and the number of candidates the Labour Party was able to field fell to 56, 42 of whom were elected. The party's manifesto was very short and to the point. 'Let all petty differences go to the four winds' it urged. 'Now is the time to unite. The poverty of one is the poverty of all. Let those who suffer join to remove their suffering. It can be removed in no other way.' Labour supported the Parliament Bill, partly because it was in favour of anything which restricted the power of the Lords, but also because the Bill included the introduction of payment for MPs, a long-standing demand which went back to Chartist days and which, Labour knew, would be the only way in which working-class people without private means or trade union support would be able to enter Parliament in any kind of numbers.

When the results came in the December election turned out to be something of a damp squib, with almost no change in the composition of the House of Commons. Much to Bondfield's relief Will Crooks was restored to his seat in Woolwich, and her friend George Lansbury, who had failed to be elected in Bow and Bromley in January succeeded in December. In the wake of the election Ramsay MacDonald replaced George Barnes as Chair of the Parliamentary Labour Party (PLP) – effectively the party leader, although the formal title did not then exist.

Once the election was over, the Liberal government was able to return to the questions raised in the People's Budget. For decades, there had been debate about what to do about the 1834 Poor Law Act, which, amongst other things, had established the Victorian workhouses. Labour and the trade unions wanted the Poor Law repealed and replaced with more humane measures which would recognize, for instance, the cyclical nature of employment in a capitalist economy. Many Liberals agreed, but there was little or no agreement on what type of relief system should replace the 1834 Act. In 1905 the government had set up yet another Royal Commission to investigate, but although it took and heard a great deal of evidence it worked very slowly and did not report until 1909, at which point its members failed to agree on recommendations and produced both a majority and a minority report. Beatrice Webb was one of the Commissioners and drafted most of the Minority Report, which argued for state provision of benefits and support. This was attacked by advocates of the Majority Report as effectively arguing for socialism, but supporters of the Minority view, including Bondfield, pointed out that if state provision of services were in and of itself a form of socialism, Britain was already well down that path since it was responsible for drainage systems and roads, which were needed for the health of the community, but which could not be adequately supplied by individuals.[3]

The lack of agreement from the Commission meant that the Liberal government felt free to ignore both sides and introduce their own measures, which is what the Chancellor, David Lloyd George, did. He began with the 1908 Old Age Pensions Act, which provided means-tested non-contributory pensions to both men and women from the age of 70. The cost was to be borne by the taxpayer, and given that, at this time, life expectancy was about 50 for men and a few years more for women, and that working-class people with harsher lives and less access to medical care were on average likely to die at a younger age, it was not anticipated that the numbers to be covered would be very high. Pensions were something Labour and the trade unions had been arguing for over many years, and their introduction was welcomed. Politically, however, the direction the government was now taking, which seemed to accept the principle that the state had a collective responsibility for the weakest in society, provided Labour in Parliament with a challenge – oppose the measures and they would look ridiculous, as well as being seen to be trying to deprive working people of much-needed help, but support them and they risked looking as though they were simply parroting Liberal policies, particularly since, before 1910, the size of the Liberal majority meant that they did not need support from any minor parties to get their measures through.

When the Lords had finally accepted the People's Budget Lloyd George had introduced the National Insurance Bill. This was the legislation intended to implement the social measures the Budget had included, and it immediately ran into stout resistance from a wide variety of quarters. It envisaged the establishment of two funds, one for unemployment and one for health costs, to which compulsory contributions would be made by workers, employers and the state. Beneficiaries of both schemes would need to meet a series of requirements, with provisions built in to prevent abuse. The Funds were supposed to be rooted in sound actuarial principles, with an anticipated unemployment rate in the industries concerned of not more than 4.6 per cent. Children were not covered by the unemployment scheme, and neither were married women who did not work outside the home. Working women's contributions to both Funds were to be lower than men's, but still compulsory.

The Bill's proposals were in many ways very reasonable and rooted in a good deal of thought and research. The part dealing with unemployment benefits was relatively uncontroversial since the provisions were restricted to workers in cyclical or seasonal trades and could be claimed for only fifteen weeks a year. There was considerable objection to the compulsory nature of workers' contributions, but a general agreement that the Fund was workable. This was much less the case with the health insurance element, which, while not necessarily covering the entire cost, would enable working people to access basic medical assistance and medication. Here objections came from all sides. The Right thought that the provisions of the Bill were socialism by the back door, while Beatrice Webb, the Fabian Society, the ILP, a number of trade unions, several MPs and various women's groups were hostile for different reasons. One of the main bones of contention was the compulsory nature of the employee's contributions; many trade unionists as well as the ILP felt that any scheme should be non-contributory and that anything else would effectively force the poorest in society to pay an extra tax for the privilege of basic treatment when they were ill. Keir Hardie's description of it as a poll tax resonated with many. For many families the few extra pennies a week that they would have to find seemed exorbitant, and although women were to pay a penny less than men their wages were also lower, so that for single women the burden was proportionally even greater. Despite the fact that contributions would not be triggered until the employee's income reached £160 a year – then the tax threshold – there was a very strong suspicion that something designed to make people's lives better would, because of the compulsory contributions, actually make them worse. For some the Bill was irredeemable and should be voted against, whereas for others, particularly the women, the priority became to amend it.

The second main line of objection related to the method by which the health benefits were to be paid. The government expected existing organizations to manage the system on its behalf by acting as 'approved societies'. These bodies would be registered and would not only administer claims but also collect the contributions. Clearly this was a role for insurance societies, but under the Bill's initial provisions charities and friendly societies could register too. Many trade unions already ran long-standing benefit funds and after some discussion these were added to the list, but this did not solve the problem of how to ensure that the approved societies did their job properly, not to mention honestly. It was easy to see that being an approved society could quickly turn into a very profitable business so that both the taxpayer and the employers could potentially be fleeced by unscrupulous or incompetent organizations.

For the WLL, the Cooperative Women's Guild (CWG) and other women's groups, however, the way in which women were treated in the Bill was so bad that that there was even some question over whether it should be supported at all. Despite being some of the poorest paid workers in the most seasonal of industries, very few women were eligible for unemployment benefit, and the proscriptive way in which the sickness benefit regulations were drawn meant that hardly any women could claim that, either. The health provisions did not cover widows or their children. Throughout there was a presumption that women's needs would be looked after by their husbands, if they had them, and a streak of misogyny undoubtedly ran through some of the thinking. When Lloyd George, expecting sympathetic male agreement, observed to Ramsay MacDonald that if married women were covered they would be constantly claiming medical costs, he was infuriated to discover that MacDonald had related the remark to his wife, who promptly repeated it in public. Lloyd George accused her of being unscrupulous, but what he really resented was criticism of a piece of legislation which he considered to be a radical innovation, and which, in some ways, was indeed exactly that. Negotiations to try to get women included were protracted and not always easy. For some reason Lloyd George took such a dislike to Mary Macarthur that, much to her irritation, she had to be left out of subsequent delegations and be replaced by Dr Marion Phillips,[4] the weight of whose erudition perhaps made her harder to dismiss.

Middle-class women took an interest in what the Bill proposed, if only because parts of it would affect them in terms of their domestic staff, but the WLL was worried that working-class women were unaware of it, or might have expectations that were not going to be met. To try to assess the problem Bondfield visited some of the poorer areas of Birmingham to listen to women's views. She recruited a team of local canvassers and went door-to-door asking questions. 'Oh!,' she reported, 'The lonely lives of these women, hidden away at the back of a network of small, mean streets!'[5] As usual, she was struck with rage and shame at the way the poorest, most hard-working women were treated, and returned with renewed vigour to the legislative battle.

Always painstaking in her approach, Bondfield now acquired detailed knowledge of the technicalities of the insurance industry, as well as the complexities of negotiating live legislative proposals, and how to analyse the effects of both on the people who had the least and were least well placed to understand them. It was through the fires of this fight and the ones that followed it that she began to develop the breadth and depth of knowledge of insurance systems that would eventually lead her, more than a decade later, into government office.

Chapter 8
The End is Not Yet

In June 1911 Margaret MacDonald, the Secretary of the WLL, cut her finger. It was a small cut, and she thought nothing of it, attending meetings and then travelling down to the family's country cottage at Amersham where Bondfield was their guest for the weekend. As the hours passed the injured hand began to swell and become painful, and both Ramsay and Bondfield were alarmed. On her return to London Margaret was diagnosed with blood poisoning – now known as sepsis – and began the long, slow decline which ended in her death in September at the age of just 41. Ramsay MacDonald was understandably devastated, and many who had never met her were grief-stricken. A huge number of letters of condolence arrived at the Lincoln's Inn Fields flat and hundreds of people lined the route of her funeral cortège. Bondfield was deeply distressed. MacDonald had known she was dying and at their last meeting had 'said "Goodbye" with a smile. I' recalled Bondfield, 'could not say anything.'[1]

Hard on the heels of this tragedy came the happier news of Mary Macarthur's marriage to Will Anderson. Anderson, with whom Bondfield had worked in the Shop Assistants' Union, was a Scot who had first proposed to Macarthur before she moved south.[2] Now himself living in London, he had left the Union shortly before Bondfield and was working as a journalist and public speaker as well as chairing the ILP. Interestingly, he was the only man for whom, so far as is known, Bondfield was ever said to have entertained a romantic feeling, and even then the suggestion was only made long after they were both dead. In 1975 Ross Davies, trying to find material for his proposed book, approached Dorothy Elliott, who had worked for Macarthur at the NFWW before spending twenty years as Bondfield's colleague at the NUGMW. When they met Elliott told Davies that Macarthur had not trusted Bondfield for two reasons; first because of her parliamentary ambitions – an idea which, as we shall see later, held very little water – and second because she had wanted to marry Anderson herself. However, within days of their initial meeting she wrote to him to say:

Thinking over our talk I am a little worried about having said anything about W. Anderson. I have gone over it in my mind and can find no evidence at all. In any case Margaret was a warm person and I was wrong in saying she was afraid of personal relations. On reflection I am sure I was wrong.[3]

Bondfield certainly kept two of Anderson's letters to her, dated August and December 1903,[4] but the tone of both is chatty and friendly with no suggestion of a man fending off unwanted attentions. Indeed, if anything, the first of his letters would seem to put the boot onto the other foot, which would make more sense in the light of Elliott's observations in her retraction. He has, he says, arranged for her to be sent 'a beautiful boxful *(of heather)* when *(it reaches)* its full flush. So will-nilly you will have to accept it, and the heather will last longer than the flowers.'[5] Nor is there any explanation as to why Macarthur should have confided to Elliott – then a very young and junior member of staff – doubts about the trustworthiness of one of her oldest and closest friends. In the absence of any other information Elliott's withdrawn story has to remain as an outlier; interesting, but unlikely to be true.

Macarthur and Anderson were a well-matched couple and their wedding was the subject of considerable press interest. They were married at the City Temple in Holborn with Bondfield and Gertrude Tuckwell as bridesmaids. Macarthur continued working after her marriage, kept her maiden name for all professional purposes, and usually earned at least as much as her husband. After the wedding the happy couple had a short honeymoon in Paris and Bondfield returned to her ever-increasing work.

When Margaret MacDonald first fell ill Bondfield had taken up some of her secretarial duties, but after MacDonald's death the WLL offered her the post of Secretary on a permanent basis. This was not the first time that the possibility of her taking this job had been suggested; in May 1910, after the death of the previous Secretary, Mary Middleton, Maud Ward had suggested to members of the Committee that Bondfield would be a good replacement. Margaret MacDonald had then written to Bondfield and gently warned her off, first because 'you would be rather hampered by the office work and position' and second that such an appointment would look like favouritism. 'Of course,' MacDonald added, 'you would be excellent for the work but rather wasted on some of it . . . '[6]

This time, however, the offer was made, and Bondfield accepted. Apart from anything else the salary would come in handy, but she was now stretching herself very thinly indeed. She was, as usual, travelling all over the country speaking and organizing, while at home things may not always have been easy. In 1908 Macarthur had described Bondfield as 'sensitive and highly-strung' and throughout the American tour there had been references to her exhaustion and need to rest. Ward was not always the most undemanding of companions, and while Bondfield probably gave as good as she got domestic conflict would not have helped. Moreover, in 1911 Ward was appointed Chief Woman Inspector under the new National Insurance Act, which made her a senior civil servant with a good salary and left Bondfield living a peripatetic life alone. However pleased for Ward she was, the difference in their fortunes must have rankled; at the age of 38 Ward had a job and a stable income while Bondfield, at the same age, was still living, if not hand to mouth, at least with very little security. She was not good at looking after herself, and she took toughness as a necessary element of her occupation. She was involved in so many campaigns and organizations that demands came at her from all sides, and she hardly ever turned them down. In October 1908, for example, fresh from her resignation from the Shop Assistants' Union, she spoke at a by-election meeting in Newcastle upon Tyne despite suffering from 'a severe injury to her right foot'. The socialist Robert Blatchford reported in *The Clarion* that 'Miss Bondfield . . . went down to Newcastle from Liverpool on the 2.10 p.m. train, spoke for the Socialist candidate, and returned by the night train to London. That is the sort of stuff our women Socialists are made of.'[7]

This pattern of constant toil could not be sustained indefinitely, and in the end the inevitable happened. On Saturday, 18 November 1911 while giving a speech for the CWG in Altrincham, she collapsed. As she spoke she simply came to a halt 'with a mind perfectly blank. It was a terrible experience. I felt lost.'[8] She was taken home to Ward, who no doubt received her with alarm. The doctor was sent for and Bondfield was diagnosed with nervous exhaustion. She was anxious and excitable, unable to do anything yet obsessed with the idea that everything would fall apart if she was not constantly active. Even sleep provided no respite, since her dreams were full of trains and meetings. The remedy for all this was some mild medication plus instructions to 'live like a cabbage, not to read, or write, or talk'.[9] In late December the doctor sent her to Penlee in Cornwall, possibly to some kind of rest home or retreat at which she could recover far removed from the causes of her condition.

The physician who issued this prescription was no ordinary doctor. Ethel Bentham was one of the first women to receive medical training in England, although she actually had to go to Paris and Brussels to qualify. She was both a suffragist and a socialist and had joined the ILP while living in Newcastle-upon-Tyne. In 1909 she had moved to London, setting up a practice treating women and children. She was a member of the WLL Executive and also provided medical services to the mother and baby clinic established to commemorate Margaret MacDonald and Mary Middleton. Her private means enabled her to underwrite its costs, which she did for a number of years. She had known Bondfield and Ward for some time, and she and Bondfield had both been ILP delegates to the TUC Congress in September. As a member of the WLL Executive, upon which Ward also sat, Bentham was technically Bondfield's employer as well as her friend and doctor. Two other WLL women, Marion

Phillips[10] and Mary Longman, lodged with Bentham at her house in Holland Park, so that from the start there was an unfortunate entanglement of people, roles and interests which was shortly to cause a considerable amount of trouble.

Ward had initially taken Bondfield to her new house in Hendon, which was larger and quieter than the flat in Camden, and where it would be easier to keep an eye on her and prevent her from trying to work. However much she tried to shield her from any source of anxiety, excitement or stress, though, she could not keep everything out. Ramsay MacDonald had tried to face his grief at his wife's death by writing an account of her life and circulating it to friends.[11] He sent a copy to Bondfield and Ward, and unfortunately Bondfield opened the parcel. She immediately broke down. Later the same day she wrote to thank him. Beginning 'Dear Mac' she plunged straight in telling him that:

> The sight of her dear face brought back so acutely the overwhelming sense of loss that they have taken the book away from me. Maud says I must get steadier before I shall be allowed to read it. But I cannot wait for that before I thank you, my friend, for sending us that gift.[12]

Soon after this Bondfield went alone to Cornwall. Her illness meant that the WLL had to find an interim secretary, and the person they chose was Marion Phillips. Phillips was a ferociously intelligent Australian with a doctorate from the LSE and excellent organizational skills and was thus an obvious choice. But her appointment complicated matters even further so that when there appeared to be a falling-out between Bondfield and Ward on the one hand and Bentham, Phillips and Longman on the other the assumption was that it was personal or perhaps caused by jealousy over the secretaryship of the League, while in fact it was the result of Ward's decision to assume control of Bondfield's treatment herself.

Dr Bentham seems to have been clear from the outset that Bondfield's recovery would take time and need patience. However, as the days wore on and Bondfield showed little perceptible sign of improvement, Ward decided that what was needed was a psychiatrist rather than a GP, and proceeded unilaterally to call one in. It is hard to be sure why she did this, particularly since, so far as is known, she had no expertise in mental health or medical understanding of Bondfield's condition. It is not impossible that Bondfield had told her about incidents or experiences that she had confided to no-one else, not even to Bentham, and that Ward therefore felt justified in seeking a more specialist opinion. This in itself might have been no more than awkward, had she not chosen not only to ignore medical etiquette by bypassing Bentham to do it, but also to decide on a male practitioner in whom Bentham did not have much confidence. Her exchange of letters directly with Ward on the matter has not survived, but Bondfield, who destroyed so much of her personal correspondence, kept the originals of five letters Bentham wrote to her between 5 and 13 January 1911.

From these it is immediately clear that Bentham was furious. She was not opposed to the taking of another opinion in principle, but, she said, it would be wrong to ask the patient to incur unnecessary expense of a specialist if one was not needed. 'Your case,' she went on:

> is as clear as noonday and could have been predicted months ago by anyone with eyes in their head. (In fact it was so predicted for I had a long talk with Mrs MacDonald which resulted in our both pressing upon the Executive that you should have a long and complete holiday. . . .)[13]

Bentham went on to explain that for Ward to suggest the calling in of a 'mental specialist' and for Bentham to agree, would:

> give you the impression that there was some dissatisfaction with your progress, or something mysterious which we needed to elucidate and this would eventually tend to dispirit you and eventually retard your progress. . . . In the second place – if such a mental specialist was really necessary you would of course have to abide by the consequences, but my experience is that such a consultation always becomes known however careful you may be and this might do great harm to your future career. You may possibly think this exaggerated, but unluckily I have seen some very unfortunate results.[14]

Bentham's apprehensions were not at all without foundation. Mental and physical exhaustion caused by overwork was a common ailment of people living Bondfield's kind of peripatetic life, and a number of Labour leaders were prone to working themselves into a state of collapse. There was relatively little comprehension of either the need for self-care or the possible long-term effects of unrelenting stress. Physicians like Bentham might counsel rest and sleep, but they were not often heeded unless or until it was too late. But mental illness was altogether different. That carried a stigma with it, and for women doubly so, since in their case any suggestion of it played into the idea of the 'female hysteria' which was assumed to be one of the contributory factors making women unfit for any role other than those traditionally assigned to them. Worse, women who lived without men, who failed or refused to marry, or who chose to live with women, were even more at risk, both in terms of the treatments some psychiatrists chose to employ and the perception of their ability to be or become fully adult. Lesbian relationships were interpreted as a sign of immaturity. Teenaged girls might 'fall in love' with one another or with older women, but it was thought that these attachments should not last and, for most young women, would soon be replaced by a 'normal' relationship with a man. Those for whom this was not the case were seen as stunted in both their mental and sexual development, never quite reaching full adulthood and always behaving as juveniles. Bentham, herself probably a lesbian, must have been acutely aware of all this, and aware too that if it got out that Bondfield had visited a mental specialist the damage to both her reputation and her future would be terminal. 'You must remember,' she wrote to Bondfield on 9 January:

> that I made Miss Ward thoroughly understand in our conversation that I would arrange with any consultant you wanted but I earnestly begged her not to influence you to choose one who was not the most useful person from a medical point of view, and whom to have been known to have consulted *(sic)* would give a very bad impression as to your mental condition – for which there was not an atom of reason or justification other than her own anxiety. This was and is natural enough, but as I impressed upon her it is not fair to sacrifice your prospects or progress to it.[15]

Had she known it, her fears were soon amply justified by the view taken of the rift by Katharine Bruce Glasier,[16] a member of the WLL Executive and herself a well-known speaker and writer. She liked neither Bondfield nor Phillips very much, and was fairly confident that she knew the root of the problem, writing to Ramsay MacDonald that:

> I wish I had Margaret Bondfield's confidence or quite understood her: but her friendship with Miss Ward which your dear wife dreaded got right between us. These violent attachments don't seem to help, or to be good servants of the commonwealth. They have in them all the disproportionate heats and chills – and passionate and impulsive actions against outsiders who touch one of the beloved one's supposed interests or dignities that belong to lovers.[17]

Bentham's final objection to Ward's behaviour was that, because the referral had been made behind her back, it constituted a 'dismissal from the position of your medical adviser, and a dismissal made in the most discourteous way possible – so much so that any consultant who was fully aware of the facts would decline to intervene'.[18] She was withering about Ward, who, she said, 'talks, not as a friend or relative, but as a med. Practitioner who has taken over the case'. Bondfield had assured her that Ward was 'in ignorance of the usual manner of conducting such things' and she 'joyfully' accepted this assurance. She was prepared to make an appointment for Bondfield with any professional she chose, but:

> must still ask you to choose some other adviser. Miss Ward's distrust of my judgement has been openly expressed and as you and she *(are)* quite naturally

so close to one another, that I should be at a great disadvantage in treating you and it would be comfortable for neither of us. No one with any self respect could continue on such terms . . . This makes no difference to our future relations in any respect. I feel no resentment against Miss Ward, but just recognize her position as one that she cannot help though it has proved a misfortune for all three concerned – for me because I regret more than I can say having to relinquish a patient in whom I took more than ordinary interest.[19]

Later, when Bondfield visited the second doctor, he concurred in Bentham's view of the case, said that he could 'find no trace whatever of organic disease and regards it as altogether exhaustion due to over-work and over-excitement . . . and has prescribed for you certain drugs which, oddly enough, are exactly what you have been taking'.[20]

By now Bondfield had taken a decision which influenced, not just her immediate problem, but also how she managed her mental health over the ensuing years. She did not like being fought over, and so simply removed herself from the situation. She resigned from her post with the WLL and returned to Penlee in Cornwall. There she stayed for several months, initially 'haunted with the sense of deserting my post; worrying about how the work was going on – a kind of inflated egotism, which makes one feel indispensable'. The WLL Executive, which was reluctant to appoint Marion Phillips permanently, had refused to accept her resignation and instead granted her sick leave on half pay, so that her anxiety about how they were managing without her was not unreasonable. After the first couple of months, however, she found that she 'had gone to the other extreme. I was not thinking or caring much about anything, but I was gaining physical strength'.[21]

At the end of April she went back to London and tried to take up the various reins again. She went to a meeting in Woolwich but found that she was 'Tired and excited before. Tired and depressed after.'[22] Once more she tried to resign, and once more the Executive declined her resignation. She took more leave and went back to the peace and quiet of the country. In July she made another attempt to return to work before going back to Cornwall and then to a house party in Ireland where she had 'a most wonderful time with a sense of complete irresponsibility. Plenty of boating and swimming.'[23]

Ward does not appear to have accompanied her on her travels; apart from anything else she was now a civil servant and could not simply drop everything and take an extended holiday. Whatever difficulties there might have been the relationship continued, with Bondfield living with Ward in Hendon while maintaining a foothold in rooms in London. Since Ward's job kept her out of politics they spent much less time together than they had done when appearing on the same platforms and cribbing from one another's notes, but Bondfield recorded social events and evenings at home with Ward (who, for reasons unknown, she called 'G') in her diary. In other respects, however, she made sure that her life changed, and that she regained some of the control that had earlier escaped her.

The WLL was still trying to hang on to Bondfield's services, but she was adamant. Apart from anything else she now encountered difficulties with relationships, writing to Ramsay MacDonald that she had decided:

> not to hold office in the League. I shall be a member of the executive committee only. For the first time I have met with people with whom I *cannot* work . . . At present my attitude divides the Executive Committee and is frightfully bad for the League. . . . I do not choose to be the nominal head without any real power.[24]

MacDonald wrote to express how sorry he was about this. 'What is the poor League to do? Are we fated to see it pass away after all? I do not know if I can do anything else to help matters.' For himself, frustrated at the way the party was going, he thought that 'I shall have to retire altogether and content myself by writing at the end of many unfinished chapters "The end is not yet . . ."'[25] In September 1912 Bondfield returned to London and finally persuaded the WLL Executive to accept her resignation. She threw herself back into other work and was soon travelling the country again. Meanwhile she kept Bentham's letters perhaps as a form of insurance against any future allegations or insinuations of mental illness. Although this breakdown would not be her last, and although she would by no means always take proper care of herself, she did acquire a better understanding of how to manage the intense stress her life increasingly came to involve and, at the very least, to accept the importance of rest and quiet to a mind constantly on the move in a noisy and demanding world.

When she returned to London from Ireland she began to work more closely with the CWG on issues relating both to the implementation of the Insurance Act and the question of maternity provision, eventually accepting a full-time post as Secretary of the Guild's Citizen Sub-Committee. She really enjoyed this job, at least in part because it got her away from the mesh of relationships which characterized the WLL, in which she remained involved, but less and less engaged. The CWG, founded in 1883, had a remit, not only of promoting the interests of women employed by the Co-operative Society, but also those of women generally and working-class women in particular. It was run by its Secretary, Margaret Llewelyn Davies, who, together with her life companion, Lilian Harris, worked from a room in a vicarage in Kirkby Lonsdale in Westmorland, and it is a testimony to her abilities that she did this successfully for more than three decades. She was one of the founding lights of the PSF, whose Executive Committee Bondfield chaired, and the two also knew one another through the ILP. Together they made what Llewelyn Davies' biographer called 'a formidable team',[26] using their joint strengths to great effect to advance the causes they cared about.

One of the most significant of these campaigns was the fight for a minimum wage for girls and women employed in Cooperative enterprises, which was achieved in 1912. The question of a minimum wage had been a very divisive one amongst Labour women generally, with one group, headed by Margaret MacDonald, arguing for it and another, led by Mary Macarthur, advocating Trade Boards which would set minimum rates industry by industry. In 1909 Trade Boards had indeed been established in four areas, including hammered chain-making, and the famous 1910 strike in that industry had been caused by the employers' refusal to implement the new minimum rate. The Cooperative's minimum wage of 18 shillings a week covered workers in both Coop shops and the factories which made the goods being sold, and was paid, as Bondfield pointed out, 'mainly to unskilled labour for which no trade union rate has been fixed. The trade union rate is always paid where one exists.'[27]

Throughout the discussions on the 1911 National Insurance Act women had fought to get proper provision for working-class women both before and after childbirth. The Act had instituted a maternity benefit (in theory) for most insured single women and for the wives of insured men. Since some people had wanted to exclude single women on moral grounds, there had been a fight to get them covered. On the other hand, there was a huge loophole in the legislation which allowed groups of employees whose employers provided their own sick pay schemes to be 'contracted out', and this resulted in thousands of married women losing their maternity benefits, which were contingent on their husbands being contracted into the government scheme. Many thousands more were married to men who, for one reason or another, were entirely uninsured. Some of the conditions in which the poorest had to give birth were truly grim; Bondfield gave the example of one woman who was 'confined in a cellar, where rats ran about on the floor. . . . a most horrible place. A maternity nurse appealed to a ladies' charity, but no help came until two days after the confinement. No maternity benefits.'[28] Even when women were in receipt of benefits the money could be withdrawn. For the period around the birth when they were signed off work 'due to incapacity' they were not supposed to work at all, and since this was interpreted as including domestic work women had their benefits withdrawn if they were found sweeping the floor or feeding existing children. Officials who visited women's homes and made decisions about eligibility were overwhelmingly male and had very little understanding of what the reality of working-class women's lives was like. 'When a man is ill,' said Bondfield, 'his wife is there to look after him. When the wife is ill there is no one to look after her.'[29] Bondfield and Llewelyn Davies also led the successful campaign to get the maternity grant paid directly to mothers rather than to their husbands, as had initially been the case.

One of the CWG's objectives was to challenge a culture in which detailed discussion of sex, pregnancy and childbirth were taboo subjects in polite society. They realized that the strongest advocates they had for this were women themselves, so in a revolutionary move they collected hundreds of letters from women detailing their experiences of birth and perinatal motherhood. These were published in a book called *Maternity – Letters from Working Women* which was instrumental in persuading both national and local government that there needed to be action. In 1914 Llewelyn Davies and Bondfield developed a national maternity scheme which proposed to revolutionize care, focusing on the women and significantly overhauling the maternity grant scheme. The extensive campaign for this plan was interrupted by the First World War, but many of its principles filtered through into post-war provision and it was one of the pieces of work of which Bondfield was most proud.

Another part of this project was to help women understand and talk about their own bodies. Ever since, in the distant Brighton days, Mrs Martindale had enlightened her about sex, she had been an advocate of giving women as much information as possible, but she was out of step with the times, which, for women, equated ignorance with virtue. But many women wanted to know about their own physiology, and, in particular, wanted to be able to explain conception and birth to their daughters in clear, unambiguous language. Dr Christine Murrell, whom Bondfield may have met through Ethel Bentham, was strongly of the view that because women knew so little of how their bodies worked they were hugely vulnerable to being persuaded (especially by male physicians) that their female anatomy made them inherently inferior. Murrell and the CWG developed a scheme which would cascade knowledge through the membership, training local leaders both to understand it and to pass it on to others. 'Many students' said Bondfield, 'were grandmothers. They heard the names and functions of their bodily organs for the first time.'[30]

Meanwhile the suffrage question continued to trouble both the Labour Party and the WLL. In 1909 Bondfield, as the WLL delegate to the Labour Party Conference, had got herself into trouble with many WLL women by unilaterally changing their amendment to the resolution on electoral reform. Amongst other things the resolution proposed 'The enfranchisement of all adults, male and female' and the WLL's amendment would have added a rider which included the requirement that 'any attempt to exclude women will be met by the uncompromising opposition of organized labour to the whole Bill'.[31] This effectively mandated Labour MPs to vote against adult male suffrage, and, with her experience of how the block vote worked, Bondfield knew that the amendment was very unlikely to be passed. She did think, however, that they might get away with it if the mandate was not to vote against the whole Bill, so she simply removed those words from the amendment. In her autobiography she said that she would not have thought of this if Arthur Henderson,[32] the party's

General Secretary, had not expressed concerns, but given her role in the adult suffrage campaign this seems unlikely, and she may simply have been using him as a shield. In the event the resolution was not passed, but the WLL was extremely annoyed at Bondfield's high-handed action. Reluctantly, the Executive voted to endorse her action, though the incident soured several relationships for some time.

In 1912 Labour revisited the whole question, partly because Labour women kept pushing it, but partly also because there had been a change in the NUWSS's political positioning. Millicent Fawcett no longer believed Liberal assurances that they would support votes for women; they had been in government since 1906 and had not used their parliamentary power to broaden the franchise to anybody, let alone women. Henderson, always on the lookout for anything that might help Labour in practical terms, saw an opportunity. The Labour Party was chronically short of funds and their electoral and organizational expertise was woeful, but they did have a voice in Parliament. The NUWSS, on the other hand, had been working in elections and by-elections for years, and had a group of highly experienced agents and campaigners as part of their team. In January 1912 they now passed a resolution which was very little different from that which had been defeated in 1909 and which included the words which Bondfield had deleted. This was followed by an agreement with the NUWSS to set up an Election Fighting Fund (EFF) giving the Labour Party access to both NUWSS funding for candidates who supported female suffrage and NUWSS organizers' expertise. The latter was as much needed as the money; commenting on the agreement the NUWSS paper, *Common Cause*, remarked that their motto had always been 'organize and organize now', but that although the 'spirit and fire of the Labour Party is wonderful, . . . you can't mobilise forces without the machine of mobilisation . . . '[33]

Over the next couple of years the EFF supported a number of Labour candidates but, most importantly, contributed significantly to the building up of on-the-ground expertise amongst both male and female Labour activists. It also had the effect of beginning to draw Labour women back together, and even the WFL backed it. Isabella Ford, a socialist and trade unionist as well as a member of the NUWSS's Executive, said that 'I feel comradeship, the real thing, is growing fast just because of this battle. . . . I feel like bursting with joy over it at times.'[34] Ford's enthusiasm may have been overly optimistic, but it did reflect a changed environment and, although the agreement had some difficult moments, it survived until the outbreak of war in August 1914 split both the NUWSS and the Labour Party and put an end to elections for the next four years.

Chapter 9
Events Beyond Control

In later years, Margaret Bondfield would look back on the outbreak of war in 1914 much as most other people did, as a horror which exploded almost without warning – 'it came upon us, as upon almost all English people, suddenly, unexpectedly, as a surprise. Probably it was not possible to be ready for it and yet innocent of complicity in its preparation.'[1] In 1913 she, Ward and Lilian Wald,[2] an American friend visiting Europe, had gone on a walking holiday to Auvergne where they admired the scenery and met local people. There was then, she said, no talk of war, and the three women concentrated on their 'various preoccupations, which seemed to all of us infinitely more urgent. . . . Our minds were almost wholly preoccupied with the details of social reforms, which we felt to be of primary importance. In this we were probably right.'[3]

This may well have been the case, but it was by no means the whole story. There had, in fact, been many warning voices, including those of socialist and pacifist women. Moreover, in 1910 Bondfield had become the inaugural Chair of the British section of the Women's International Council of Socialist and Labour Organizations, a body founded as part of the Second (or Socialist) International, which had existed since 1889, and which, despite being predominantly Marxist in policy and outlook, included many social democrats as well as those who occupied the contested ground in between. She must have heard some talk of war at conferences and in correspondence, though it is also entirely possible that, like many other people, she thought the apprehension of it overblown and the likelihood of it improbable.

By 1913 she was an experienced internationalist, having attended her first conference abroad in 1904 when she, Macarthur, Margaret MacDonald and others attended the International Congress of Women in Berlin. There she met women from many other countries and was introduced to new ideas, but although she very much enjoyed the travel, the company and the work in the sessions on women in industry, she also felt rather like a fish out of water. Most of the 1,000 women present were from the middle or upper classes, and very few had actual shop floor experience. The social functions seemed over-luxurious and the conference sessions were rather intimidating to women who had not had much formal education. 'Mary and I' she said:

> felt very strongly that this was no place for us. . . . nearly everyone *(who spoke)* was a professor or a Doctor of Law or Medicine or Science, Mary and I agreed that even so, salvation for the workers would not come that way – that leadership must come from themselves.[4]

The main thing she had taken from Berlin was a commitment to internationalism which never left her. Towards the end of her life, after the Second World War, she wrote that 'international cooperation . . . furnishes the only possible basis upon which a solid and enduring peace may be built'.[5] She had a consistent internationalist outlook, even when, during the 1930s, the rise of fascism drove her to modify her pacifism. She believed that world peace was achievable and that it was within the power of humanity to achieve it, provided that they kept talking to one another. Despite the severe provocation of two world wars, she never wavered from this faith.

The International Women's Suffrage Alliance (IWSA), representing about twelve million women from twenty-six countries around the world, had its headquarters in London, and as the War loomed closer and closer, women's organizations and international socialists began desperately to try to avert it. In July 1914 Millicent Fawcett and Chrystal Macmillan,[6] both officers of the IWSA, drew up an International Manifesto of Women which was sent to the Foreign Office and all embassies in London. It was an impassioned plea for peace, appealing to the governments of the world on behalf of politically powerless women 'to leave untried no method of conciliation or arbitration . . . which may help to avert deluging half the civilised world in blood.[7]

On 1 August the British Section of the International Socialist Bureau issued an 'Appeal to the British Working Class' calling upon workers to 'stand together for peace . . . '[8] The following day a huge demonstration in Trafalgar Square was addressed by Keir Hardie, Arthur Henderson, Margaret Bondfield, Mary Macarthur, Charlotte Despard and many others. Bondfield 'in a burning speech called upon the men and women of Britain to fight Jingoism with every ounce of intelligence they possessed'.[9] After the demonstration ended Ramsay MacDonald went to Downing Street to find out what was happening. Other speakers went to his third-floor flat in Lincoln's Inn Fields. Hoping against hope they waited for news, but 'When he *(MacDonald)* came he had no good news to give them . . . *(he)* had to report to those who so anxiously awaited him that it was going to be war.'[10]

Three days later a large women's protest meeting was held. In speech after speech an international platform of women denounced what was coming, but it was hopeless. As they emerged from the Kingsway Hall they found that, in Bondfield's words, 'the Guards were on their way to Dover. The die was cast. We were at war. Events had got beyond control.'[11]

With alarming rapidity people began to choose sides. Some women became enthusiastic supporters of the War, often because they thought that if women were seen to support it they would be rewarded with the vote when it ended. Millicent Fawcett took this view: 'Women, your country needs you,' she wrote, 'LET US SHOW OURSELVES WORTHY OF CITIZENSHIP!'[12] The WSPU enthusiastically backed the War and its paper, the *Suffragette*, was renamed *Britannia*. The NUWSS membership split to reflect both sides. Isabella Ford's lifelong Quaker pacificism set her firmly against the conflict, but this tested and sometimes broke old friendships. 'I do not think,' she wrote to Fawcett, 'that war ever destroyed war – & real salvation can only come to people and nations from within.'[13]

In March 1915 the German socialist Clara Zetkin[14] drew together an International Conference of Socialist Women in Berne, in Switzerland. Throughout the War, women would keep trying to work together for peace across national boundaries, often in dangerous circumstances and usually without success. In the case of the Berne Conference Britain was represented by Marion Phillips, Mary Longman, Ada Salter and Bondfield herself. Delegates from seven other countries also attended, passed resolutions intended to promote peace, and returned home full of hope that something might be done.

Meanwhile the IWSA was organizing a conference in the Hague for April. A committee including Bondfield, Macarthur and Phillips organized a national women's conference in London to 'discuss the basis of a permanent peace settlement' and as a result at least 180 women applied for passports to travel to the Hague. By now, however, the government was growing wary of allowing women to meet 'the enemy' and all the applications were refused. Eventually it was agreed to grant 24 permits to a group of women which included Bondfield. Despite this Winston Churchill, then First Lord of the Admiralty, was determined that they should not go and when the women arrived at Tilbury they found the shipping lanes closed to all traffic. Rather than concede defeat they settled down and hung on to see what happened next, but Churchill simply waited until the conference had ended before removing the blockade. The delegation was, Bondfield wrote, 'marooned. . . by the Government's decision to suspend all passenger service boats from Tilbury as long as we besieged Tilbury dock'.[15] The newspapers were fully on the government's side, with the *Daily Express* sneering that 'A dismal group of Peacettes are waiting at Tilbury for a boat to take them to Holland for the International chirrup with the German fraus.'[16]

The advent of War presented the Labour Party with a dilemma. Belgium was a neutral country but when Germany invaded it in August 1914 there was general public outrage, and many people who had opposed war only a few days earlier now changed their minds. After a very difficult meeting the Parliamentary Labour Party decided to support the government in the war effort, and MacDonald resigned as its Chair, effectively relinquishing his role as party leader and moving to the back benches. Arthur Henderson was elected to replace him. The ILP's National Administrative Council, to which Bondfield had been elected in 1913, was plunged into heated discussions about the stance to be taken but remained opposed to the conflict, convinced that it was the result of 'secret diplomacy' between elites across the continent at the expense of the working classes.

The result of this view was the establishment of the Union of Democratic Control, an organization founded by Ramsay MacDonald and others which was as much about how to prevent wars in the future as how to end them in the present. Women's organizations like the WLL affiliated to it, and Bondfield and Macarthur joined it as individuals. Because most of the people involved in it were moderates rather than extremists and included negotiators who understood the need to keep channels of communication open, it was able to maintain conversations which would otherwise not have taken place, but it was unsuccessful in stopping the War. Its argument for a negotiated peace at the earliest possible opportunity made it look out of step, not only with the public, but also with large sections of the trade union movement. Its commitment to democracy in foreign policy, international courts, self-determination and disarmament sounded impossibly idealistic to many people, even those who agreed with them. MacDonald devoted the war years to laying the foundations for peace and paid a high price for doing so. He became the target of hatred and derision for the right-wing patriotic press, who attacked him mercilessly, at one point even publishing his birth certificate. Since illegitimacy was still considered a stain upon both mother and child, this was embarrassing and humiliating. He was described as the 'libeller and slanderer of his country' and the 'illegitimate son of a Scotch servant girl', and this together with some confusion over his legal name (he had been registered at birth as James McDonald Ramsay) was alleged to render him unfit to be an MP.[17] By the end of the War he was a hero to the Left and an undiluted villain to the Right, who continued to pursue him long after peace had been achieved.

For most working people, however, the challenges of war were more immediate and practical. Women employed in non-essential or luxury industries were soon laid off, but as men went off to the Front many jobs in industry were backfilled by women, raising all kinds of questions about skills, facilities and pay. Moreover, the immediate development of voluntary groups making clothing and other items for men at the Front meant that the women who had made these things for a living began to be laid off. As war production for the military took hold, women were extensively employed in the manufacture of munitions, an occupation which could be very dangerous and sometimes even fatal.[18] When, in March 1915, the Board of Trade announced that women should register for work it had become apparent that they would need both organization and representation too. There had been no planning for what might happen when increasing numbers of women entered manufacturing industries, and the NFWW regarded the Board of Trade's announcement as irresponsible because, Bondfield said, it 'threatened to flood the labour market with volunteers willing to take employment on any terms, regardless of the consequences to the normal wage earner'.[19] Decades of work to reassure men that women would not undercut their wages or put them out of work could be undone almost overnight.

To deal with some of this the Labour and trade union movement created the Workers' War Emergency Committee which brought together all the disparate parts of the movement. In the wake of the Board of Trade's announcement the Committee held a conference, chaired by Macarthur, which agreed a series of demands. Broadly speaking, these were that joining a trade union should be a condition of employment for women coming into war work, that there should be equal pay (thus negating the undercutting issue), that women should receive a living wage, that suitable training should be provided, and that, after the end of the War, women being replaced by returning men should be guaranteed other employment. Added to this was a demand for women to be represented on Advisory Committees and on the Court of Arbitration, which dealt with industrial disputes, and, tucked in at the end, '(in extremely polite but quite unmistakable words)' a demand for the franchise for all women.[20] Many of these demands were successful, though the franchise took some years to achieve and equal pay remained a fraught issue both during the War and for decades afterwards. The NFWW's workload now increased exponentially, and Bondfield left the CWG to become Macarthur's Organizing Secretary. This work was important, and she was very happy to be with Macarthur and to be back in a trade union environment, but, whatever impression she gave later, her work in the peace movement occupied at least as much of her attention as the NFWW.

To address the problem of volunteers the Central Committee on Women's Training and Employment brought together allies as unlikely as Mary Macarthur and Queen Mary[21] to support working women by providing workrooms where goods could be produced and skills developed. This was all well and good, except that the minimum wage was set at a rather meagre 10 shillings, and although meals were provided and women with children got extra, the rate was still well below anything the NFWW would have demanded in industry, causing Sylvia Pankhurst to describe the workrooms contemptuously as 'queen Mary's Sweat Shops.' Bondfield was the supervisor of one of the larger facilities at Park Street but also worked on a variety of issues relating to women in industry as well as returning to involvement in the wider trade union movement. The NFWW's membership increased by leaps and bounds as more and more women entered factories and workshops, and as a consequence the staff increased also. By the end of the War a core of experienced women, including future MPs Susan

Lawrence and Dorothy Jewson, had developed linking together the NFWW, the WLL and the CWG, with Bondfield an integral part of all three.

All through 1915 a furious debate raged over the government's introduction of conscription, a measure which Labour members largely opposed. However, a handful of the party's leaders were now involved in government, in Arthur Henderson's case as a member of the Cabinet, and they were committed to conscription as an inevitable part of the war effort. In January a special Conference of the Party 'urged' Labour MPs to oppose it. The NEC then decided that Labour ministers should withdraw from the government, which they duly did, though Henderson was furious and swore to vote for conscription whatever happened. At the end of January the party's Annual Conference affirmed the decision to oppose conscription but not the decision to withdraw from government. The ILP issued an Appeal to the Organized Workers asking them 'to take action against the conscription proposal at once'. Bondfield was a signatory to this and also moved the ILP's resolution calling for a drastic overhaul of the Act in order to protect workers who, once conscripted, could find their wages and conditions reduced. Conscription for unmarried men came into effect in January 1916, but as the year wore on the casualties on the Front built up, and in May Lloyd George introduced conscription for married men, too. 'One of the great scandals' said Bondfield '. . . was the attitude of mind . . . which regarded human life as the cheapest thing to expend.'[22]

Throughout the War Bondfield continued to appear on peace platforms and on committees organizing demonstrations and events. These were the subject of increasing hostility from the press and suspicion from the government, so that by the end of the War she was regarded as almost an enemy of the people. As the Women's Peace Crusade grew in strength around the country a committee of ILP women – Bondfield, Katharine Bruce Glasier and Ethel Snowden – drew up guidelines on how to organize and canvass as well as a directory listing Peace Crusade Committees which grew steadily. Women's marches were attacked, meetings were disrupted and rallies cancelled by the police at no notice. Nevertheless, though always a minority opinion, support for a negotiated peace continued to grow.[23]

Despite the suspension of the suffrage campaign at the start of the War, the issue had not entirely gone away, and by 1916 it was clear that some decisions needed to be made. There was a general agreement that the working-class men who had fought and suffered in the trenches had more than earned the right to vote but although there was some acceptance that women had also earned consideration, universal suffrage still seemed a distant prospect. In August 1916 a Parliamentary Speaker's Conference was convened to consider future franchise arrangements, but the failure to include any women in its membership was alarming. The Conference's report, published in January 1917, proposed (by a majority of one) that single women over a specified age (30 or 35) should have the vote, as should the wife of any man who was on the Local Government Electoral Register. The ensuing 1918 Representation of the People Bill enfranchised all men from the age of 21, but for women set the age limit at 30 and specified a property qualification. The debates in Parliament were fierce, with strong opposition in some quarters to enfranchising any women at all, and even some resistance to allowing working-class men to vote. Despite this, the Act received royal assent early in 1918. The next general election would have women electors. A separate Act allowed all women over the age of 21 to stand for Parliament.

For universal suffrage campaigners this was a bitter-sweet victory. As always, working-class women would be last in the queue, and it seemed particularly unjust that although they had kept industry, munitions factories and much else going during the War they would be forced out of work once the men came home and, in many cases, not even allowed to vote. 'Most of the Adult Suffragists,' said Bondfield '(certainly Mary Macarthur and I) felt that it was a mean and inadequate little Bill, creating fresh anomalies which had to be overcome.'[24]

Soon after this the Russian Revolution burst upon the world to be hailed by socialists and the wider Left with absolute joy as a huge victory over a reviled and detested Tsarist regime. For decades socialists and trade unionists had regarded the Russian empire as embodying everything that they wanted to fight against. Russian émigrés were welcomed and their stories of imprisonment and torture heard with sympathetic outrage. The overthrow of the Tsar and the installation of Alexander Kerensky's revolutionary government was greeted with wild and sometimes unwise enthusiasm. There were celebratory rallies and events with pro- and anti-war speakers coming together to celebrate the new dawn. Margaret Bondfield was a member of the Standing Orders Committee for the National Labour and Socialist Convention in Leeds on 3 June,[25] where the speakers included Ramsay MacDonald, Philip Snowden, Charlotte Despard, Will Anderson, Ethel Snowden, George Lansbury and Sylvia Pankhurst as well as Bertrand Russell and the future Foreign Secretary Ernest Bevin. Many speeches were made and several resolutions passed. MacDonald moved one entitled 'Russia Hail!' which congratulated the Russian people on overthrowing 'a tyranny that resisted the intellectual and social development of Russia' and liberating 'the people of Russia for the great work of establishing their own political and economic freedom on a firm foundation . . . '[26] Will Anderson moved the resolution to establish 'Councils of Workmen and Soldiers' Delegates for initiating and co-ordinating working-class activity . . . to work strenuously for a peace made by the peoples of the various countries, and for the complete political and economic emancipation of international labour.'[27] Later in the year the October Revolution ejected Kerensky's government, which the Convention had welcomed so fulsomely, and ushered in Lenin, Trotsky and the Bolsheviks. However, although this made some on the Left wary, most remained supportive as well as deeply curious to know what was happening in Russia and what the implications of events would be for the post-war world when it came.

As the Leeds Convention was meeting, Arthur Henderson was visiting revolutionary leaders in Petrograd (formerly St Petersburg). A debate had been going on in Britain as to whether or not the Labour Party should participate in a controversial international conference in Stockholm, and part of Henderson's remit was to make an assessment of the Russian position. When he returned the messy debate over the Stockholm conference continued, with the party, Henderson and Lloyd George, who was determined that British representatives should not attend, locked in a three-way battle so bitter that it eventually resulted in Henderson's resignation from the Cabinet. Now free to focus on the party, and convinced that mass democracy was the way forward, he began the internal structural re-organization which resulted in the 1918 Labour Party constitution including, amongst much else, the nationalization policy known as Clause Four and the admission of women as individual members.

The WLL had also begun to think about its next steps and, in particular, to worry about the prospect of a 'Women's Party'. In April 1917 they noted that women should not be drawn into the 'separate women's organisations which are bound to be set on foot. It is most important that, as workers, they should join with men and not form a special women's party.'[28] After some negotiation it was agreed that the WLL should become the core of the Labour Party's new Women's Section, with Marion Phillips as its first National Woman Officer and a team of female organizers to be recruited and run by her. The WLL understood that power resided in those parties which were likely at some stage to be able to form a government, and that where power was, there women should be. For his part Henderson understood that the introduction of votes for even some women meant that they would have to be included in the party's structure. Phillips and Henderson got on well and were in agreement that women as a whole were politically ignorant and would need 'educating' before they could play a full part in the political life of their country. The same view was not expressed about the millions of working-class men who were enfranchised at the same time, who were thought more likely to have had the advantage of trade union activism or educational schemes and in any case to have taken more interest in politics generally throughout their lives.

The WLL wanted a separate National Women's Conference held on an annual basis to provide a space in which women could 'have opportunities of discussing special women's questions or problems from the women's standpoint'.[29] Henderson was resistant to this, seeing women's role as secondary so that they would be supporting men 'not only with their votes, and with work at election times, but in helping to form the policy of the party and in the way of political education'.[30] A Women's Conference was eventually established, however, but throughout the 1920s and beyond its status remained a bone of contention and it was rarely able to influence policy in any meaningful way. There was also an ongoing debate about how the four reserved women's places on the NEC should be elected; women wanted to elect them directly themselves but lost the argument and had to accept them being chosen by the men as well as women. The first four women to sit on Labour's NEC were Susan Lawrence, Ethel Snowden, Ethel Bentham and Florence Harrison Bell, a WLL Executive member from Newcastle. Macarthur replaced Bell in 1919. Lawrence and Bentham would both go on to be MPs, and in 1929 Lawrence would become the first woman to chair the Labour Party. The Standing Joint Committee of Women's Industrial Organizations, which Phillips had set up in early 1916 to bring all the relevant women's groups together, became the party's Women's Advisory Committee with Phillips in the Chair. On 14 June 1918 the WLL ceased to exist. Labour had moved into the next phase of its life and the WLL had moved with it.

By mid-June 1918 Bondfield was exhausted and went to Penlee in Cornwall for a holiday. She stayed with Mrs Barnett, who had looked after her in 1912 after her breakdown, so there may have been some concern over her health. It is possible that there were difficulties in her private life, but if so her diary gives no indication of it. As always on holiday she walked long distances, but she also spent quite a lot of time in bed, reading and resting. On 20 June she received a letter from Ward ('G' in her diary). 'Very upset. Mrs Barnett most kind. *illegible* G. Wrote to MRM *(Mary Macarthur)*, G, and WEO *(Rev W. E. Orchard)*. Walked to Happy Valley. Most miserable. Late for dinner.'[31] The following day she stayed in bed, and the day after swam in the sea and walked. The next day she received replies from Macarthur and Orchard which 'much comforted' her. Ward's reply did not arrive for another two days, and Bondfield recorded its arrival without comment.

It is actually not clear from the wording of her diary entry whether it is she who is 'very upset' or Ward. There are at least two interpretations of what happened, the most obvious ones being either that Ward was breaking the relationship off by letter, or that Bondfield had done so before retreating to Cornwall and that Ward's letter was a reaction. It's even possible that the letter did not relate to a break-up at all, but to some completely different set of circumstances. Bondfield's behaviour, however, makes this seem the least likely option, if only because rather than rushing home to deal with whatever the crisis was she decided to stay in Cornwall. At the beginning of July she visited Chard, where she preached in the Congregational Church, finally only returning to London on 8 July on her way to a conference in Paris.

After this there is relatively little mention of Ward in her diary, though it is clear that they kept in touch. They seem to have spent a weekend together in September,[32] though where or in what circumstances she did not record. The address Bondfield wrote in the front of her 1919 diary is a new one in St. George's

Road, SW1.[33] It does seem that, after twelve years, the most significant personal bond of her adult life was severed, at least in the sense in which it had existed since 1906. As a friendship it continued, but as an intimate relationship it was over. By 1921 Ward was living in Surrey with a woman called Eleanor Welton. At the age of 45 Bondfield was now alone and, despite many close and rewarding friendships, would remain without a settled partner for the rest of her life.

Travel usually cheered Bondfield up, and the trip to Paris was the result of a series of events which had greatly pleased her. She had returned to the TUC as a delegate for the NFWW in 1916, and in 1917 topped the list of those failing to be elected to the Parliamentary Committee. In 1918 one of the successful candidates died, and she stepped up into the vacancy, becoming, after all, the first woman to sit on the TUC's governing body. At Congress that year she stood for re-election and succeeded easily, more than doubling her vote and coming in just ahead of the Miners' Federation candidate. She was now unquestionably one of the most senior trade unionists in the country with a voice at tables she had once only been able to dream of.

Her path to Paris, however, was not straightforward and followed yet another stand-off with the British government over passports. In April 1918 she had been appointed as one of two TUC delegates to the Minnesota Convention of the American Federation of Labour, due to take place in June. Bondfield's application for a passport was refused, and when the TUC queried this they were informed that 'women were not to be permitted to travel to America'.[34] The other delegate, the miners' MP Fred Hall, said that if Bondfield could not go then neither would he. The TUC wrote to Balfour, the Prime Minister, and were informed that 'there were no circumstances . . . such as would warrant the issue of a passport under the Admiralty regulations prohibiting women and children from travelling abroad'.[35] When the whole question was debated at Congress later that year the view was that not only had Bondfield been insulted, but also the whole of the TUC. By then, however, the position had changed, and Bondfield's application for a passport to attend the French Confédération du Travail conference in Paris in June 1918 had been granted. Before she could travel, however, the French government required her to sign an undertaking that: 'I have no desire to exceed my mandate in any way. I undertake to make no difficulties nor to make any "defeatist" propaganda.'[36]

This was Bondfield's first opportunity to travel since 1915 and she made the most of it. There were an impressive number of women delegates at the Confédération, but meetings tended to be rowdier than in England, with fights between delegates and missiles being thrown at speakers.[37] In France, as in Britain, workers were simultaneously anticipating peace and fearing what it might bring. The Russian Revolution, years of a debilitating war and near-famine conditions in some parts of Europe were causing widespread unrest, some of which erupted into violence. Delegates were divided over what the next steps should be, with some advocating direct action and the establishment of soviets as the 1915 Leeds conference had done, and others absolutely opposing (yet more) violence. Meanwhile, the War dragged on, and even as the Confédération met the city of Paris was being bombarded by the German army. Bondfield was very proud of the fact that her hands 'kept steady when Big Bertha dropped a shell outside our café at the moment when I was making salad dressing in a tablespoon, and I did not spill a drop'.[38]

In 1918, after her election to the TUC General Council, she decided to leave the ILP's National Administrative Council and concentrate on her trade union work. Ramsay MacDonald was not impressed. 'The ILP' he wrote to her:

> needs to be kept with its head to the wind or the wind will blow it over. Now you, my dear friend, will only get small in the Trade Union movement if you confide your activities to that. We need moving in Labour and Socialism a big generous free spirit, but a spirit withal that deals with real things and does not subsist on slops . . . if the ILP goes I shall . . . vegetate for the rest of my days and watch you waste on Trade Unionism (I mean exclusively on Trade Unionism) what was given for Socialism.[39]

Philip Snowden, who shared MacDonald's scepticism, wrote to her after her re-election in 1919 that he congratulated her on her 'magnificent vote . . . tho' when I see your colleagues I am not sure if it's condolences you need'.[40] Despite their long friendship, the trade union movement would always be a dividing line. Neither MacDonald nor Snowden ever understood her commitment to it and she never understood their ambivalent view. But it is also the case that for many years she felt pulled between Labour and the trade unions in a way that she never felt pulled between the Labour movement and women's groups. She believed in the progression of women's interests and would fight hard for it, but her heart was in organized labour and she always believed in it as the best route through which working-class women could advance.

Chapter 10
Isn't It Glorious!

In November 1918 the War finally came to an end. Three days later, Lloyd George announced that there would be a general election on 18 December. Labour had already withdrawn from the Coalition government and did not allow its candidates to accept the government 'coupon', or statement of support made to candidates standing with its backing. For the first time, all working-class men and about 60 per cent of women would be able to vote, even though the election was called so quickly that many men were still at the Front and thus effectively disenfranchised.

In August, in anticipation of an election, Mary Macarthur had become the first woman to be selected as a Labour parliamentary candidate when she was chosen for Stourbridge. Inevitably, there was speculation about what Bondfield might do, but none of it seemed very realistic or came to anything. Labour Party selection processes at this time were much more decentralized and ad hoc than they later became. Selection committees drew up shortlists of candidates they liked the sound of without necessarily having any contact with them, so that when, for instance, a Yorkshire newspaper reported that Margaret Bondfield, Ethel Snowden and Isabella Ford were 'before the local Labour Selection Committee for the Scarborough and Whitby Division'[1] it is unlikely that any of the women named had any idea that they were being considered. Candidates were also routinely selected in their absence, so that although Bondfield was later successfully selected to fight various seats a total of eleven times between 1921 and 1942 she very seldom attended or spoke at selection meetings. Moreover, if she had had parliamentary ambitions in 1918 she would not have chosen to pursue them in Scarborough and Whitby, which Labour had no prospect of winning. This is not to say that she was not tempted by the prospect of Parliament, and the fact that she stood in a by-election at the first available opportunity suggests that she very definitely was, but she does not seem to have sought selection in 1918 and instead spent several weeks in Stourbridge working for Macarthur.

Macarthur was widely expected to become Britain's first female MP; that she did not was down to a combination of factors which coalesced against her. For one thing, the returning officer insisted that she should appear on the ballot paper under her married name of Anderson, a name which she had never used professionally and by which she was unknown. She was also short of resources, some of which were diverted to nearby Smethwick to help defeat Christabel Pankhurst who was standing for the Women's Party on a platform which included both women's rights and the abolition of trade unions. Added to this, there was very strong public feeling against anti-war candidates, whose activities were viewed in some quarters as close to treasonable. Any one of these factors on its own Macarthur might have been able to overcome, but not all three together.

Three other women – Charlotte Despard, Emmeline Pethick-Lawrence and Millicent Mackenzie – also stood for Labour and were duly defeated. Across the country almost every Labour candidate who had been associated with peace campaigns or was believed to be 'soft' on Germany was beaten, even Arthur Henderson, who had been a member of the War Cabinet and had supported conscription. Will Anderson lost his Sheffield seat, which grieved Macarthur almost more than her own defeat. MacDonald was ousted in Leicester East and Philip Snowden in Blackburn. Despite the hostility and losses, however, Labour representation rose from 49 in 1914 to 62. More significantly, its share of the vote rose from a pre-war 8 per cent to a new high of 24 per cent. Although this was largely achieved by the piling up of votes in Labour areas, it was also true that there were now more of these areas, and even the resistant coal field constituencies were beginning to turn in Labour's direction. This suggested, first, that in another election without the Coalition coupon Labour might do much better in terms of seats, and, second, that the split in the Liberal Party was well worth trying to drive a wedge into in future elections.

Lloyd George's Coalition government, which was perceived as having got the country through the War to victory, was returned with a huge majority. Margaret Bondfield noted that pro-peace candidates had been defeated by 'methods which do not now bear the test of inspection', adding that the 'Liberal majority that had ruled England so long, and had hurried us into war in 1914, was the real casualty of the Khaki election'. The new government had 'an ample majority pledged to no principles and to no programme but with an unlimited zeal against the defeated powers which it could interpret at its own will'.[2]

There was scarcely time to draw breath after the election before, in January 1919, the Allied powers gathered in Versailles to sort out the peace treaty. It was entirely a conference of the victors and intended to reinforce their victory. Although there was a strong desire to create a Europe in which a major war could not happen again, the defeated powers were not invited to attend, nor was there to be any question of Germany or Austria refusing the terms they were offered. Despite the Armistice, the blockade which had been imposed at the start of the War was maintained to 'encourage' them to sign whatever was agreed as rapidly as possible. In Germany, there was also the threat of the Allied armies entering Berlin, with all the possible consequences (for women in particular) that that could entail. Since the blockade included food and medical supplies as well as military materiel, the effect on civilians was severe, and hunger had already turned to famine. The Armistice agreement conceded that the victorious powers needed to 'give consideration to the provisioning of Germany during the armistice to the extent recognised as necessary',[3] but the definition of what 'necessary' involved was very tightly drawn. In practice very little was done except through charity and whatever else could get through, which could hardly hope to meet the monumental need created by hunger and disease across Eastern Europe.[4] The human cost of defeat, particularly for women and children, was thus very high. Estimates of deaths caused by the blockade as a whole vary, but they certainly numbered in the hundreds of thousands, with hundreds of thousands more children suffering from the long-term psychological and developmental after-effects of prolonged malnutrition.

Economic collapse in Germany and Austria also contributed to the unrest which broke out in both capitals. In Vienna the fall of the imperial monarchy produced an elected social democratic rather than a communist government. In Berlin, however, in a city stalked by hunger, disease and despair, the struggle between the social democratic-led government and the new Communist Party founded by Karl Liebknecht and Rosa Luxemburg became an armed uprising during which Liebknecht and Luxemburg were arrested and murdered. Socialists across Europe were horrified, regardless of whether or not they supported violent revolution. Ramsay MacDonald, who had known them both for years, spoke for many when he wrote sadly in the Glasgow weekly paper *Forward* that:

> Rosa . . . was a born revolutionist, a bundle of restless energy. Her face, . . . was the mirror of a mind always on the attack. . . . They have both gone down to the grave and to history together . . . Those who read of it can but shudder, and do their best to see in the noise and horror a transition to peace. For the moment it will add to Europe's frenzy . . .[5]

MacDonald wrote this against a background of strikes in Glasgow and Belfast which were panicking parts of the government, both local and national, into believing that an uprising was about to break out in Britain. In Glasgow the local civil authorities were encouraged to ask for military assistance, but on 31 January violence broke out before the military arrived. In what became known as the Battle of George Square strikers and police fought in the streets for hours. The Secretary of State for Scotland described the situation as a Bolshevist uprising and greatly exaggerated the number of strikers involved. The strike leaders were arrested as the fighting broke out and by the time the army turned up the battle was over, though soldiers remained in the city for another two weeks and the atmosphere continued to be tense. In Belfast the strike only collapsed after the military were brought in in mid-February following considerable civil disturbance. In neither case were the strikers successful, but both raised the spectre of revolution to minds made deeply apprehensive by events in Russia and Germany.

Thus, for socialists all over Europe, including in Britain, one of the main questions for them to answer was whether or not they supported democracy or dictatorship, and, in either case, what that actually meant. Another was the vexed problem of blame for the War. Pro-war sentiment had developed into a demand for retribution against Germany in particular, but pro-peace campaigners thought that this would not help reconstruction in either the short or the long term. In her address to voters in Stourbridge during the 1918 general election the first of Mary Macarthur's Fourteen Points had been that: 'THERE MUST BE NO MORE WAR! . . . The Peace settlement must be based on Justice and Equity between the nations.' Many Coalition candidates, however, supported public calls for punitive reparations. Internationally socialists were deeply divided with many, particularly some factions of the French parties, believing that German socialists should be made to admit their guilt and apologize for their complicity in what had happened before any other issues could be considered.

Another challenge was how to rebuild international socialist and trade union structures, and how to position the British Left within them. The Second Socialist International, founded in 1889, had effectively disintegrated at the start of the War as socialists in many countries, including Britain, abandoned internationalism and lined up behind their governments. In many cases, again including Britain, socialist parties had split, although unlike most other parties the British Labour Party had contrived to restrict the split to internal disagreement rather than the forming of new parties. By 1918 Russia was establishing the Third International (later the Comintern) which would draw together socialist and communist parties which advocated armed revolution and accepted the authority of the Soviet Union.

Both MacDonald and Henderson were determined that the ILP and the Labour Party should stand with the Second International and reject the Third. This was also Margaret Bondfield's view, not only as a pacifist but also as a socialist and trade unionist. The British Left had not yet sorted out its attitude to the new Russian regime, however, and there were many people who supported affiliation to the Third International. Ramsay MacDonald correctly understood that such was the general fear and loathing of communism that if Labour lined up behind the Third International (and therefore Bolshevik Russia) the consequences for it would be terminal. Despite this, however, the position was complex, and there is no doubt that Bondfield, like many other Labour leaders, was far more sympathetic to the Russian Revolution than she would be later. In 1919 there was still hope that something great might come of it, and distance combined with a lack of detailed knowledge made that hope seem much more reasonable than it did with the advantage of hindsight. There was also a very strong feeling on the Left that the West should not be intervening militarily in Russian affairs, and there was a vocal 'Hands Off Russia' campaign. Though the War had ended in Western Europe it was still going on in the East, and even people who were very wary of the Bolsheviks nevertheless felt that military intervention by the victorious powers would achieve nothing.

From a pragmatic political point of view Labour apprehension about being too closely connected with communism and Russia was entirely sensible. Henderson's general election loss had been at least in part because he was believed to have 'shaken hands with a murderer' when he went to Russia and met Lenin in 1917, and prominent pacifist candidates like MacDonald, Lansbury and Macarthur were thought to be little more than pro-German Bolsheviks. People were relieved that the War was finally over, but they still saw enemies everywhere. They wanted Germany to be heavily punished and they wanted Bolsheviks – who they thought might murder them in their beds at any moment – suppressed. An almost entirely right-wing press was perfectly happy to feed both of these sentiments, and Lloyd George himself had been by no means averse to promoting them. One of the results of the general election was that he was able to go to Versailles with what he considered a clear mandate for punitive reparations.

Thus when Margaret Bondfield left London in late January to attend the Second International conference in Switzerland she left behind an uneasy political mood. As always, however, travel energized her, and the prospect of international socialism being able somehow to rise above the quagmire of the peace negotiations seemed to her like 'a rift in a black sky'. Mary Agnes Hamilton, who saw Bondfield on the day of her departure from Victoria, said that Bondfield was: 'as jolly as a child going off on holiday, her eyes sparkling with animation, alertly open to take in everything presented to them. . . . She was not bothering about luggage, passports, or the fatigues of the journey: her mind was on what it all meant for Europe.'[6]

Ethel Snowden,[7] who was travelling with her, also recalled Bondfield's joy.

'Isn't it glorious!' shouted Margaret Bondfield . . . as we shot swiftly into Folkestone station. 'Isn't what glorious?' I asked, thinking she meant our first view of the sea . . .. 'Why, that we can travel once more, and that we are flying as fast as we can to see the comrades from whom we have been separated so long.' . . . Margaret's bright face beamed with happiness . . . She was like a bird set free from the cruel cage that had held her for four tormenting years.[8]

This description of Bondfield, while accurate in the sense that she loved travel and was never happier than when on the move, was also slightly disingenuous in that Snowden must have known that she had been to Paris the previous July. However, Snowden often wrote for effect rather than strict accuracy, so that her accounts of both this and the Russian expedition the following year are more entertaining than Bondfield's. As a journalist, Snowden often looked for the story before the politics, whereas for Bondfield the politics invariably came first. In addition, Snowden's personal political outlook was to the right of Bondfield's, and this also affected her selection of what to report and how.

The journey from London to Berne took four days and was anything but smooth. The trains were slow and over-crowded and the hotel arrangements at the various stops haphazard. As always, Bondfield appreciated the good things she encountered, particularly the coffee. The landscape was snowy and picturesque and Berne, when they finally arrived, as beautiful as she remembered, though Snowden observed that it was also full of gangs of spies, operating fairly openly, and reporting everything said in even the most casual conversation back to somebody somewhere.

The Berne conference was the first post-war attempt to rebuild the Second International, and Bondfield described it as 'the Peace Conference of the Socialist movements of the world', considering that:

> Its limitations, its success and its failures exactly indicate how much force remained to the international Socialist Movement after the catastrophe of war, and what force had been let loose in Europe, not only against this country, but against those very principles of civilization upon which Britain, as well as all other European nations, was ultimately founded.[9]

In fact, the attempt to rescue the Second International was doomed. Although 26 nations did send representatives to Switzerland the Americans were absent, and there was a deep rift between French and German socialists. There were profound disagreements over how to reconcile support both for armed revolution and gradualist social democracy within one movement. However, this did not mean that nothing constructive came out of it. Margaret Bondfield's remit was to get the Conference to pass the Labour Charter, which would effectively create the International Labour Organization (ILO) to work parallel to the putative League of Nations and represent the interests of workers. At the beginning of the Conference a Commission was set up to agree a draft document to be put to the full meeting; Bondfield, representing Britain, was the only woman on it, as she was on the Trade Union Sub-Committee. The resulting document was passed without dissent by both trade union and socialist sections of the Conference, and the ILO would go on to become an integral part of Bondfield's international activities. Her friend and former NFWW colleague Sophy Sanger[10] later became the head of the ILO's legislative section, bringing her formidable legal mind and experience to bear on the first phase of its work.

Elsewhere matters did not progress so well. The French contingent, led by Albert Thomas, wanted the German and Austrian delegations to accept their guilt and even advocated the proscription of groups considered to have collaborated with capitalist and imperialist powers. Bondfield found the aggression of the French approach disheartening. At one point she noted in her diary that she felt 'very sick at the abortive tactics of the French Minority group. Albert Thomas seems a warlike influence.'[11] The Commission tasked with producing the report on responsibility for the War took an inordinate amount of time to reach agreement, with the French alleged to have spent three hours wrangling over one word. Eventually it appeared and was accepted by the Conference, with the French delegation splitting its vote and Albert Thomas abstaining.

There was also a long debate about dictatorship and democracy, in which MacDonald made what many people thought was the finest speech of the Conference in support of parliamentary democracy and peace. The resolution endorsing democratic socialism and declaring revolutionary dictatorship incompatible with it was eventually passed, but not until after a fierce debate.

Women delegates had arrived at Berne determined to make their voices heard, or at least to develop a plan for how to do so within the emerging post-war structures. Friendships disrupted by armed conflict were resumed, both at conference sessions and through more informal routes. The British women hosted a dinner for other female delegates and on one evening Bondfield noted that she had 'Rosika *(Schwimmer)* to dinner. She talked scandal most of the time, to my delight.'[12] Bondfield had known Schwimmer in London before the War and liked her, but neither she nor Ethel Snowden felt able to support Schwimmer's idea of formalizing the various meetings and discussions into a conference of women which, they thought, would be meaningless in the absence of the Americans amongst others.

Despite this, Schwimmer persisted, and eventually the Swiss section of the Women's International League for Peace and Freedom organized a conference attended by about 40 women from nine nations. This was held after the end of the main conference, and Bondfield was very tired and already worried about the logistics of the return journey to London, while Snowden, who had to speak, was unwell. Bondfield attended the morning session but left at lunchtime. This was a mistake since it meant that she missed the discussion about what action the group should take and was extremely irritated to find that they had decided to send telegrams to several Prime Ministers, including Lloyd George, asking them to 'receive Mrs Snowden, MacDonald, Madame Duchêne and self to convey resolutions!' What annoyed her most was the political ineptness of this; she described it as an 'Absurd lack of appreciation of difficulties and exaggeration of importance of this scratch gathering.'[13] When the British women saw Gabrielle Duchêne in Paris on the way home they were relieved to find that she shared their view. Bondfield, whose route into almost all her political activity had been the tough realism of the trade union movement, rarely had much sympathy with the more dramatic ideas of some feminists, and had a very accurate assessment of exactly how much notice men were likely to take of women's voices. This sometimes made her unpopular in feminist circles but also saved her from some of the more impractical plans into which efforts were made to drag her.

The four-day homeward journey was slightly delayed in Paris by problems over visas, but in the end all was well and Bondfield arrived home on 17 February. Two days later she heard ominous news; Will Anderson, Mary Macarthur's husband, was ill with Spanish flu. In early 1919 Britain was in the first stages of the third wave of a global pandemic which eventually killed more people than the War, and, in the absence of an accessible health service or an adequate government strategy for combatting the disease the prognosis for anyone contracting it was not good. By 21 February Bondfield was writing in her diary that 'Anderson is worse. Great anxiety. All meetings cancelled.' The following day she heard the news that Kurt Eisner, the leader of the Bavarian socialists and a man whom she had particularly liked and admired at Berne, had been assassinated in the street on his way home from the Conference. 'Have cancelled engagements for today and tomorrow,' she wrote, 'I must be quiet.' On 23 February, however, she reported a 'frantic search for nurse and oxygen for Will Anderson'[14] and the next day was spent desperately telephoning everyone they could think of to get help. Eventually oxygen was found, but it was too late. Will Anderson died on 25 February 1919.

Anderson had been widely liked and generally respected, and his loss was a blow to the movement as a whole. For Bondfield, however, it was personal. She had known him for nearly twenty years, and he had been part of her early days as a trade unionist, a supportive, friendly presence and, she said, a 'splendid comrade'. For Macarthur, now left a widow with a small child, it was devastating. She was persuaded to take a three-months' break from her work at the NFWW which, taking little Nancy with her, she spent in America touring, attending conferences and giving lectures about peace. Margaret Bondfield, who knew a thing or two about the relationship between trauma and rest, thought this ill-advised, but was powerless to prevent it.

In May she herself went to the United States to attend the AWTUL conference where she had arranged to meet up with Macarthur. She crossed the Atlantic together with a group of American women trade unionists including Rose Schneiderman, whom she had not seen since before the War. As always, Bondfield found the company of American women liberating. The ship was almost a holiday in itself; in her diary she described it as 'a floating palace of luxury. Palm Court, lift, Library, reading rooms, all kinds of baths, electric light bulbs, band, great stretches of promenade decks'.[15] At one point the American

Plate 1 Margaret Bondfield aged 7 with siblings Katie and Frank.

Plate 2 Margaret Bondfield aged 14.

Plate 3 Margaret Bondfield in 1912.

Plate 4 Margaret Bondfield in animated discussion in Russia in 1920.

Plate 5 Margaret Bondfield entering Parliament to be sworn in in 1924.

Plate 6 Margaret Bondfield in her ministerial office in 1924.

Plate 7 Bondfield speaking at a May Day Rally in 1926.

Plate 8 Arthur Henderson, Margaret Bondfield and Ramsay MacDonald at Labour Conference, Margate, 1926.

Plate 9 Labour women MPs elected in 1929.. (Front, l to r, Cynthia Mosley, Susan Lawrence, Margaret Bondfield, Ellen Wilkinson, Jennie Lee. Back, l to r, Marion Phillips, Edith Picton-Turbervill, Ethel Bentham, Mary Agnes Hamilton.)

Plate 10 Bondfield with Ramsay MacDonald in the garden of 10 Downing Street, 1929.

Plate 11 The Second Labour Government, 1929.

Plate 12 Campaigning in Wallsend in the 1931 general election.

Plate 13 With Frances Perkins, Washington DC, 1933.

Plate 14 Tea with Ellen Wilkinson *c.* 1946.

Plate 15 Margaret Bondfield aged 80, March 1953.

women tried to persuade her to participate in a champagne breakfast, which, despite being a lifelong teetotaller, she found both exciting and amusing. One way and another they had a very pleasant crossing before travelling in a hot train to Philadelphia, where the AWTUL conference was due to take place.

Mary Macarthur arrived on the first day and Bondfield soon saw that her apprehensions had been amply justified, noting in her diary that Macarthur was 'Still terribly unnerved; all this travelling and excitement is not helping her . . . more settled work is best at times of such grief.'[16] Later, after a very hot meeting ('audience one great waving fan') she added 'M.R.M. not her natural self. Good speech in substance, but suppressed hysteria and fatigue patent to me. She had a great reception.'[17]

After the AWTUL conference Bondfield moved on to Atlantic City to the American Federation of Labor, which was the main event of her visit. 'I am very excited,' she wrote in her diary, 'because this is the first time a woman has been sent as the fraternal delegate from the British Trades Union Congress, and I am thrilled that it should be my opportunity . . . '[18] She spoke on the fourth day of the conference to much acclaim, and the *Baltimore Sun* reported that:

> Easily the most impressive performance of any of the speakers . . . was the address of Miss Margaret Bondfield . . . It was an astonishing effort – tactful, logical, forceful and fired with conviction. . . she gained enthusiastic applause from the whole body of delegates, although a large majority of them are out of sympathy with the extreme views which she holds.[19]

During the conference Bondfield was impressed by the Black delegates who spoke, but dismayed when the hotel where the AWTUL women were holding a tea-party refused to allow in a Black woman who had been invited. For a time it looked as though the meeting would have to be abandoned, but in the end the woman (who sadly remains nameless in Bondfield's account) was smuggled into the building without incident. Bondfield had a long conversation with her and pronounced her 'a most intelligent and practical woman, *far* superior to some of the shallow girls of the party'.[20] A few days later the same problem arose at a restaurant where the women delegates were having tea, and again the Black woman was smuggled in, though this time she had to sit in a dark corner. Bondfield sat there with her and had a very enjoyable afternoon. She was impressed with all the Black trade unionists she met and particularly interested in the 'exceptional' education many had received, but recognized that when they joined unions they had 'first to push open the door'. In Washington she stayed with her friend, the home economist Professor Caroline Hunt, who was still working on racial equality and wanted to build 'a bridge of real communication between white and coloured (*sic)* people'.[21] Casual racism was endemic at all levels of British society at this time, but Bondfield's approach seems largely to have been one of interest and inquiry rather than prejudice. If her thinking on race issues was not very deep, it does seem to have sprung from an underlying sense of sisterhood, particularly with working-class and trade union women, and she was clearly dismayed by segregation in both the north and the south.

After the conference had finished Bondfield went on a two-month speaking and lecturing tour, visiting old friends and, as always, making new ones as she went. She spoke at trade union meetings and women's meetings and lectured at colleges. She spoke at churches, met groups of workers, advised on organization and explained socialism to sceptical audiences. She was interviewed often for newspapers and magazines and met people from all walks of life. On one occasion when she was in New York to address a strike meeting in Brooklyn she was invited to meet the Irish republican leader Eamonn de Valera at a lunch being given at the Waldorf Astoria. Her perennial curiosity about people meant that, despite misgivings, she decided to attend. She was dismayed to find herself seated next to him but nevertheless attempted to make conversation. She asked him a question about the co-operative movement in Ireland, but he 'blandly said that he was not interested in economics. After that,' she observed, 'there was nothing more to be said.'[22]

On 14 August she left New York for the voyage home, arriving back in London nine days later. On the ship she read John Reed's *Ten Days That Shook the World*, an American journalist's recently published account of the Russian Revolution. She admired the book, but could hardly have thought that less than a year later she would be in Russia herself.

In late October she and Macarthur were back in America for the International Labour Conference to agree the ILO's conventions on various aspects of industry and employment, an event which was to be followed by the first International Congress of Working Women. Macarthur, Bondfield noted in her diary, was 'not at all well' and by the time they arrived at New York 'very ill'. This did not, however, prevent her from participating and both women worked hard to get good maternity provision into the conventions. Perhaps Bondfield's most effective intervention, however, was on behalf of Indian child workers, who had initially been omitted from the proposal to ban children working under the age of 14. Bondfield was outraged, and, against considerable opposition, she got the clause changed so that Indian children were recognized as being 'entitled to the same safeguards as those which had proved so essential in Western industry'.[23] She returned to Britain in time for Christmas, which she spent at Chard, before returning again to London.

On 19 March 1920 the National Liberal Northampton MP Charles McCurdy was appointed as Minister of Food Control in the Coalition government. MPs newly appointed to ministerial roles had to seek re-election to Parliament in their constituencies, a provision which had been in force in one form or another since the turn of the eighteenth century and which would not finally be abolished until 1926. As a result by-elections were common; Northampton was the tenth that year and in the whole of 1920 alone there would be a total of twenty-four. McCurdy had a majority from the 1918 general election of over 7,000 and there was no obvious reason why he should be in any danger of losing. Newly appointed ministers did sometimes lose their by-elections – most notoriously, perhaps, in 1906 when Winston Churchill had been ousted in Manchester North West – but it was rare and since the Conservative Party was not intending to field a candidate the general view was that he would have a clear run.

Quite why Margaret Bondfield chose this particular by-election for her first parliamentary outing as the candidate is not clear. The local party in Northampton do not seem to have shown any reluctance about selecting her, and indeed there may well have been some excitement since Bondfield brought with her not only seniority and profile as Britain's foremost female trade unionist and public speaker, but also national and international experience as well as the ability to get Ramsay MacDonald to come and launch her campaign. Moreover, people liked her. She was, said the *Daily News*:

> simply capturing the hearts and minds of every man and woman with whom she comes into contact. . . . Indomitable energy and unfailing good humour are useful assets for any candidate, but she has more qualifications than these. Her profound knowledge of social and industrial questions, her wide view and comprehension of international problems, are making a striking effect on her hearers. . . . I do not think I have ever seen in a candidate the same vitality, charm, and captivating clearness of exposition.[24]

The *Daily News* was a left-leaning paper, but even if their account of Bondfield's qualities as a candidate is a little overdone, it does reflect what many people thought. She was a natural networker, she liked people and was interested in them, and she was never one to discard them once they had ceased to be of use to her. Long after she had moved on from Northampton she remained in touch with the local Labour Party and the people she had met in the town, and they remained proud of her. As late as 1948 she would still be invited back to speak at a school prize-giving, a legacy of the relationships she built during the early 1920s.

Polling day in the by-election was set for 1 April, a day after two others in Camberwell and Basingstoke. In Camberwell the candidate was Susan Lawrence, Bondfield's colleague at the NFWW, who faced a three-way contest in a seat where, in 1918, the Coalition Liberals had achieved a narrow majority. In 1920, however, the electorate was still supportive of the Coalition government, and despite both Bondfield and Lawrence roundly attacking it it was an uphill task to take votes from it. In Camberwell the incumbent National Liberal won, but

Lawrence came a close second. In Northampton Bondfield got the majority down to 3,300, and there was a view on the Labour side that had she had another week to work at it she might have won. Though disappointed, she was on the whole upbeat, writing to a friend that: 'we are all very cheerful and quite satisfied that we can wipe out the rest of the majority in the general election'.[25]

Chapter 11

Are You Really Going to Russia?

Disappointed though Bondfield may have been, there was not much time to dwell on the defeat, since within weeks a new adventure arrived.

Most socialists, including Bondfield, were still broadly supportive of the Bolshevik regime and felt that Russia should be given the chance to sort out its own affairs. The British government, on the other hand, broadly agreed with Winston Churchill that communism should be 'strangled in its cradle' and had maintained a blockade on Russia, depriving it of food, medicines and basic items such as soap. In April Poland launched its own offensive against the Red Army, and in May dockers in the East India docks, believing that the government was sending assistance to the Poles, refused to load munitions onto the *Jolly George*. By then, however, the TUC and the Labour Party had decided to send a joint delegation to Russia to investigate what was happening and to inform their decisions about what attitude to take to the whole question of intervention and the blockade. 'What precise right,' said Bondfield, 'we had to intervene in Russia was not clear. What useful purpose was fulfilled by intervention was equally obscure. Knowledge was wanted.'[1]

As usual the government created difficulties over passports, but eventually they agreed to allow a delegation of thirteen to travel. Ethel Snowden, a member of Labour's NEC and part of the party delegation, was the only other woman, and Bondfield may have correctly surmised that Snowden intended to write a book about the trip as she had done about the conference in Berne the year before. Although she got on well with Philip Snowden, Bondfield seems to have had a slightly more distant relationship with Ethel. Nevertheless, both had been elected to the most powerful bodies in their respective wings of the movement, and both brought to the Delegation female presence and political experience and authority.

In 1920 relatively few British people had been to revolutionary Russia, and the expedition was an exciting prospect. MacDonald, who would very much have liked to go himself, wrote to commiserate over the outcome of the Northampton by-election, and asked:

And are you really going to Russia? I am very disappointed. I could not leave until the middle of May. . . . Will you explain to . . . Lenin why I am not with you? Say I was most anxious to go and say I have asked you to give them assurances of my most friendly interest even if I cannot agree with them altogether but that I am most anxious to learn on the spot how they are getting on. Warn them from me of the utter ridiculousness of their friends here posing as people of influence. . . . I might come and see you off . . .[2]

The main group embarked in early May, but Bondfield did not go with them. Mary Macarthur was now very ill with ovarian cancer and underwent dangerous surgery at the beginning of the month. Bondfield refused to leave until she was sure that Macarthur would survive it. Then she sailed a week after the rest of the Delegation, going by ship from Newcastle to Sweden and then to Reval (now Tallinn) in Estonia. At Hungar in Finland they had to pause for the night to avoid crossing a minefield in the dark. The passengers dined late and saw the Northern Lights, a 'wonderful glow in the west, merging into a green-blue sky which in turn was lost in velvety starlight – a breath-taking picture of beauty'.[3] When, at seven in the morning, they set off again it was foggy, and the ship crawled carefully through the minefield, stopping frequently. Finally they arrived safely at Reval, where Bondfield was delighted to be met by British officials with a car. 'Find all arrangements made for me to proceed tonight with the Courier to Petrograd. Hurrah!'[4]

Her late arrival meant that she missed all the formal events laid on for the rest of the Delegation, but she did not mind. Instead she investigated the food supply and noted how empty the shops were and how high the prices. She was also fascinated by a process, invented by a Mr Lovell, for turning peat into a coal substitute, and was very happy when she was allowed to try the experiment for herself. Mr Lovell, however, turned out not to be quite as nice as he appeared; when departure was delayed because the Courier's coach was too heavy for the engine drawing the train he shouted at the railway workers trying to sort the problem out. When Bondfield 'mildly remonstrated' with him he explained to her that '"this is the only way they understand, and they want my fuel."' It was, she said, a 'very humiliating experience.'[5]

After crossing the border into Russia they arrived at Gatchina, where they met some German prisoners being returned home. The men had been captured early in the War and had only the haziest idea of what had been happening beyond the overthrow of both the Tsar and the Kaiser. While waiting on the platform for a connection Bondfield gave some chocolate to a child who, in return, came back with a huge bunch of lilac for her. Once they got going again the train was very slow, and when they arrived at Petrograd (now St Petersburg) it was to find that their connection to Moscow had departed minutes earlier. It was a public holiday, so all the shops were shut, but the churches were open so Bondfield went to see the cathedral. She did not take to Petrograd much; the streets were clean but the people looked half-starved and the city seemed lifeless. Red Army soldiers on their way to the Front looked 'not at all fierce, but are tired men living hardly, just taking one day at a time'.[6] Ethel Snowden had stayed longer in Petrograd, sharing a room in a confiscated Palace with Bondfield's friend Angelica Balabanoff[7] and conjuring up the ghosts of the departed, both Tsarist and revolutionary. Bondfield, on the other hand, sat up until two in the morning eating black bread and cheese, drinking tea and having a 'fierce discussion' on policy.

The journey to Moscow took over twenty-four hours but there was plenty to see on the way and she enjoyed talking to the young Russian Courier, who was very enthusiastic about Trotsky and certain that the Poles would be defeated. At Moscow, where they arrived at 11 pm, she found the rest of the Delegation 'rather depressed, suffering a little from the black bread'.

After a night's rest her first visit was to the Ministry of Health, where Dr Nikolai Semashko,[8] the People's Public Health Commissar, was struggling against enormous odds to develop a new health service. Both Bondfield and Snowden found Semashko to be impressive; Bondfield thought him 'an exceptionally able statesman and a fine character' and Snowden called him 'one of the most admirable and devoted men it has been my lot to meet'. Both she and Bondfield were horrified by the scale of the task which confronted him. Apart from anything else there was a typhus epidemic raging across the country, yet according to Snowden:

> Against the most appalling sanitary conditions left by war, poverty, pestilence and famine, this heroic doctor is putting up a magnificent fight. He and his band of gallant helpers have few means with which to work. They are almost entirely lacking soap and disinfectants . . . but in spite of this he is doing marvellous things and rapidly stamping out some of the epidemic diseases which have raged all over the country . . .[9]

That afternoon Bondfield went to visit a facility run by the League for Saving the Children, a non-communist charity which was alleged to be selling girls into prostitution. When she raised this with the people running the school they 'most indignantly repudiated the suggestion as slander' and were emphatic that there was 'not any encouragement of immorality, but entirely the contrary'. Food, particularly milk, was in short supply, but the children had fruit and seemed as well cared for as they could be under the circumstances.

Throughout their stay the Delegation was accompanied by government officials who took copious notes and reported back to unknown superiors. Despite this the Delegation asked difficult questions, although not everyone chose to answer them, or felt that they could. In some places, even the questions were tricky. On 26 May, the whole Delegation was taken to the headquarters of the Moscow Soviet to have the new system of government explained to them, and in the afternoon they were introduced to Lenin. Snowden described having to pass through considerable security to reach his room where he was sitting for a sculptor who was making a bust of him. His way of talking to visitors was, she said 'clever. He has the most engaging frankness. He suggests by his manner a more or less confidential exchange of opinions. But when the interview is over, it is found that he has told you far less than you have told him.'[10]

Whether or not Bondfield gave Lenin the message that MacDonald had given her for him she did not say, but throughout the meeting he was quite clear and straightforward about the ruthlessness he considered necessary to preserve the revolution. Peasants who opposed the communization of land must be dealt with, and there must be 'merciless war on the bourgeoisie'. There were, said Bondfield:

> no freedoms either of Press or speech for the enemies of the Revolution. . . . No one could possibly accuse Lenin of wishing to mislead the Delegation either as to the nature of his Government or the ruthlessness of his policy in dealing with the opposition. 'War is war and no quarter can be given.'[11]

Snowden thought that he showed very little knowledge or understanding of the British Labour movement, imagining the influence of communism to be much greater than it was and appearing to believe that revolution in Britain was imminent. He regarded pacifists with contempt and seemed indifferent about the chances of peace with Poland or the raising of the blockade. He conveyed, she said, 'the impression of an awful sureness of himself, of an immovable and overpowering self-confidence.' Both women were depressed by the experience, though for rather different reasons. Snowden found the ruthlessness dispiriting and thought that Lenin was essentially the same type of person who had landed the world in the Great War, while Bondfield was more conscious of 'the guilt of the democracies . . . which had suffered their governments to continue a policy so blind and so remorseless as the policy which had driven Russia to this position'.[12]

That evening she ran into Angelica Balabanoff just as the latter was going to deliver a lecture to a Communist Party meeting about the aims and ideals of the Revolution. Bondfield went with her, and although she presumably did not understand much of what was said, she enjoyed herself immensely, being almost as interested in the audience as the speaker. When she returned to the hotel she was met by a woman who wanted to give her a volume of plays written before the Revolution but predicting it in quite a lot of accurate detail. By the time she was able to sit down to supper at 11 pm she was very tired indeed.

Most of the days followed this kind of pattern, being filled with activities both planned and unplanned with very little time to think or write. Snowden found this a ridiculously pressurized work rate, but Bondfield was more accustomed to it and thought little of it. She talked to everyone who wanted to talk to her, and listened to their stories with interest, and although, with the advantage of hindsight, some of her judgements were mistaken she was by no means alone in that at the time. Throughout this early Soviet period many Labour and trade union people were torn between what they wanted to see and what they increasingly suspected might be the truth, and even when the truth was laid out very clearly before them they still chose to look for hope.

One such meeting was with the Extraordinary Commission, the body charged with carrying on a 'merciless struggle against those trying to overthrow the Soviet system; against sabotage, espionage and speculation'.[13] Led by Felix Djerjinsky, who was not available to meet them, it is better known as the Cheka, a covert and much-feared police force with a reputation built on secrecy and brutality. The Delegation was welcomed as though to any other arm of the bureaucracy, and the Commission's procedures were explained to them, though the use of torture and the sheer scale of the executions were omitted. The Delegation asked various questions about freedom of speech and the right to dissent and were given reassuring if not entirely comfortable answers. Bondfield's colleague, Alfred Purcell, himself a communist and an official of the Confederation of Shipbuilding and Engineering Unions, said that the Delegation had been told that when the British left there would be arrests. Djerjinsky's deputy, with whom they were meeting, said that '"Nobody will arrest anyone unless they have committed a crime, as sabotage, espionage, treason, and official dereliction of duty."'[14] This was fairly typical of the kind of evasive, if superficially open, reply the Delegation was given to most of their questions. Bondfield asked about the position of conscientious objectors and was told that if they had declared themselves to be so before the Soviet they were freed. This said nothing about those who had refused to take up arms after it, and Bondfield must have realized that. She recorded the meeting in her journal without much comment and published it in full in her autobiography.

Ethel Snowden, however, whose hopes and expectations of the new regime were much lower than Bondfield's, was disgusted. She asked why so many people were afraid to meet the Delegation or speak openly to them and was told that perhaps people were suspicious that the English would tempt them into counter-revolutionary activities. It was, said Snowden:

denied that any conscientious objector had been shot. It was denied that anybody had been shot without trial. It was denied that any great tyranny was exercised. It was declared that the object of the Extraordinary Commission was to protect perfect liberty of speech outside of those who were fomenting armed opposition to the Republic.[15]

She came away from the meeting 'cold with horror and dislike' and related several stories of the Commission's activities, many of them against innocent people or those whose offences were very minor. Bondfield, with her pacifist convictions and detestation of violence, must have had much the same feeling, and indeed Snowden did say that the whole Delegation lived 'hourly in a spirit of hot hate of the cruelties and tyrannies which met us at every turn'.[16] Bondfield was less likely to be directly critical in this way, but she was certainly aware of what was happening. On one occasion, when they were at the opera, a woman asked to borrow a pencil from her and used the excuse to say, very quietly, that she wanted to come and talk to her. Bondfield, equally quietly, suggested that she telephone the hotel at 10 am the following morning. No call was made, and she never heard from the woman again.

There were a small number of British prisoners being held in Moscow, and the Delegation visited three of them – two men imprisoned for spying and a woman, Lily Burand. The men – one confined in a camp and the other in a prison – were relatively cheerful and said that they were being well treated, though Bondfield was suspicious of this and observed of the journalist Edward Keeling that: 'There seemed to be something extraordinarily artificial about the whole atmosphere *(he)* created . . .. It seemed much more like a comic opera than a real prison.'[17] This was in stark contrast to Lily Burand in the Women's Prison. She was ill with typhoid, 'very wretched and hysterical' and 'unable to reconcile herself to her position'. The tour of the prison seemed on the face of it to show a clean, modern facility, but one of the prisoners who could speak English told Bondfield that the prisoners were not happy because there was not enough to eat, though they were still better off than if they had been free. 'She said Moscow nearly died last winter; it will quite die this winter unless the blockade is lifted.'[18]

By the end of the tour Bondfield felt ill and had to be taken back to the hotel. She blamed the sour smell of the bread in the bakery, and that may well have been a factor, but she may also have been affected by the increasing understanding that, if the blockade was not lifted, famine was inevitable. Talk of food, and anxiety about the availability and price of it, was everywhere except in the higher echelons of government. Bondfield was a country woman by origin, and she knew how crucial agriculture was both to the economy and to the lives of ordinary people. As the Delegation visited farms and food processors she took a considerable interest in what was being grown, how much of it there was, what livestock was kept and so on. Like several other members of the Delegation, she knew exactly what it felt like to have no idea where her next meal was coming from, and to be close to fainting in the streets with hunger. The memory of those first months in London were, she said, 'the shadow of a nightmare', and she had never forgotten them. Now she was surrounded by thin, anxious faces in a city in which people told her that prison was better than liberty because at least there they would be fed. It was perhaps not surprising if she was unwell. She was supposed to be going to visit the Volga region but decided instead to remain in Moscow and recuperate. Angelica Balabanoff looked after her, bringing her food and taking her out for a walk to see more of the city. They found an illicit tea shop where they were overcharged for coffee and a pastry. They talked about some of the challenges and contradictions of the situation, and Balabanoff explained that for her it was important that 'The poor people will now openly say that they want more bread. Before, under the old regime, they would not dare to express themselves.'[19] In the evening they went to hear an Act of *La Bohème* and then walked back through mild evening air. The following day she felt well enough to resume her programme with a visit to a stud farm and a village school.

There were not many old friends like Balabanoff to be met with in Russia, but one of them was the anarchist Prince Peter Kropotkin, now in his late seventies and living in the town of Dmitri near Moscow. Bondfield had first met Kropotkin during the heady early years of her trade union life, having been introduced to him by an anarchist member of the Shop Assistants' Union. Kropotkin had long since come to the conclusion that violence would not achieve anything, rejecting 'propaganda of the deed' in the belief that 'a structure based on centuries of history cannot be destroyed with a few kilos of dynamite'.[20] The new Russian regime had allowed him to return after the Revolution and regarded him as a hero, though he was critical of their methods and had refused a cabinet seat. When Bondfield saw him at Dmitri she was impressed with his vegetable garden and once again the talk was as much about food as politics. When she was invited to address the workers in the nearby village she accepted, but confessed to: 'a feeling of almost terror at the continued reiteration of that question, "Why do you want to fight us; why do you not let us have Peace?"'[21] Kropotkin's daughter, Sasha, was highly critical of both the government and the Western powers, but 'was satisfied that there was no other course open to any of the dissentient groups in the country except to support the existing Government as long as any attacks were made from without . . . '[22]

As a long-standing co-operator and member of the CWG, Bondfield was very interested in hearing about what was happening to the Russian co-operative movement. Under communism all co-ops had been taken over by the state and merged into the All Russian United Co-operative Movement. The plan was that this body – known as Centrosoyu – would take over all matters connected with food, including distribution. There was a complicated structure for decision-making and control for both monopoly items (mainly everyday essentials plus building materials) and non-monopoly goods, which meant everything else. The inevitably unwieldy nature of this system was already causing problems in the food-supply chain and would go on to cause many more the following year. Another layered system governed the allocation of agricultural land to small local co-operatives. Shares and the dividend had been abolished, and the main benefit people got from joining the Co-op was access to food. Since anyone who did not join had to depend on speculators if they were to eat, membership was fairly high. Money wages for the workers were being phased out and replaced by payments in kind. Given how many years Bondfield had spent trying to eliminate truck payments this must have struck her as ironic, though she did also admit that the devaluation of the rouble put rather a different perspective on the question. As a trade unionist, Bondfield was particularly interested in the wage structures and how they were developing to reflect the reduction in the use of money. Factories which exceeded their targets were paid a cash premium which the workers' representatives distributed as they saw fit. Troubles with the rouble meant that here also the Centrosoyu was looking at converting the cash payment into kind. Free meals were already being provided and there were plans to expand this to the point at which most workers ate all their meals in the communal canteens.

Needless to say, not all co-operators of the old variety had been happy with the changes, and when Bondfield and Purcell met the Chairman of Centrosoyu they raised with him the question of arrests and worse. He denied that anyone had been arrested, apart from six men who were in prison on suspicion of sabotage. Nobody had been shot. Everyone who had been part of the old co-operative movement was now working willingly for the new one, and it was all going very well. Even Bondfield, keen as she was to hear the best, suspected that this masked another story altogether.

Like co-operatives, trade unions had also been absorbed by the state, and strikes were illegal on the grounds that the workers could not strike against themselves. As an illustration of the effects of this Bondfield recorded a strike of tobacco workers whose premium (or bonus) of cigarettes was being reduced. In this case the workers' wages were so low that they claimed they could not live on them and had therefore been selling the cigarettes in order to buy food. When the premium was reduced they were furious. However, the decision had been made by their own trade union Committee, which, by the convoluted thinking which the Revolution had brought into being, was now the representative of both the employers and the employees. With nowhere to turn the operatives had no option but to accept the decision.

All this was fairly depressing, but a much more encouraging field of inquiry was the improvements to the lives of women, especially working-class women. This work was led by Innessa Armand, the Head of the Women's Department of the Central Committee of the Communist Party, a determined and influential woman who ran a body which had considerable powers, including the right to legislate. This she had used to some purpose. Divorce and abortion had been legalized, and childcare was now free for all working women on either a daily or a residential basis. The children were well fed and educated and those at the residential facilities saw their parents every day. This arrangement meant that women were able to take up their full role in the economy. Armand told her that

'In the old days the poor woman in Russia had to lock her children in the house while she went out to work for bread. Now they can take their children to the kindergarten or leave them at the residential schools, knowing that the children will be well cared for and kept clean and safe.'[23]

By the time Bondfield met her in June 1920 Armand was already suffering ill health due to overwork, but, as Bondfield herself so often did, was working on regardless.[24] Her remit was very wide, and the two women discussed prostitution, the high incidence of venereal disease, illegitimacy (which had been abolished) and marriage as well as childcare and working conditions. The concept of the family wage, which in Britain bedevilled attempts to get equal pay – or even decent pay – for women had been removed in Russia, and women were expected to take a full part in economic activity from the age of 16. Given this, childcare was essential and should be provided by the state. 'The story,' said the Delegation in its final report 'that women are "nationalised" in Russia is a stupid libel without foundation.'[25]

The main aim of the Delegation was to advise on both the blockade and what the Labour and trade union movement's posture on intervention in the Polish war should be, and a small group, including Bondfield, travelled to the Front to take a look for themselves. There they met both senior officers and soldiers, spoke to Polish prisoners, and listened to many more interminable speeches. They came away impressed with the spirit and discipline of the Red Army and with their opinion of the military situation unchanged.

When the Delegation returned to London it reported back to both the TUC and the Labour Party. Two Interim Reports had been sent before their return, both opposing the blockade and the British government's policy. The appalling famine conditions, and the public health emergency caused by the lack of access to soap and medical supplies, meant that the crisis Russia faced was beyond anything seen so far, and the Delegation believed that forcing Russia into an isolated corner of starvation and disease could only be detrimental, not only to the country itself, but also to British prospects of trade in the future. Despite reservations about some of the more repressive aspects of the regime, therefore, the Delegation's conclusion was that:

> Peace now and at once – that is the great need of Russia and of the world, and in the name of the humanity of the world, we call upon our nation to insist that peace be made now and Europe be allowed to turn from the terrible spectres of war, famine and disease to a rebuilding of its homes and a reshaping of its shattered civilisations.[26]

The Report was accepted, and the Labour NEC, the TUC Parliamentary Committee and the PLP agreed to set up a Council of Action to organize against and hopefully prevent military intervention, using any methods up to and including a general strike to achieve their aims. In the event the government decided not to intervene and involvement in the conflict was averted, but Ramsay MacDonald was alarmed by the impression of force that the Council of Action had seemed to advocate and warned that: 'In the imaginations of our people there is an unlimited supply of bogeys. Mr Lloyd George can extract them as a magician takes rabbits out of a hat.'[27]

Bondfield herself obviously found her expedition to Russia intensely interesting, but in a different way to her American visits. For one thing, Russia was business, with a clear remit and an audience at home. America, on the other hand, even when she was being paid for lectures or help with recruitment, always involved a gathering of old and new friends, women whose lives were committed along similar paths to hers and who, even when they deeply disagreed with their own government, did not have to fear what the consequences of that disagreement might be.

Careful though she was not to express a direct opinion in her diary or anywhere else it is evident from her account of her conversations with Angelica Balabanoff and Sasha Kropotkin that she was perturbed by their acceptance of one evil to mitigate another. Although she and Ethel Snowden, through different lenses and to differing degrees, both accepted that sometimes this was the only choice available, neither was comfortable with it. But Bondfield was also carried through by the hope that the Revolution had brought, and the belief that somehow Russia would get past this unfortunate stage and move into a freer and less oppressive phase of socialism. Moreover, the Tsarist regime, which had been gone for only a few years, had been a byword for cruelty and oppression, and even Ethel Snowden, outspoken about the evils of communism, recognized that the reality was more complicated than it might seem on the face of it. 'All dwell in an atmosphere of suspicion,' she remarked:

and the Red Terror is a terrible reality. And it is no consolation for me to learn, as I did, that the White Terror was even worse. I am absolutely satisfied, on the evidence I have seen, that where the Red Terror has slain its thousands the White Terror has destroyed its tens of thousands.[28]

If Bondfield's attitude now seems equivocal it was representative of a broad spread of opinion at the time, when there still seemed to be some hope that repression was a phase and that true socialism would win through. Ethel Snowden's opposition was very much a minority opinion and was a major factor in her failure to get re-elected to Labour's NEC in 1922, particularly as it was seen as feeding the apprehensions of Labour's opponents and thus playing a part in the party's electoral challenges. The debate over the Labour Party's approach to both communism and Soviet Russia would endure for many decades and play a key part in the party's electoral struggles during the 1920s and 1930s.

If Russia took up a good deal of time and effort, another conflict nearer home was also causing considerable disquiet. In Ireland the War of Independence had been raging since January 1919, with the Irish Republican Army conducting guerilla operations against both the British Army and the Royal Irish Constabulary (RIC). The RIC, facilitated by the British government, had recruited thousands of demobbed soldiers who were known, notoriously, as the Black and Tans. Alongside them there was also the RIC's Auxiliary Division, run by former British officers, which was technically a counterinsurgency unit but was actually employed on punitive attacks carried out mainly against civilians. Between them the Auxiliaries and the Black and Tans – sometimes working together and often viewed as interchangeable – were responsible for atrocities of all kinds, sometimes with the blessing of the government in London and sometimes without. The Labour Party demanded an investigation into the situation and sent across its own inquiry team, including Arthur Henderson and J. R. Clynes.[29] The government remained indifferent to the public unease, and even outrage, at what was being done in its name. When a large public meeting at the Albert Hall threatened to get out of hand it was Bondfield who, in an eight-minute speech, changed the mood. 'Our honour' she told the crowd,

> is lying in the mud. Every section of the British people is responsible for what is happening. . . . What can we do? Shouting is not enough. We can all do something. If we could only send down the sales of some newspapers it would be something. . . . I am utterly opposed to murder and reprisals, but I ask you, which are the murders and which are the reprisals?[30]

She made, according to one journalist who was present, 'a flawless speech. She was never asked to speak up. She was heard breathlessly . . . The audience felt she was speaking her heart and mind.'[31] The *Westminster Gazette* called it 'The turning point of the meeting' and the *Daily Herald* said that she 'repeatedly rose and bowed her acknowledgements, having little effect, however, in reducing the storm of applause.'[32]

Any exhilaration she felt at the time was quickly extinguished. She went straight from the Albert Hall 'to see Mary *(Macarthur)*. We talked about the Irish Question. It was our last meeting.'[33]

Chapter 12
An Unprecedented Double

As soon as Bondfield returned from Russia she realized that, despite the operation, Mary Macarthur was not going to survive. Macarthur herself remained hopeful and was busy working with her friend J. R. Clynes to merge the NFWW with his union, the NUGMW. Macarthur was to become the Union's first National Woman Officer with a remit to organize and represent women workers as well as keep an eye on insurance matters. Bondfield visited her regularly, anguished at her visible decline yet unable to let her go. By the end of the year Macarthur was confined to bed at her house in Hampstead and on 1 January, as the two unions merged, Mary Macarthur died. She was forty-one years old.

Her death was a great blow generally, but for Bondfield it was a profound grief. She had loved Macarthur more or less since the moment she first saw her on the station platform in Newcastle nearly twenty years previously, and whatever the nature of that love or the form its expression did or did not take, she had remained loyal and loving ever since. But she may also have felt an uneasy sense of guilt. The NUGMW had appointed her as their National Woman Officer instead of the dying Macarthur, and although Bondfield was bereft without Mary, she had also inherited her ideal job. In her autobiography she referred to it as 'a bitter cup'. The combination of grief and guilt, however mild, was toxic and plunged her into a spiritual and mental depression so profound that it lasted for over a year. Unlike in 1911 there does not seem to have been an actual breakdown and she kept working throughout, but she did find herself unable to shake off a disabling melancholy and a sense of sin and unworthiness that went well beyond imposter syndrome. 'This year of 1921,' she wrote in her diary at the end of it 'has been full of failures and disappointments. I have had nearly a year of spiritual darkness and of a desire to press forward towards the spiritual life being constantly thwarted by petty sins and vices – sloth, pride, jealousy and anger constantly tripping me up.' She had had 'a wonderful holiday full of physical enjoyments, of lovely scenery and good company – but when back at work I felt no deepening of the spiritual life . . . ' She kept going to church 'when work permitted' but neither this nor prayer seemed to help. She was obsessed with the idea of self-deceit and wrote lists of the many forms she thought it took, castigating herself for ambition, false humility, conceit, complacency, and much else besides. At one point she wrote, perhaps revealingly, and certainly inaccurately: 'Great minded men have few secrets.'[1] She wrote lists of things to do to fight self-deceit, most of which centre on struggle, self-denial and resolutions to be tranquil, calm and quiet. 'The Eye of God,' she wrote, 'emancipates from the tyranny of human respect.'

She spent an unhappy Christmas at Torquay but early in 1922 she started to read James Moffatt's *New Translation of the New Testament*, a work by a Scottish academic and clergyman which aimed to make ancient texts more accessible to the modern reader. In Bondfield it seems to have struck a chord which had an almost immediate effect. 'On Jan 17th,' she wrote, 'the inner light returned and I had great happiness – I could pray once more with a sense of reality. . . . It seems I have been trying to save myself and wipe out my own sins but find grace alone is enough and love alone can cleanse.'[2]

There would be other spiritual crises and other periods of depression and at least one more breakdown lay in the future. This long dark period in 1921, however, is the only one she recorded in such detail, and is therefore useful in gaining some understanding of the complex mixture of self-loathing and self-confidence with which she approached life. Nowadays she would be advised to find a good therapist, but in 1921 Ethel Bentham's advice to be careful who she consulted still held good. As a woman of deep faith it was natural for her to look for a spiritual answer to her difficulties, but by the time she found one she had probably already begun to mend. That her faith sustained and fed her is beyond question; unfortunately, that it tormented her when she was already depressed or anxious is also all too evident.

During the year of her misery she had had to deal with challenging political and industrial developments. Early in 1921 Will Crooks, for whom she had spoken in the first 1910 general election, had resigned his seat in Woolwich because of ill health, and the ensuing by-election was bitter and deeply unpleasant. The candidate was Ramsay MacDonald, restlessly seeking a way back into Parliament, and the right-wing press and the supporters of the Coalition attacked him mercilessly. The atmosphere was intimidating, and inevitably there was violence and rioting. Humiliatingly, Labour lost. Nevertheless, there were some hopeful indicators. MacDonald himself had been unpopular and the campaign very dirty, but despite both these factors the Conservative majority was only 683. If there was little enthusiasm for MacDonald there was not much for his opponent, either, and people had had to be scared into voting Tory. The Coalition government's support was beginning to fray at the edges and, dogged though Labour was by accusations of communism and red menace, there was every prospect of increasing its representation at the next general election.

Meanwhile her new job at the NUGMW was also providing challenges. Despite the promises made to the NFWW and the Workers' War Emergency Committee at the start of the War, women had been forced out of employment to make room for returning men with very little prospect of alternative jobs. Women's unemployment had risen rapidly since 1918, benefit arrangements were inadequate or non-existent and many women were at their wits' end how to pay the rent and feed their children. Young, single women were forced into domestic service, for which they had neither appetite nor, often, aptitude, while others found themselves offered only poor jobs at very low pay. Macarthur, Bondfield and the NFWW had found themselves inundated with complaints, many from angry women who rightly felt that they had sacrificed much during the War and were now being cast ignominiously aside. This failure to adjust to seeing women as workers as well as, and sometimes instead of, home makers would be part of the problems which developed during the 1920s and Bondfield's views on them would often prove controversial once she was in government.

The wider trade union movement, also, was having to adapt to the challenges of peace. In 1914 the mining, transport and railway unions had come together to form a Triple Alliance of mutual support, especially during industrial disputes. This had not come into play much during the War, but after it, when there was a debate about the role of direct action in politics and industrial relations, it was a different matter. In the wake of the Russian Revolution there was fairly widespread support for strikes, with even MacDonald arguing that, if Parliament was not representative, the workers were entitled to act. In March 1921 a miners' strike tested the Triple Alliance and found it wanting. On 15 April (known subsequently as Black Friday) both the rail and the transport unions decided not to call strikes in support of the miners, over a million of whom were locked out following the industry's return to private hands after nationalization during the War. The Triple Alliance's collapse caused disquiet and outrage across the movement, but also provided an early warning as to the limits that industrial solidarity might have.

In October 1922 the Coalition government collapsed, brought down by a revolt of Conservative MPs led by Andrew Bonar Law and Stanley Baldwin. The coalition had been unsteady for some time, with increasing discontent in the Conservative ranks, and when a by-election at Newport resulted in an unexpected Tory victory, Conservative MPs decided that the party should fight the next general election on its own rather than as part of a coalition. A number of Conservative ministers then resigned from the Cabinet, and Lloyd George and the rest of his government immediately followed suit. The King asked Bonar Law to form an administration, which he did, before calling a general election for 15 November.

For Labour, this was a clear opportunity. Twelve years earlier in 1910 they had been able to field only 56 candidates; now they were able to stand 411, more than ever before, and in more seats which they judged they had a reasonable chance of winning. There were ten Labour women candidates, including Susan Lawrence in East Ham North. Bondfield raced back to Northampton with high hopes of overhauling the majority she had so effectively reduced in the by-election in 1920. MacDonald was standing in Aberavon, a South Wales ILP seat with much more sympathy with his anti-war stance than Woolwich had had.

The Liberals, meanwhile, were in complete disarray, with Asquith and Lloyd George leading a faction apiece. This did not prevent candidates from the two wings collaborating either with one another or, in the case of the Lloyd George Liberals, with the Conservatives. Some Asquithian Liberals were so far to the left that they were almost in the Labour Party; within a couple of years some of them actually would be. Labour stood four square on a socialist programme, though the Leader, J. R. Clynes was soon forced to back-pedal on the proposed capital levy (similar to a wealth tax) and many candidates, including Bondfield, were attacked on the grounds that they were, or were at any rate as bad as, Russian communists.

In Northampton she went through the three-week election period with her usual energetic attack. She spoke at several meetings a day, knocked on voters' doors, visited schools, factories and markets and gave interviews. Her leaflet was headlined 'Make M.B. your M.P.' and included forthright criticism of the Liberal McCurdy's record in Parliament. Her election address, with the slogan 'The Labour Policy is the People's Welfare,' took the issue of Labour's attitude to red revolution head on. 'You will be told,' she said:

> that Labour is out for violence and destruction because it is a Revolutionary party. I am opposed to all forms of violence whether organized by the proletariat or the capitalist government. I believe in the policy of a peaceful revolution by mental processes – a revolution of the mind and heart – the substitution of service for self-interest, of cooperation for competitive individualism – of putting the public well-being before individual privilege and profits . . .[3]

Unfortunately this appeal was not enough. Once again there was no Conservative candidate but there were both varieties of Liberal, and between them they mopped up the Tory vote. This was the first real post-war election, with no voters still waiting to come home from the battlefields, 60 per cent of women able to vote and, following the 1921 Treaty and the founding of the Irish Free State, only a handful of Irish seats. Turnout in Northampton was up by nearly 20 per cent, and while Bondfield's numerical vote rose, the percentage share fell. This was not the most encouraging of results, especially when elsewhere friends and colleagues were elected. MacDonald was successful in Aberavon and soon replaced Clynes as Leader. Major Clement Attlee won Limehouse and Woolwich was regained for Labour. Susan Lawrence came within a whisker of winning in

East Ham North. Only two women were elected, the Conservative Nancy Astor and the Liberal Margaret Wintringham.

By far the most striking outcome of this fractious election was the further implosion of the Liberals and Labour's leap up to 142 seats, making them the official opposition for the first time. The overall Tory majority of 36 seats meant that, all things being equal, there would not be another election for some years, but Labour had now decisively broken through. As Bondfield returned once more to union work she must have reflected that perhaps it was time to give up on Northampton and try to find somewhere more winnable. George Bernard Shaw certainly thought so, having written to her earlier in the year to inquire: 'why Northampton? You are the best man of the lot, and they shove you off on a place where the water is too cold for their dainty feet . . . and keep the safe seats for their now quite numerous imbeciles.'[4]

In September 1923 Bondfield made the first of the three big cracks in the glass ceiling that she achieved within the space of the next four months. She was elected Chairman (*sic*) of the TUC's General Council, a post which she correctly described as 'the supreme position in the industrial wing of Labour'.[5] She took over in difficult circumstances. One of the by-products of the post-war slump was a drop in trade union membership as members became unemployed, and that impacted on union funds, thus making industrial action less likely. There were also a variety of organizational problems which meant that any action that took place was often disjointed and likely to fail. When Bondfield took office almost the first thing to land on her desk was the boilermakers' dispute, which had been going on for most of the year with no prospect of a resolution. Bondfield had served on the TUC's Disputes Committee since 1918 and now had considerable experience of dealing with such situations. By deft use of good leadership, a persuasive approach and honed diplomatic skills she managed to get an agreement by mid-November. She was immediately deluged with praise, much of it based on her sex rather than her abilities.

> A woman has settled a devastating strike which has paralysed industry for seven months, defying the attempts at mediation of the best male brains in the country. Miss Margaret Bondfield, Labour's woman leader, . . . has put an end to . . . a national calamity which has cost £10,000,000 and involved 70,000 workers.[6]

This kind of coverage did not entirely please her, if only because in her view the success was the result of a collective effort which she had done little more than lead. In this she rather underplayed her role, perhaps so as to avoid irritating the 'male brains' with whom she now had to continue working.

However, there was little more time to spend on TUC affairs since the next opportunity now thrust its way in. Soon after he took office as Prime Minister it transpired that Andrew Bonar Law had throat cancer, and in May, after just six months in office, he resigned. He was replaced by Stanley Baldwin, who, given the parliamentary majority he inherited, should have been able to continue for a full term. Instead, however, he chose to call a general election.

Along with his majority in the House of Commons the new Prime Minister inherited steadily – and alarmingly – rising unemployment. The brief boom after the end of the War had not lasted, and an economic downturn had inevitably resulted in job losses and thus more pressure on the government's Unemployment Fund. The unemployment benefits system was creaking and some benevolent societies were already warning that they would soon be unable to pay out. The only answer was to put more money into the system, and the only way Baldwin could see of achieving this was to strengthen the economy. The mechanism he turned to was protection of trade through tariffs.

He could hardly have come to a conclusion more likely to enrage large parts of both the body politic and the electorate. The one thing that could have united the warring Liberals was their belief in free trade and detestation of protection, while Labour had been from the beginning a party of free trade which believed that tariffs would increase prices and put basic foods out of the reach of working people. Moreover, what united the Liberals divided the Tories, with many opposed to tariffs on principle. Knowing this, and knowing also that Bonar Law had included a promise in the 1922 manifesto not to bring in tariffs, Baldwin decided that the only thing to do was to go to the country for a mandate. There had been some speculation about an election, but most people, including his own MPs, were still astonished when Baldwin announced to Parliament that there would be one on 6 December.

Margaret Bondfield was immediately thrown back into campaign mode. Having called an election over tariffs Baldwin seemed to have very little idea of what they might mean for the economy as a whole, which left the field wide open for opponents to interpret them on their own terms. Bondfield had no difficulty detecting the jugular and going for it. Her campaign launch, at which Ramsay MacDonald again spoke, was held in a cinema which was so full that there was a huge crowd outside and Bondfield had to make an impromptu speech standing on a chair. Inside she attacked Baldwin alleging that 'it was a monstrous insult to the intelligence of the country to imagine that working people could be hoodwinked by the nebulous, unexplained proposals which Mr Baldwin has put before the country'.[7] She was for free trade, the abolition of all taxes on food and other basic necessities, nationalization of the railways, the mines and power stations, action to relieve rural poverty and (countrywoman as she remained) allotments for all. The capital levy, a form of wealth tax intended to pay off the war debt, had been played down by Clynes in 1922, but MacDonald took it head on and defended it. Bondfield had borrowed a red Ford car and toured the constituency relentlessly in an endless round of meetings, speeches and visits, pausing only to consume 'the ideal candidate's supper' of onions stewed in milk,[8] which seems more like a throwback to her Chard childhood than the kind of sustenance she really needed. Her speeches and literature were policy-heavy and some of her more middle-class election workers were worried that they were too 'highbrow' for working-class audiences. As an experiment they stopped a labourer in the street and asked him if he understood what the candidate was talking about when she said that the country was in chaos. '"Why yes," said the man, "she meant it was in a bloody mess."'[9] Bondfield's own life may well have moved some distance from her working-class roots, but she was still well able to resent working people being patronized by other classes, well-meaning or otherwise.

On polling day turnout was high – 84 per cent in Northampton – and counting took a long time. Many seats did not declare until the following day. For the first time, the results were reported on the radio and Baldwin and his inner circle were able to gather at No 10 Downing Street to listen to their majority melting away. In the end they suffered a net loss of over 88 seats. The combined Liberals gained over 70 and Labour 49. The House of Commons was now hung, with the Tories still having the largest number of seats but unable to form a government without support from another party and Labour within sight of being able to form a government if they went into some kind of coalition with the reunited Liberals. This resulted in fevered speculation as to what might happen next and rumours that Britain might now turn socialist were rife.

In Northampton, where Bondfield had finally won with a majority of just over 4,000, there was jubilation. Her supporters drew her round the town 'perched on the high seat of a big charabanc, men hauling on the ropes for two hours round the wards and ending up in the Square.'[10] The *Daily Mirror* hailed her victory as 'one of the greatest sensations' of the election, noting that since she had also been elected 'president of the Trades Union Congress some months back she has brought off an unprecedented double.'[11] Letters and telegrams of congratulation poured in from all sides. Nor was she the only Labour woman elected; Susan Lawrence had won East Ham North and the trade unionist and suffragist Dorothy Jewson had taken Norwich. Trains going to London were full of cheering, waving new Labour MPs and their supporters.

The question now was what was going to happen next. Baldwin remained in office for the moment but could be brought down at any time by a vote of confidence. He could only form the next government if one of the other parties would work with him, and neither was prepared to do that. On the other hand, they were not at all inclined to work with one another either, and certainly not to form a coalition. The Liberals had to decide whether to support Baldwin, whose protectionist policies they detested, or MacDonald and Labour, who agreed with them on free trade but were now a real threat to them electorally. Labour had to decide whether to go it alone, form a minority government, and see what came next, or to do a back-room deal with the Liberals which would put them into office without the need for a coalition. Some in the ILP thought that Labour should try to force another general election immediately, but everybody else dismissed this as an unviable option. The party could hardly afford another election so soon, and Henderson, who had again lost his seat, needed time to build the finances back up before facing another expensive electoral outing. MacDonald and others thought that if Labour did take office the most it would be able to do was demonstrate that it was competent and would not plunge the country into the arms of Bolshevism. Beyond that, most senior Labour figures were extremely apprehensive about the prospect of office, and regarded it, however it came about, as a difficult and possibly unpleasant duty which would have to be endured.

On 13 December the TUC General Council (chaired by Bondfield) and Labour's NEC met in adjacent rooms to consider what their position should be. To both, MacDonald was clear that there was no option but to try to form a government with Liberal support. He said the same to the Parliamentary Party when he met them. Bondfield herself was very much opposed to doing any kind of deal with the Liberals; she had fought long and hard to defeat them at Northampton and she did not feel at all inclined to go into government with them now. She was by no means the only person to feel this, but pragmatism prevailed and all three meetings warily agreed to back MacDonald. Apart from anything else, there would have to be Liberal cabinet ministers, and this would need careful negotiation. The different wings of the Labour Party would all have to be included, in itself no mean feat. Henderson was of the opinion that MacDonald should not be left to do this alone, but in the end the party gave its Leader a free hand to do whatever he thought necessary. The question of whether or not the Liberals would participate was clarified when Asquith addressed a meeting of his MPs before Christmas and suggested that since a Labour administration seemed inevitable it might be a good idea to let them try now, effectively under Liberal supervision so that any damage could be limited.[12]

Thus when Bondfield left London for Christmas it was in the knowledge that there would almost certainly be a Labour government and that there was a serious possibility that she would be in it. The newspapers were full of speculation that she would become the first female Cabinet Minister within weeks, probably as Minister of Health. This was viewed as a popular and deserved possibility, and Bondfield was described as 'well-known, not merely for her flashing energy and broad human sympathies, but as a woman of considerable intellectual power'.[13] One newspaper even went so far as to speculate whether, if and when she was made a Privy Counsellor, Bondfield would have to wear the white knee breeches which were part of formal court dress. At this time women did not wear trousers, and the term 'wearing the breeches' when used of women was usually derogatory, meaning one who behaved in an unnatural, masculine or domineering way. The prospect of a short, rather round fifty-year-old woman in them was almost too much for the journalist to bear. 'The question at once arises' he (or she) asked 'what kind of breeches, if any, will Miss Bondfield wear? . . . No doubt *(she)* would look charming . . . she is a very charming woman. But will she? If not, what will she wear?'[14] Away from this kind of nonsense MacDonald spent Christmas at his home in Lossiemouth planning his Cabinet and may or may not have had any conversation with Bondfield about her possible role.

On 9 January Margaret Bondfield was sworn in as the Member of Parliament for Northampton. This was (and remains) a formal occasion with a religious tone for which women were normally expected to cover their heads. Women in the 1920s wore hats as a matter of course both indoors and out, and especially in religious spaces or in the presence of their social superiors. Bondfield and Jewson habitually wore hats, and indeed the photographs of Bondfield entering Parliament on the day of her swearing-in show her wearing what was described as a 'brown satin toque'. Susan Lawrence wore hats much less often and seems not have worn one at all on that day. At the door of the Commons, however, Bondfield removed her hat and went in to take the oath bare-headed. This caused some comment in the press; the *Western Daily Press* reported that:

> Miss Bondfield created considerable comment by appearing without a hat – looking very nice, too, for she is a handsome woman with beautiful hair, very simply dressed. If she decides not to wear a hat in the House some of her feminine colleagues will probably follow her example, for it is so tiring to wear even a light weight hat for many hours a stretch, especially in that notoriously stuffy and superheated atmosphere.[15]

When, sometime later, Nancy Astor began leaving her hat off in the Chamber the tiring nature of wearing one was indeed the excuse she gave, but Bondfield was made of sterner stuff and mere discomfort would not have been sufficient to make her take a step which she must have known would cause comment. She herself did not provide an explanation but she very probably agreed with the Duchess of Atholl, one of the newly elected Conservative MPs, who, at a dinner honouring the eight women MPs, said that she had:

> one ambition that I have not yet divulged, and that is that I may find it possible to do my work in the House of Commons with my head uncovered. (Laughter.) I am ready to obey the wishes and teaching of St Paul as I enter a divine building, but when I enter the House of Commons I am prepared only to recognise the authority of the Speaker and the rules of the House.[16]

Later, the Duchess was interviewed about her first week in Parliament, and when asked about the 'great "hat or no hat" problem . . . which has given Parliamentary gossips much material for their paragraphs' she credited the Labour MPs with setting her the example, though in this case she too suggested that hats made her tired. 'Nobody', she said

> has so far taken any objection, so that the Labour members and myself are making full use of our freedom. . . . I had hoped before coming to London that hats would not be worn, and when I heard the Labour lady members had adopted the practice I at once followed suit.[17]

Five years later, when she was sworn in as a Privy Counsellor, Bondfield would again decline to wear a hat for the occasion, even though the idea of a woman not covering her head in the presence of her King was almost scandalous. Despite all her private self-doubt and anguish, she considered herself, as a working-class woman and representative of her class, inferior to nobody.

On the evening of her swearing-in she spoke at the party's Victory Demonstration at the Albert Hall where she was given 'an extraordinary reception'[18] and on the Friday evening of that week she attended a function hosted by Nancy Astor at which guests were greeted by all eight female MPs lined up like a receiving party at a wedding. A correspondent for the *Yorkshire Post* described Susan Lawrence as 'grey, humorous and shrewd, she seems to be inwardly assessing values all the time' and Bondfield as 'a tiny figure, in a dark blue dress, who presently darts to and fro among the crowd and is hailed with congratulations by people of all parties'.[19]

The eight women members were likely to get to know one another pretty well, since they had to share office space in one room opening off the Terrace. Described later by the Labour MP Edith Picton-Turbervill as a 'boudoir or underground dungeon',[20] the room had to accommodate both the MPs and their secretaries, if they had one, and the noise and crowding made it difficult to work there.[21] Lady Astor used her office at home, and others found alternatives if they could. In Bondfield's case, she was able to use the secretarial services of the Union, and later the Ministry, but it was a deeply unsatisfactory way of working. There were lavatories reserved for 'Lady Members', but none of the bathing or changing facilities that were available to men. Neither was the culture of Parliament particularly welcoming to female members. Few had much use (or time) for the shooting range, and teetotal temperance supporters like Bondfield were not likely to frequent the bars and restaurants, even had unaccompanied women been welcome. Thus women MPs' interactions with their male colleagues were often restricted to the lobbies, the Chamber, and a very small number of the catering facilities, making the internal politics of both their parties and the House as a whole even more difficult for them to access.

On 15 January the Debate on the Address (the King's Speech at the Opening of Parliament) began in the House of Commons. On the third day Clynes moved an amendment to the Address stating that 'The present advisers of His Majesty have not the confidence of this House.' Since everyone now knew what the outcome was going to be the ensuing debate did not have the fire that it might otherwise have done, but it was momentous nevertheless. The Labour Party, which had existed for less than a quarter of a century, was about to bring down the government by democratic means in a peaceful and traditional setting. Revolutions might rage elsewhere, but in Britain change would be both gradual and within set rules of engagement. Outside Parliament there was some apprehension – and even scaremongering – in more conservative circles, but on the whole there was an acceptance that, by the end of the process, the dreaded socialists would be in power.

Susan Lawrence made her maiden speech on the evening of the second day of the debate, beginning with an 'apology for speaking so soon' but going on to regret the absence of education from the King's Speech. Bondfield had to wait until the late afternoon of the fifth day to make her intervention, and when she did it was not a success. She knew this herself and must have been rather perplexed by the failure at the time. She could hold a crammed Albert Hall in the palm of her hand, but she found it hard to achieve anything like the same effect in Parliament. Her speech was perfectly competent, but competence in public speaking was well below the standard she expected of herself. Like Susan Lawrence she began with an apology for intervening and then went on to attack the government for their record on women's unemployment, retraining and support. These were areas she knew well and had worked hard on, and she was determined to speak about working-class women in her maiden speech. She did so concisely and fluently, but it was the wrong place in the debate to do it and, in retrospect, she understood this. At the end of her speech, she criticized the Conservative Party for its misrepresentation of socialism and reaffirmed her belief in it. In the context of the debate her intervention seemed out of place, as though she had written it in advance and was unwilling or unable to alter it on the hoof. It certainly got her maiden speech out of the way, but it did nothing for her reputation.

One of the problems was the transition from speaking on a public, often open-air, platform to the enclosed setting of the Chamber of the House of Commons. Bondfield had never been a speaker who shouted, but she had had to learn how to make her voice fill a large hall or carry across market squares. The Chamber was very different, and there was criticism. One journalist rather cruelly said that:

> Her matter was excellent, and she addressed herself to subjects of which she is master. Her manner, however, was defective. She spoke in a high, shrill voice, which indicated that she is accustomed to speaking in great spaces. She was difficult to hear, and failed to grip the attention of the House.[22]

Another unsympathetic commentator reported that she

> spoke in a high pitched voice, with a strident open air orator emphasis, and used too much gesture. . . . Miss Bondfield is exceedingly fluent. Probably forty or fifty words a minute faster than most masculine orators. She betrayed little nervousness . . . She wore no hat, and, of course, occasionally touched her back hair with one hand to feel that was all right, slapped her notes at the crescendo passages, and wore a red blouse which went with her declaration that she was Socialist of 30 years' standing.[23]

Bondfield comforted herself that one journalist had told her that 'It was the first intellectual speech by a woman the House had ever heard,'[24] but there was no concealing the fact that her first Parliamentary outing had not been the success she might have hoped.

On 21 January the no-confidence amendment was passed and Baldwin resigned the following day. MacDonald accepted the King's invitation to form a government and was immediately sworn in as a Privy Counsellor. He was the first working-class Prime Minister, the illegitimate son of a farm-hand who, in the space of just six years, had gone from being the most hated man in the country to holding the highest political office it could offer. But more, and more importantly, Labour had arrived at and passed through the gates of power. There was no turning back.

Chapter 13
A Strange Adventure

On 23 January Margaret Bondfield was chairing a meeting of the TUC General Council when a message was brought in asking her to have a word with the MP Tom Shaw. Shaw was secretary of the International Federation of Textile Workers and joint secretary of the Labour and Socialist International, a fellow trade unionist and internationalist. Bondfield had known him for years and although in her memoir she rather disingenuously suggests that she did not know why he wanted to speak to her she must in fact have had a fairly good idea. Shaw had just been appointed Minister of Labour, and his first job was to appoint his Under-Secretary. He had a high opinion of Bondfield, describing her as 'a woman of rare charm, dignity and administrative ability'[1] and she was, at that point, the most senior trade unionist in the country. Accordingly, and probably with at least an inkling of what he wanted, she went down to the lobby see him. 'We shook hands,' she recalled, 'and then he said without any preliminary: "I want you as my Parliamentary Secretary of the Ministry of Labour, and can you come at once?"'[2]

Bondfield gives no indication as to whether or not this offer was a disappointment. She must have known by then that the much-trailed Cabinet post was not going to come her way, and that the need to balance all the competing interests was not going to leave a seat for her, or for any other woman. There may well have been an initial plan to include her, but her very publicly expressed opposition to any kind of coalition with the Liberals would not have helped her case. MacDonald would have had no option but to sacrifice her on the altar of keeping the Liberals – with whom Labour was now in an 'arrangement' rather than a coalition – onside. George Lansbury later suggested that Bondfield was actually offered a cabinet post but declined it.[3] It is hard to see why she would have done this, if only because doing so would have run counter to her decision-making style for most of the rest of her life; her instinct was always to take whatever opportunity offered and to see what happened next.

This is certainly what she did with Tom Shaw's request. She explained to him that she was chairing a meeting and would come when it was finished. She returned to the meeting and explained the position to them; again, it was one which they must have anticipated and there must have been discussions about how to handle it when it did. The TUC's own rules prevented her from holding both offices, and therefore she was forced to choose. That she chose government can hardly have surprised anyone, but there do seem nevertheless to have been a few grumbles that she had not shown sufficient gratitude for the honour the trade union movement had bestowed on her. There is no denying that the timing was poor, but then it is also true that a male TUC Chairman appointed to ministerial office would have had to make the same choice. Certainly she could have turned Shaw's offer down, but there is no reason why she should have done, and few men would even have considered doing so.

Nevertheless, it was a wrench, and she was 'both sad and glad; I was leaving the greatly prized Chair of the industrial world, of which I knew something from the inside, and I was going on a strange adventure.'[4] Like other trade unionists going into government, however, Bondfield retained her union employment and would be able to go back to her job if she lost her seat.

Generally speaking, the appointment was popular, but there was some annoyance that she was not in the Cabinet. The Conservative MP Nancy Astor was particularly cross about it and used a meeting organized by the National Union of Societies for Equal Citizenship to say so. 'I am certain,' she said:

> that if any man had done as much work for his Party as Miss Bondfield he would have had a place in the Cabinet. Some people say that she has been omitted because she has had no Parliamentary experience. I know the Cabinet pretty well, and there are some men in it whose Parliamentary experience is not to their credit. . . . Why, Miss Maggie Bondfield is worth twice some of the men. Everything she has done has been a credit to her.[5]

The Ministry of Labour was situated in Montagu House, a huge, rambling Victorian mansion which had been built in the 1850s in the style of a French chateau.[6] In 1917 it had been taken over by the government, and although the main rooms offered splendid offices for ministers and senior civil servants, the rest of it was a rabbit warren of poky little rooms and dark corridors. Years later, when visiting Washington DC, Bondfield would be very envious of the light, modern office space occupied by the Department of Labor. In Montagu House her office was 'a beautiful room with a most elaborately painted ceiling, but no cloakroom accommodation whatsoever'.[7]

The new government was now the subject of intense press interest. It was unlike anything Britain had seen before, and there was a huge amount of speculation as to how its members would behave. Alongside Liberal and former Liberal peers and grandees there were men who had left school as children and worked in manual trades. A few, shockingly to many people in the 1920s, were illegitimate, and that this number included the Prime Minister only made it more remarkable. There were moderates like Clynes and J. H. (Jimmy) Thomas but also firebrands like John Wheatley, the socialist ILP leader of the Red Clydesiders. For one of the very few times in political history the press became fixated on what men were wearing, or rather, on what they would be wearing on their trip to the Palace to be sworn in as Privy Counsellors. MacDonald thought that they should adhere to whatever was traditional, but the King had waived the requirement for formal dress and the new Ministers therefore turned up in a variety of attire depending either on what they had, what they could borrow, or what they thought would inspire confidence. Clynes, in a tweed coat and scarf, found himself 'marvelling at the strange turn of Fortune's wheel, which had brought MacDonald the starveling clerk, Thomas the engine driver, Henderson the foundry labourer and Clynes the mill hand, to this pinnacle beside the man whose forebears had been Kings . . . We were making history.'[8] He was not the only one to find it all rather poignant. Isabella Ford, writing to Millicent Fawcett, said that she was 'greatly moved' to see people she had known for so long in power, though she heard from Snowden, in particular 'how immense their difficulties are – both amongst their own MPs & constituents & the other parties . . . their inexperience makes things hard. I feel Miss Bondfield is a great asset.'[9]

Clynes himself was now Lord Privy Seal, Henderson Home Secretary, and Snowden Chancellor of the Exchequer. MacDonald had, after much deliberation, decided to be his own Foreign Secretary. Given his extensive international contacts and experience as well as the importance, in the new post-war world, of the role, there was some logic to this, but it made for an enormous workload at a time of crises in every direction, and there would be problems further down the line. The Ministry of Health, with which Bondfield's name had been connected, went to John Wheatley on the grounds that somebody from the Left of the party had to be included and, for various reasons, MacDonald was determined that it should not be Lansbury.

The new government had taken office at a time of post-war economic slump with rising unemployment and an uneasy international situation. Not expecting to be in government, Labour had made all kinds of promises in its election manifesto, many of which would be unachievable since they needed Liberal support and were unlikely to get it. Of the new Cabinet, only Henderson and Clynes had previous government experience, and that was during wartime, when conditions were very different. There were many new MPs, some of whom, like Bondfield, were trying to get grips with ministerial office as well as parliamentary procedure. The PLP itself was a disparate group of men (and three women) from very different political quarters of the movement. There was a group of ILPers and Clydesiders, led by men like Lansbury and Wheatley, who thought that the new government should seize the moment and be as radical as possible as quickly as it could. Then there were former Liberals, some of whom had joined Labour from conviction and some of whom had moved across because they saw which way the wind was blowing. The trade unionist MPs, including Bondfield, were often more pragmatic than most other elements of the PLP, understanding that time might be limited and that the new government should achieve what it could and not try to be revolutionary. This was a difficult mix to knit together and keep moving in the same direction, and there were frequent disagreements. Meanwhile, outside Parliament there was the bulk of the Labour Party, which had its own expectations and wanted them to be met, and the ever-present press and newspapers, who had column inches to fill and were always on the lookout for problems. Almost all of the major newspapers were hostile to Labour, although some were more so than others, and sometimes even the Labour *Daily Herald* preferred sniping from the sidelines to providing consistent support.

When Bondfield took up her ministerial post she had been an MP for a little over six weeks and had spoken in the Chamber just once. Now she was responsible for, amongst other things, all issues relating to women's employment, a subject on which she knew a great deal, but had never had to deal with from the point of view of government. She was, as many people had noted over the years, a very able administrator and a good negotiator, and she was quick and decisive when faced with problems. But she could also be obstinate and opinionated, and this could be a drawback in a political world where flexibility could sometimes be an advantage. All of these traits would be a factor in her ministerial career.

However, there was very little time to sit and reflect on the situation. Two days after her appointment MacDonald sent her to Geneva to help to resolve some problems at the ILO. Her friend Sophy Sanger, who she had known since the days of the NFWW, was now the head of the ILO's legal section, and Bondfield was delighted to see her again. Sanger's partner, Maud Allen, was also a close friend who kept Bondfield up to date with Geneva news in long, chatty letters. Allen usually, for some reason, referred to Bondfield as 'Bongy', and their friendship was of long standing. It took several days to deal with the ILO problem and after she had returned home the Secretary General, Albert Thomas (whose 'warlike' approach had saddened her at the 1919 Berne conference), wrote to MacDonald to express his 'warm appreciation' of her work. 'I just send this line to you,' wrote MacDonald to Bondfield, 'to let you know what pleasure it has given me personally to hear of your success.'[10]

She returned to London in early February to find mountains of work awaiting her. Apart from Departmental documents for her to read, correspondence came at her from all sides. It began with a 'fairly heavy' 8 am delivery of post at home, which was now a flat at Adelphi Terrace a few minutes' walk from Montagu House. More post had to be collected from the Post Office in the House of Commons lobby, and more still waited for her in the Department. On top of this she had to read reports, proposals, legislative bills and digests as well as attend meetings, be in the House when required, and look after the needs of constituents, some of whom would arrive at Parliament expecting attention and a personal tour. She did not mind dealing with letters and requests from her own constituents, but 'when these letters come in from people outside one's own area, who could perfectly well write to their own member . . . it is rather an imposition upon the woman MP, notwithstanding the flattering implications!'[11]

On her return from Geneva she also found herself plunged into debates about unemployment insurance and training schemes for women and young people. A month after her maiden speech she became the first woman to speak from the despatch box in the House of Commons. In the intervening period, and between travelling, reading herself into the job, responding to letters and receiving deputations, she had worked on both her voice and her delivery, and this time her contribution had a much better reception. Although she had 'hitherto very modestly tucked herself out of sight at the end of the Treasury Bench that is hidden by the Speaker's Chair' she was agreed to have given her answer 'in a clear, well-pitched voice . . . Everyone in the Chamber could easily hear her, and she well deserved the cheer that came from all sides of the House.'[12] The *Daily Express* was of the opinion that she was 'evidently going to be a parliamentary success'.[13] Another observer noted that, although she had 'given a lesson to her colleagues in the art of clear, precise and audible answer' her lack of height 'was against her, and as she could hardly look over the Treasury box she had to place her notes on the table'.[14] This may have been an exaggeration, but certainly the House of Commons was not a space designed for small women.

The problems of both male and female unemployment levels and unemployment insurance with which Bondfield and Tom Shaw were faced were enormous, and would have been daunting to experienced ministers, let alone those who were complete novices. After a brief post-war boom unemployment had escalated rapidly as the economy faltered, and the forcible replacement of wartime workers with men returning from the Front had only served to increase female unemployment even further. As a result, pressure on the Unemployment Insurance fund, which, according to Bondfield, had had a surplus of £22 million at the end of the War, was intense. By 1924 the government had begun what she rather bitterly called its 'rake's progress of borrowing', a progress which would be a contributory factor to the waiting disaster of 1931. 'The coffers,' she said:

> were empty; the industrial anarchy was in full swing . . . the financial crisis in Europe was germinating and the figures of unemployment were steadily rising. Nearly all the leading figures in the financial world were out of sympathy with the Socialist programme, and knew how to be politely obstructive.[15]

Getting anything done was, despite a 'helpful' civil service and a considerable degree of political will, very difficult. It did not help that, on the whole and in the general view, Bondfield was better at her job than Shaw was at his. The problem of unemployment, which was stubbornly stuck at 10 per cent, seemed to baffle even the best brains in the government. Worse, responsibility for alleviating it was split between several departments with very little effective coordination between them. Sidney Webb, who was reckoned – and who reckoned himself – to be an expert chaired the Cabinet's Unemployed Committee but seemed to have little more insight than anyone else. A slight upturn in the economy, while welcome, had almost no effect on the unemployment figures.

By March the scale of the task had become clear. A number of palliative measures had been taken, including abolishing both the three-week waiting period before unemployment payments could be claimed and the much-hated condition for unemployed women that they should be prepared to accept domestic service whether they wanted to or not, but these did nothing to resolve the underlying problems and satisfied nobody. Outside Parliament, and particularly in the ranks of the ILP and some unions, there was considerable impatience at the apparent absence of any real action. Inside it was becoming clear that Shaw was out of his depth. On 10 March he found himself in the Chamber defending the fact that almost every measure being proposed had originated under the previous government. Irritated by the heckling to which he was subjected from the Conservatives, he unwisely demanded: 'Does anybody think we can produce schemes like rabbits out of our hat?'[16]

Bondfield's speech on this occasion won her wide praise. According to one newspaper it was 'the best speech that has yet been made from the Treasury Bench' and the writer opined that Tom Shaw would have done better to stay at home and 'leave Miss Bondfield to do all the defending of the Government. Not only is the House in sympathy with her when she speaks, but she has shown herself a keen debater, as well as a most practical and skilful exponent of facts and figures.'[17]

For Bondfield, the problem was not so much a lack of ideas as an inability to implement them. Sub-Committees like the one on unemployment had to get Cabinet agreement before they could actually do anything, and Bills arising from that process had to go through the Home Affairs Committee to make sure that there was no duplication or overlapping. This created a bottleneck in which proposed legislation could languish for weeks. Getting anything at all onto the Statute Book was a painfully slow process, especially since, for any significant piece of legislation, they had to get support from the Liberals or, failing that, from enough Conservatives to get them over the line. 'We were a new team,' she said '. . . with gigantic masses of papers to be read and – what I regard now as the great weakness – no real focussing point for action on any one thing because of the multitude of things to be attempted.' In these circumstances she thought it amazing that 'the first Labour Government made so few blunders and reaped so many successes'.[18]

On 22 May there was a Commons debate on unemployment which was anything but edifying. There was much reference to rabbits, and even Bondfield was drawn in. The government's aim was to talk an opposition motion out, and to this Bondfield contributed by saying as little as possible for as long as she could. She:

> rapped her lorgnette with dangerous emphasis *(on)* the Treasury Box, and heroically endeavoured to repair some of the blunders of her chief. She is pleasant in voice, manner, and appearance, and speaks with lucidity, as well as devastating fluency. On this occasion, though her speech was long, she had not much to say.[19]

A week later the opposition tried to reduce Shaw's salary but were defeated. Bondfield may well have felt sympathy for him but there must also have been a degree of frustration. There were some successes, but overall it was not a particularly easy or happy position to be in.

One of the issues which was to cause Bondfield a considerable amount of trouble over the next few years – some of it self-inflicted – was the question of the employment of women and of married women in particular. Like most people at the time, Bondfield believed that most married women preferred being at home, and she was extremely interested in how working conditions there could be developed so as to provide a better environment. She thought that there should be health and safety requirements for homes just as there were for industry, and she supported women's campaigns to improve the standard of housing. The 'homes fit for heroes' promised by Lloyd George had not materialized, but Labour had come in with a promise to build as many of them as possible, and since housing at that time was regarded as a public health issue the responsible minister was John Wheatley. His Housing (Financial Provisions) Act of 1924 turned out to be the only major piece of legislation that the first Labour government managed to get through, leading to the building of tens of thousands of new homes until the National Government repealed it a decade later. Labour women believed that the housewives who would have to work in these buildings should have a say in their design and had been working on this since before the War's end. In 1919 Marion Phillips and Averill Sanderson-Furniss, an architect and WLL member, had coordinated the production of *The Working Woman's House*, a book which was the result of wide consultation, and which made many recommendations which, if implemented, would have changed ordinary women's lives in far-reaching ways. In March 1924 Bondfield herself invited suggestions from working women as to what they wanted in the modern house. Unfortunately, Wheatley paid no attention to any of this, and the new houses were all designed by men who would never have to work in them.

One issue in which Bondfield was considerably interested was the provision of training and education for women workers. This included training for domestic work, which, despite her own aversion to it, she believed should be viewed as skilled. This idea had a variety of origins, including the prevailing social view of domestic work as essentially female and menial, and may also have been influenced by Maud Ward's experience of teaching cooking before the War. Bondfield may not have done much in the way of housework herself, but she had huge admiration for those who did. She also saw clean, well-kept houses as an essential contribution to the fight against disease and recognized that young women who had probably been at work since their mid-teens had had very little time or inclination to acquire domestic skills. She thought that professional training would not only give women marketable skills which they could use in both their working and their private lives, but would also make a significant contribution to the overall health of the nation. Inevitably, many middle-class women took exception to the idea that domestic work had or should have the kind of value Bondfield wanted to put on it. Working-class women's feelings were more mixed, but on the whole much less hostile and the home training centres Bondfield established were generally popular. The whole question of women's domestic role would be a theme of Bondfield's politics for a long time to come, and at points would prove highly contentious, as it still does now.

If the idea of professionalizing working-class women's domestic skills was controversial, the notion that they should be able to control their own fertility was even more so. Middle-class and aristocratic women already had access to some forms of birth control if they wanted it and could pay for it, but working-class women had very little. The result was poverty, deprivation, and damage to the health of both the children and their mothers. Most Labour women were strongly in favour of making birth control, or at least information about it, available to working-class women, but many trade union men saw the answer as an adequate family wage, better housing and improved health services which, in their view, did not include women having either the right or the ability to control the size of their families. Many, like Wheatley, had religious objections, while others, who did not themselves object, were worried about offending the Catholic vote in the North West of England and parts of Scotland. The Labour Party conference passed no resolutions supporting access to contraception, and since Wheatley was responsible for health there was no hope of getting any change to birth control provision through the 1924 parliament. Neither Bondfield nor Susan Lawrence were able to be publicly supportive while they held government posts, and in Bondfield's case taking Wheatley on at a time when she had to work with him on employment issues in the building industry would not have been wise politically. Given her long support for contraception and for women to understand their own bodies this must have caused her some disquiet, and there were doubtless conversations behind the scenes. Her appearance of neutrality was not always well understood, however, and certainly undermined her with those who wanted female politicians to act as women first and Labour politicians second.

Much of Bondfield's first period in government was turbulent, but there were some compensations. In February she was the guest speaker at a dinner given by the Society of Somerset Folk in London. 'When I hear the good old Somerset dialect,' she told them, 'I feel it is good to be alive, and my heart leaps.'[20] Even more gratifying, perhaps, was her presence at the Drapers' Chamber of Trade dinner in March. Her speech to them was serious and about trade issues, but she must have had some quiet satisfaction in her progress from insignificant shop assistant to the guest of honour at a dinner at the Trocadero restaurant. In July she was the guest speaker at Charlotte Despard's eightieth birthday party. In that month also the veteran Isabella Ford died, and Bondfield spoke at her memorial meeting. 'The workers accepted her,' she said, 'not as a middle-class woman, but as one of themselves.'[21] From Bondfield, even now that she was so far removed from her roots, this was still the highest possible praise. As she whirled from one engagement to another her diary was rarely clear, but it was all energizing and the problems, though huge, were there to be solved. People continued to note her vitality and zest for life, and despite everything she enjoyed her job.

One of the issues which came under Bondfield's remit was emigration. This was a question which interested many people in both the Labour movement and the trade unions, partly because it offered opportunities to working people that they could not have at home, but also because it was seen as one of the answers to over-population and unemployment. There were many schemes for promoting and managing emigration, and people could go – or be sent – to most of the colonies in one way or another. There were also various programmes for sending orphaned children to new homes in places like Canada and Australia, some of which were very dubious, and there were some serious allegations of abuse and exploitation. The Colonial Secretary, Jimmy Thomas, was keen that these should be examined and addressed, and asked Bondfield to lead an investigation.

Since this necessitated travelling to Canada she probably did not need much persuasion to go, and she and her team set sail in mid-September. They were to examine three main areas: the settlement of families; the position of unaccompanied women; and child migration. The Delegation conducted many interviews with people involved at all stages of the emigration process and came to some sensible conclusions. While other reports set child migration in the context of imperial trade, Bondfield considered it from the point of view of the children themselves, and as a consequence recommended an immediate end to child migration under the age of 14. Later, in a slightly different context, she remarked that she knew 'from bitter experience what it is to be hustled suddenly out of one environment into another totally different . . . '[22] When the Report was published the following year this recommendation was accepted, though by then Labour was out of office and Bondfield herself was out of Parliament.

Things had not been going well for the government over the summer, although there was, at that stage, nothing to suggest that they would so quickly go so badly that they could bring the government down altogether. As Parliament broke for Recess ministers felt that they had got to grips with their departments, had started to work out how to make things happen, and were beginning to see progress. But then a small scandal broke out over the gift to the Prime Minister of a car and some shares, the dividends from which were to pay for the vehicle's upkeep, and matters began to go downhill. MacDonald had very little in the way of private means and could not afford a car. The state did not provide one and it seemed ridiculous that the Prime Minister could not move around the country with some privacy. This had not been a problem for his predecessors, all of whom had been men of some wealth. The donor, Alexander Grant, was a friend from MacDonald's youth who was in a position to help and did, but MacDonald might more easily have been able to defend himself had Grant, who was the Managing Director of the biscuit company MacVitie and Price, not been given a baronetcy in the King's Birthday Honours. The whole situation then began to look corrupt, and the press had an understandable field day.

After that one thing began to follow another. Earlier in the year the government had recognized the Soviet regime; given the situation in Russia this was probably inevitable, but it caused a good deal of anger amongst people who were already terrified of a Bolshevik takeover. In July a commercial loan to Russia was approved, which again caused outrage and the negotiation of which dragged on for weeks. Suspicions began to grow that Labour was more under Russian influence than they claimed, and while some people had always believed this to be the case, others who had given the party the benefit of the doubt began to change their minds. This process was greatly accelerated by the case of J. R. Campbell, the editor of the Communist *Workers Weekly*, who had been charged with inciting police and troops to disobey orders after he urged them not to fire on strikers. It soon turned out that, in addition to being a Communist, Campbell was a disabled War hero and Labour members and MPs protested loudly at his prosecution. The Cabinet decided that political prosecutions needed its approval, following which the prosecution was withdrawn. Nobody came out of it well, but Ministers looked particularly bad, and the feeling that Labour was dancing to a Communist tune intensified even further.

On 8 October the Conservatives and Liberals combined to attack Labour over the whole affair. MacDonald, asked about what he had known about the dropping of the case was, at best, evasive and there were allegations (which he denied) that he had lied to the House. A vote of censure, which MacDonald chose to regard as a vote of no confidence, was passed by a large majority. The following day he went to the Palace and asked the King for a dissolution. The first Labour-led government was at an end and a general election was called for 29 October.

Far away in Canada Margaret Bondfield, though aware that all was not well, had no idea that the end was so near and was in Edmonton when she heard the news. Appalled, and already believing that her seat would be very hard to hold, she scrambled back to England as fast as she could, but, like Will Crooks in Woolwich in 1910, she was vulnerable to attack from opponents accusing her of wasting time and public money abroad. Northampton Labour Party adopted her as the candidate in her absence and other people had to speak for her at public meetings and events. On 17 October, two weeks before polling day, her agent in Northampton received a cablegram which said: 'Have raced across the provinces of Alberta, Saskatchewan, Manitoba, Ontario, and Quebec. Encouraging hopes expressed throughout for return of Labour to power. Confident Northampton will support MacDonald. Leaving today on Carmania.'[23]

The *Carmania* docked at Liverpool six days later and Bondfield rushed to Northampton. Much as she loved travel, the long journey home from Canada was probably one of the most stressful she ever undertook. Despite her misgivings about the outcome she put everything she had into the remaining days of the campaign. She arrived in Northampton to a great welcome and a parade round the town, and she seemed to be as popular as ever, but all too soon more than just her unplanned absence was against her. Two days after her arrival the *Daily Mail* published what became known as the Zinoviev letter, a forged missive purporting to come from Grigory Zinoviev, head of the Comintern in Russia, to the Communist Party in Britain instructing it effectively to lay the groundwork for a Bolshevik revolution. Had the letter come out of the blue it might not have been so damaging, but coming hard on the heels of the Russian loan and the Campbell case it was the last straw. Opinions vary as to what effect the letter itself had, but the cumulative effect was too much. On polling day the Conservatives gained a majority of 209 while Labour lost 40 seats, including Margaret Bondfield's at Northampton. Her first taste of public office was over.

Chapter 14
That Detestable Affair

The 1924 general election resulted in a decisive victory for Stanley Baldwin's Conservatives. The Liberals lost 118 seats and Britain returned to being a two-party democracy. For its part, Labour had learned lessons from its brief time in government. There was a better understanding of how the machinery worked as well as of how long it took to get anything done. Now there was time to think, reflect and plan.

Once she had recovered from the disappointment of the election result Bondfield returned to her job at the NUGMW. As a former government minister, she still had status in the movement and in any case she was good at her job. She remained in demand as a public speaker, and although there was already some hostility to her from the ILP and others on the Left, on the whole she retained her popularity. In November 1925, however, she made an error which would change this and which would be the foundation for some of her later troubles.

The Conservative government, now struggling with the same problems of unemployment and unemployment insurance that Labour ministers had, set up a Committee under Lord Blanesburgh to look at the issue. The Unemployment Insurance Acts were due to expire in 1927 and there was no clear idea about what to do next. Costs had to be kept down, but on the other hand unemployment was still high and even the Conservatives did not, at this stage, believe that the benefits system should be abolished altogether. Blanesburgh was a Scot, a judge, and a law lord who enjoyed detail as much as Bondfield did. His remit was to 'consider, in the light of experience gained in the working of the Unemployment Insurance Scheme, what changes in the scheme, if any, ought to be made'. For a variety of reasons, Bondfield was invited to join the Committee. The other two Labour members were Albert Holmes of the print union, and the miner Frank Hodges. All three accepted in a personal capacity.

With hindsight, she conceded that her acceptance was 'rather rash'[1] but at the time it seemed an unexceptionable decision. She thought that her trade union experience would be useful, she thought that the working-class woman's voice should be heard, and she had a detailed knowledge of the Unemployment Insurance system going back to its inception before the War. Additionally, she was encouraged to accept the appointment by her own union, with Clynes writing to her that he hoped 'you can find time to serve on the Unemployment Insurance Committee – not only because of the experience we have had, but of the probable effect of any extension on the future position of trade unions'.[2] The NUGMW circulated a questionnaire on the issues to its branches and districts and collated the responses, and other unions, too, collected and submitted evidence. There was a great deal of detailed examination of statistics and cases which was exactly suited to Bondfield's very meticulous way of working, and the final report would be over a year in the making.

In the meantime she resumed trade union work, organizing women, negotiating pay and conditions and representing the union at national level. Her life fell back into the usual pattern of travelling round the country, attending conferences and getting abroad whenever she could. She spent her summer holidays in the West Country walking, swimming in the sea, and playing golf, a game for which she had acquired a liking. She was keen to get back into Parliament, and was waiting for a by-election to come up, but this time she was prepared to hang on for something rather safer than Northampton. Susan Lawrence and Dorothy Jewson, who had also lost their seats, were similarly thinking about how to get back; Lawrence succeeded in April 1925 when the candidate who had defeated her died. Conservative and Liberal women tended to have safer seats, if only because several of them had stepped into the breach when their husbands died or when, as in Nancy Astor's case, they were elevated to the House of Lords. Labour women had to fight their corners with everyone else, and even Margaret Bondfield, senior as she was, could not be sure that she would ever get a safe seat. Nor were men entirely immune to this problem; Arthur Henderson never had a safe seat either, representing constituencies all over the country and losing them with monotonous regularity.

While she waited for what would happen next, however, there were other problems to deal with. The industrial situation, always difficult in the 1920s, continued to rumble ominously. The trade union movement was believed, both by the Conservative government and many of its own leaders, to be a revolutionary powder keg waiting to explode, while the Labour Party, smarting after its loss, was full of uneasy grumbles which periodically broke out into open argument and dissent. Writing to the Labour Chief Whip, MacDonald noted that: 'There is a great deal of mischief about. People do not seem able to settle down and contribute, without thought of personal advantage, what they can to a common cause, and the power of the whisper and private comment is really wonderful.'[3] As often when faced with a long period of opposition the party had difficulty finding its feet in the new political environment; ten months in government had fundamentally changed it.

The trade union powder keg may not have been revolutionary, but it was certainly likely to explode, and the mining industry soon provided the spark. Falling coal exports had led to the closure of hundreds of pits, and many of those that were left were running at a loss. The mine owners thought that increasing hours and reducing wages would stop the rot, a line which was always bound to encounter strong opposition. Demand for British coal was further reduced when Winston Churchill, as Chancellor of the Exchequer, returned Britain to the gold standard in 1925. Miners' pay had been falling steadily for some years, and when the employers gave notice of their intention to abandon the guaranteed minimum wage many foresaw levels of poverty which they had not experienced for decades.

There now followed a stand-off in which the government blinked first. Faced with the prospect of a general strike, which the TUC General Council had this time said it would back, Baldwin announced a Royal Commission on mining in July. This was to be chaired by Sir Herbert Samuels, and subsidies were to continue in the meantime. Few people can seriously have thought that this would solve the problem; there had been other inquiries over the years and none of them had been able to propose anything really new. Nevertheless, Baldwin had staved off industrial action for the moment and bought some time in which to prepare for it.

In August Bondfield went to Marseilles as part of the British delegation to the first meeting of the International Conference of Labour and Socialist Women, and when she returned in September she was re-elected to the TUC General Council at the Annual Congress meeting in Scarborough. However, there had been a change in the organization of seats, and women were now in a section of their own called 'Women Workers' from which two women were to be elected. Bondfield duly topped the poll but her apprehensions that this separating out of women would have the effect of making all the other sections into male preserves proved all too prophetic. It would be decades before more than two women sat on the General Council, and although it is certainly true that, had there not been reserved places there might have been none, Bondfield's view that women who did not have the support of both women and men would find real power harder to get was not entirely wrong either.

As the Samuels Commission on the mining industry took evidence and came to its conclusions both sides made their preparations. By the time it reported in March 1926 each was well dug into a bunker and a strike seemed inevitable. The Commission had, it is true, recommended that the industry be re-organized, but insisted that there would first have to be a cut in wages. The mining unions adamantly opposed this. The employers then added fuel to the fire by insisting on the abolition of nationally negotiated agreements, something to which they must have known that the unions could never agree, and when they reluctantly withdrew the demand it was only to go back to insisting on an increase in hours, which the unions could not agree to either. A general strike was scheduled to begin on 4 May, and though negotiations continued there was not much hope that they would succeed.

On Saturday 1 May Bondfield spoke at the May Day rally in Northampton before returning to London to speak at the London Labour Party's May Day event at Kingsway Hall. The following day the Cabinet met in an almost permanent session. Late in the evening the entire TUC General Council, to whom powers of negotiation had been delegated by the individual unions, was summoned to Downing Street in a last-minute bid to avert the strike. As they arrived in small groups the police had to clear a way for them through the huge crowds that had gathered outside. Bondfield and Mary Quaile,[4] the other female member of the Council, were the first to get there, and 'conversed animatedly outside until the other members of the Council made their appearance'.[5] Inside negotiations went on until after midnight, when the government terminated them after compositors at the *Daily Mail* unilaterally refused to set the type for an editorial which equated the general strike with revolution. The die was now cast, and the strike began at midnight on 4 May.

The response from workers was huge. Over one and a half million people came out in support, far more than the unions had anticipated and thoroughly alarming the government. As Bondfield pointed out, the vast majority of workers had 'no direct interest . . . they merely acted to draw attention to . . . the wrongs of the miners, and to the unfair action of the Conservative Government'.[6] Speakers from the General Council toured the country to check organizational strength and motivate the strikers while a negotiating committee remained in London. Bondfield was dispatched to the West Country where she spent eight of the nine days of the strike on the road. What press was being published took a considerable interest in her progress, even reporting on her flying visit to Chard for tea with her brother Frank. There was not much time for socializing however, as she met local committees, spoke at several rallies a day and whirled from place to place in a car and driver lent for the purpose by Lady de la Warr, a Labour member and trade union supporter whom Bondfield had known since de la Warr's involvement with the EFF in 1912. Her reputation, her organizational skills and her ability as a public speaker meant that she was welcomed wherever she went, but by the time she arrived at Yeovil on 10 May she could detect an 'anxiety to end the strike'.

This anxiety was increased when, on 11 May, a high court judge ruled, in a case brought by the National Sailors' and Firemen's Union, that for everyone except the miners' unions the strike was illegal, and that individual unions could therefore find their assets seized. The strike was now unsustainable, and on 12 May the General Council, including Bondfield, returned to Downing Street to indicate that, under certain conditions, they were willing to end the strike. The miners, who now felt doubly let down by the movement, stayed out alone for another six months, but other trades went back. The unions had asked that there be no persecution of strikers, but the government said that it could not guarantee this and as a result victimization was widespread. Worse, the pressure applied in mining areas to force the men back was extreme. A Women's Committee for the Relief of Miners' Wives and Children had been set up, with Margaret Bondfield, Marion Phillips and Susan Lawrence, amongst others, as members and the MP Ellen Wilkinson in the Chair. They collected money, food and clothes for distribution in the affected areas but were appalled when the value of these were deducted from outdoor relief and other benefits. In an open letter to the press members of the Committee explained that the women and children were 'now in desperate straits. Long periods of short time and low wages have exhausted their resources, and the lock-out finds them facing actual starvation. Some of the mining valleys . . . are now practically famine areas.'[7] This situation continued well after the miners were forced back, with some being summarily sacked and not working again for years. The after-effects of the strike were to be felt for decades to come.

There were also legislative consequences. The following year the government brought in the Trades Disputes and Trade Unions Act which, amongst other things, criminalized secondary and mass picketing, and attacked union funding of the Labour Party by requiring individual workers to contract in positively to their union's political levy. This Act was widely regarded as revenge for the General Strike and infuriated both the unions and the party. Resentment over it certainly fed the increase in the Labour vote in industrial areas but the reality was that it achieved both its aims both cooling industrial action and reducing Labour's access to funding.[8]

Towards the end of June the MP Patrick Hastings, who had been the Attorney General during the brief Labour government and had been much criticized over the Campbell case, resigned his Wallsend seat. Although he had remained on the front bench after the election he had taken little active part, and by mid-1926 he had had enough. As the party's General Secretary Henderson immediately offered the candidacy to Margaret Bondfield. Hastings had had a majority of just 1,600, but Henderson was sure that a good campaign with an energetic candidate could improve on that. Despite Bondfield's complete lack of connection with either the North East generally or Wallsend in particular, the constituency Labour party adopted her as their candidate at a hastily convened and rather rowdy meeting at which she was not present. Will Thorne, the NUGMW's General Secretary, wrote to wish her success and to ask that, since the union was footing the lion's share of the bill for the campaign, she keep the costs down.[9] The main thrust of her message was roundly to attack Baldwin's government on the grounds that it was making 'the rich richer and the poor poorer',[10] and the ensuing battle was hard-fought and at times bad-tempered. The Conservatives complained about Labour hecklers at their meetings, and the Tory press reported that on polling day their candidate had fewer cars available owing to 'Red Threats'.[11] The longer the campaign went on, however, the more sure Bondfield became of a good victory. In the event she was correct, increasing the Labour majority to over 9,000 and triumphantly returning to Parliament to join Ellen Wilkinson, who had been the only Labour woman elected at the 1924 general election, and Susan Lawrence.

Now that she had a seat that she could reasonably expect to hold for some years, the question arose of who should be her agent. At this time, and for some decades to come, a constituency agent had organizing duties well beyond simply running election campaigns, and the post often came with a salary paid for by fundraising and trade union support. Agents were expected to be a bridge between the MP, the constituency and usually, in the case of Labour MPs, whichever trade union was sponsoring them. They had to have diplomatic and political skills as well as organizational ability, and good agents were worth their weight in gold.

Claude Denscombe, was, like Bondfield, originally from the West Country, though he had been working in South Wales, where he was described as 'a born organizer and an acceptable platform speaker'.[12] It is easy to see why Bondfield would have wanted him for the job. She needed someone who could both keep an electoral machine going and look after her interests, and since this applied to the internal workings of Wallsend Labour Party, a notoriously difficult body with bad-tempered meetings which occasionally erupted into fisticuffs, it needed to be someone with good political instincts as well as the ability to impose his authority. All of these qualities Denscombe seemed to have in abundance, and the partnership between the two would last for the next fifteen years.

Having made sure that her back would be well-watched in Wallsend, Bondfield now set out for a holiday in America, sailing on the *Celtic* on 18 December. Intriguingly, the name above hers on the passenger list is that of Sir William Beveridge. Beveridge, who would later produce *Social Insurance and Allied Services*, popularly known as the Beveridge Report, was the Director of the London School of Economics, founded by the Webbs and other Fabians in 1895 as a centre of economic and social research. He was considered an expert on unemployment and related issues, as was Bondfield, so it would be interesting to know what they discussed on their voyage, but there appears to be no record. As usual, her time in America was filled with meetings, speeches and visits, as well as days spent with friends like Jane Addams in Chicago and Rose Schneiderman in New York. She visited Canada again, staying near Montreal and admiring the scenery and the skiers on the mountain. At the end of January she set sail for home, arriving back on 5 February rested and refreshed and ready for whatever came next.

She might have hoped that, having regained her seat on the General Council and got back into Parliament, what came next would be a period of calm.

Unfortunately this was not to be, and in fact she embarked on a period of turmoil and controversy which would provide the basis for the later decay of some of her reputation. Some of the choices she made in this period seem extraordinary and did so to many observers at the time. Her ability to make good decisions rapidly seemed to desert her, and her belief in the rightness of her own opinions, which had hitherto been expressed as a firmness which gave people confidence, now began to make her seem out of date and out of touch. The mistakes were not yet so great as to cost her her career, but undoubtedly she made enemies she did not need to make and lost friends that she needed to keep.

It began with the publication, early in 1927, of the Blanesburgh Report, signed by all the members of the Committee including Bondfield. In her view, she had done a good job in mitigating some of the more unacceptable ideas put forward by other members and, while she did not think that the report was by any means perfect, she did believe there was enough in it to deal with a number of the problems she foresaw. She also thought, as did the other Labour members of the Committee, that compromise was necessary in order to achieve some of their main objectives. This was – initially at least – recognized in some quarters. *The New Statesman* noted that the 'Labour representatives must have been well aware that, if they presented a Minority Report, there was no possible chance that the Government would carry it out.'[13] As Bondfield explained, 'in order to get the things which I regarded as really vital . . . I have had to give way on other points which I regard as unsatisfactory. The result of my putting in dissenting notes to the things I don't like would have been that other people would have put in dissenting notes to the things that I cared most about.'[14] The Conservative government would need to legislate on a new Unemployment Insurance Scheme before the end of the Parliament, so that there was no prospect of Labour being able to control what was in it. She acknowledged that there might be questions but was convinced she was right. 'Some of my friends,' she said, 'when they heard that I had signed a unanimous report with a number of Liberals and Tories, sat up and scented trouble. But I knew perfectly well what I was doing.'[15]

Many of the Report's recommendations were, in fact, acceptable to the movement, and some had arisen from Labour and trade union evidence. But others were more dubious, while others still were simply mis-reported. As always in these situations some of the people criticizing had not read the report, while others were so focused on their own particular concern that they failed to see the wider picture. The allegation, for instance, that the Report recommended reducing all women's unemployment benefit from 15 shillings (s) to eight was inaccurate, since the cut was proposed only for young people between the ages of 18 and 21. The principle of this was also hotly debated, as was a more general cut in benefit, the provision of training schools for young people, and the concept of 'genuinely seeking work'. Signing the Report may or may not have been a wise move, but the furore it raised seems to have taken her by surprise and was much greater than she had anticipated. She attributed this to the movement's 'angry and restless mood, sensitive to the slightest suggestion of enmity, or even of neglect'. It was, she said, 'a golden moment for mischief-makers, when it would be easy to sow mistrust and disbelief'. She saw the opposition as personal, offering her enemies the 'opportunity for more than merely revenge. They had a real tactical opening by which it was possible to wreck my influence in the Party – and they seized it. Perhaps,' she reflected, 'I had a little underestimated the opportunity it gave to serious opponents.'[16]

However, if there was one feature Bondfield had in abundance, besides (whatever she sometimes confided to her diary) faith in her own judgement, it was courage. Deluged by criticism, much of it deeply hostile and some of it personal, she stood her ground. The suggestion was made that she had signed the Report without understanding what was in it; this she angrily denied. Demands that she withdraw her signature she met with contempt; 'They had greatly mistaken me if they thought I was the kind of person who signs reports in a fit of inadvertency, and who hastens afterwards to apologise for it.'[17] There were demands for her resignation, including from the ILP in Wallsend, and she was condemned by women's groups and trade unions alike. She was now in a full-on fight for her political survival, having to conduct 'a very exhausting campaign throughout the country' as part of 'much the most severe battle I ever fought.'[18]

In April the Wallsend Labour Party held a conference to decide their position but decided to postpone taking a view until after a National Joint Council (of the Labour Party and the TUC) Conference in London on 28 April. This was the one she most needed to win. She could rise above criticism and motions of censure but she could not afford to lose the confidence of the whole movement gathered in one room. She had agreed to accept whatever verdict the conference came to, and although it is hard to see what else she could have done, she cannot have been sure of the outcome.

In the event, it turned out to be a triumph. She had already begun to feel that the tide was starting to trickle in her favour and so it proved. She was heard, if not with enthusiasm, at least with respect, a reception which was much better than she had had at some other meetings. When the vote was taken it came out in favour of supporting her action. Armed with victory at a meeting with whose decision she had agreed to abide, she was now able to see off the attack in Wallsend. She continued as a member of the General Council, representing the TUC at the ILO meeting in Geneva in June. She remained in demand as a speaker on platforms across the country.

In September she had to defend herself against a motion of censure at the TUC meeting in Edinburgh which described the Report as 'despicable' and called upon the TUC to 'guard against such people in future representing the workers on important issues'.[19] This censure was directed against Hodges and

Holmes as well as Bondfield, but the focus was on her rather than them and she was the only one of them who spoke in the debate. She rose 'wearing a light pink jumper and a very determined expression and sailed into her critics with great vigour'.[20] She did not win the day and probably did not expect to, but the vote was closer than might have been anticipated. After this, however, many people felt that everything that could be said had been and that it was time to move on to the next phase of the fight.

This took the form of the debate on the Unemployment Insurance Bill, which was introduced into Parliament in November. The Government had cherry-picked items from the Report and to Bondfield's disappointment some of the things she had fought hard to get included, and for which she had almost sacrificed her career, were not in the draft. She was particularly annoyed at the exclusion of training provision for young people, especially those leaving school without work to go to. 'You cannot' she said in the debate:

> get these young people into industry unless you set up a comprehensive, nation-wide system of training. You may call it advanced education; you may call it what you like. . . . You can teach them algebra, geography, dancing or singing. What you have to do is to bring them into a position where they will have occupation for the mind and proper physical exercise and care for the body. . . . It is not the point of who is keeping the children, it is the point that these children are not being prepared for life in a civilised community in a manner in which we have a right to expect they should be prepared.[21]

She pledged to fight the Government as far as possible, and more than a few people were either amused or infuriated by the position in which she now found herself. Right-wing papers such as the *Daily Express* were particularly mocking. Suggesting that her speech in the House was heard in silence, their correspondent remarked that: 'Hatred is long among Socialists. It radiated in waves around the gesticulating figure of Miss Bondfield in the House of Commons last night.'[22] Other papers were more sympathetic, but they all caught a mood. Bondfield's support was now more partisan, more on the Right of the party, and easier to disappoint. Ultimately, there may have been something in her view that the attacks on her were personal as well as political. Although the other two signatories were also criticized it is her name alone that is associated with the obloquy of the Blanesburgh Report. 'Unforgiven' said the *Daily Express* headline, and in some, though by no means all, quarters of the movement this would indeed always be the case.

In 1928 Parliament passed the Act enfranchising all women over the age of 21. At last the adult suffrage campaign had achieved its objective, though by then there was such wide acceptance of the idea that it was much less controversial. Still there remained people who thought that 'uneducated' working-class women should not be able to vote. Speaking in the debate, Bondfield refuted this. 'I think' she said:

> in connection with the political work of our country we can take the experience of the workman's wife and daughter, educated in the university of experience, who have had to face the hardships, ugliness and suffering which surrounds so much of our social conditions to-day. They have the experience that very few people who have passed through universities have. We want, to bring into our political life and into the general pool of experience that kind of education.[23]

Thus when the long-awaited general election finally arrived in May 1929, it was the first under universal suffrage. Despite its huge majority the Conservative government was unpopular. Unemployment was still rising, the general strike was still raw in the minds of many working people, and ministers seemed to have run out of ideas as to what to do next. Despite this, Labour was not going to have a clear run. The Liberals still had enough support to give them several dozen seats, and turning over a Conservative majority of more than 200 was a very tall order for a Labour Party that had more than enough troubles of its own. In Wallsend Bondfield was readopted by a more united local party but found herself with a Communist opponent as well as a Conservative. As usual, she was tireless during the campaign, though she was irritated by the Communists who followed her everywhere and shouted at her about the Blanesburgh Committee. Eventually, she said, 'cries of "What about the Blanesburgh Report?" . . . were treated as jokes. . . . The Communists had worked it to death.'[24]

On polling day (30 May) the Communist candidate lost his deposit and Bondfield increased her majority. Labour's national result was good, but not quite good enough. They gained 136 seats and, with a total of 288 MPs, were now the largest party in the House of Commons. The green benches suddenly had far more working-class men on them, and about a third of the PLP were trade unionists of varying degrees of experience and independence. Most were inclined to support the leadership, and Jennie Lee,[25] who certainly was not, described them as 'decent, well-intentioned, unpretentious . . . In the long term it was they who did the most deadly damage.' They were infuriatingly difficult to motivate, on every occasion reacting like 'a load of damp cement'.[26] Labour had consolidated its base in the north of England, gaining 70 seats there, many of which they did not lose again until the collapse of the 'red wall' in 2019. Nine Labour women were elected, including Susan Lawrence, Ellen Wilkinson, Mary Agnes Hamilton, Dr Ethel Bentham (at 68 the oldest woman elected so far) and Lee, who at 25 was the youngest. The Liberal increase to 58 seats meant that, despite the lack of an overall majority, Labour should be able to form a minority administration without a coalition. Government beckoned once again.

This time there was to be no drawn-out series of meetings and the decision was made very quickly. Two days after the election MacDonald met Henderson, Snowden, Jimmy Thomas and Clynes and they agreed to take office. Baldwin resigned on 4 June and the next day MacDonald went to Windsor to see the King, a trip from which he returned as Prime Minister. In his house at Hampstead he now began to put together his Cabinet. Snowden became Chancellor again, Henderson (after a tug of war with MacDonald) Foreign Secretary, and Clynes Home Secretary. Arthur Greenwood, who had been an effective shadow Minister for Health, took that job, and Susan Lawrence became his Parliamentary Secretary. Tom Shaw, Bondfield's Minister in 1924, was Secretary of State for War, and George Lansbury the First Commissioner of Works. On the whole it was a Cabinet made up of a group of people who knew each other very well. This could have advantages, but in the pressure cooker of government could also produce an element of group-think, while the inability in some quarters to leave old enmities behind also had unfortunate results.

Immediately after the election Margaret Bondfield had gone to visit friends in Brighton, and it was not until 5 June that she returned to London. In 1924 there had been much speculation about the possibility of a female cabinet minister but now there was relatively little. There was a widespread assumption that there would be one regardless of who won the election, and if there was a Labour administration she was the obvious candidate. When the Labour leaders met to discuss Cabinet posts there was a brief discussion about whether or not to appoint a woman, but MacDonald and Henderson, though they disagreed about much else, were insistent that they should and their view prevailed.[27] Philip Snowden recalled that:

The question arose of giving Miss Bondfield a Cabinet post. Henderson was strongly in favour of doing this, as he thought it would be a popular thing to do . . . Both *(J. H.)* Thomas and I took the line that a person should not be appointed to the Cabinet because of sex but on merits and qualifications. Miss Bondfield had already held *(a minor post)* . . . in the previous Labour government and she had fulfilled her duties with outstanding ability. On her own merits she was entitled to Cabinet rank. MacDonald was in favour . . .[28]

Thus when Bondfield arrived back in London she was met by a message asking her to meet MacDonald in Hampstead, and by the end of that afternoon she had accepted the post of Minister of Labour, thus becoming Britain's first female Cabinet Minister and taking on a job which, from start to finish, was to prove both an honour and an almost intolerable burden.

Chapter 15

Some Woman was Bound to be First

According to Bondfield, her reaction to the offer of a Cabinet post was to ask MacDonald 'if he was quite sure that he had made the best choice in myself'. MacDonald replied 'very decidedly that he was quite sure'. Later, when asked if she had felt nervous, she answered that she was not, because 'it presented itself as only another and rather wider aspect of the work I had been doing for thirty years, and largely with the same team'.[1]

Privately, however, Bondfield was by no means so sanguine; now that the moment had really arrived she was filled with self-doubt. When she went to clear her union desk she was met by jubilation and piles of congratulatory letters, but 'they did not fit my mood, which was one of depression. All yesterday and today I have been oppressed by the complexity and difficulty of this post. . . . That I *should* be able to do it seems clear, or the opportunity would not have come my way . . . '[2] In fact she was so depressed that she uncharacteristically went home and did some housework, a task she normally detested. The following day she met the union executive and was (again) granted leave of absence. 'Once more I am torn up by the roots from official Trade Union work which has been such a large part of my life.'

If this seems a curious mood in which to greet being made a Cabinet Minister, it was also understandable. The Ministry of Labour was generally agreed to be one of the hardest and least rewarding jobs in government, if only because the issues it had to deal with were more complex and intractable than most. Snowden described it as 'arduous and unpopular'[3] and Bondfield herself knew that it was not going to be easy. Looking back from the 1940s she said that it was 'a big and unsatisfactory job with more kicks than thanks . . . Not glory, but hard work and deep anxiety, was my portion.'[4] Very few people had a thorough grasp of the multiplicity of detail involved, and ominously many trade unionists made it clear that they would not accept cuts at any price. Against this, the Conservative Party, many employers and, as would become evident, most of the financiers and bankers from whom the government had to borrow, were equally adamantly in favour of deep cuts as soon as possible. Caught between these two implacable and equally impossible demands, Bondfield was justifiably apprehensive. Her reputation had already been damaged by 'that detestable affair' of the Blanesburgh Report, and people who might otherwise be allies could be at best suspicious and at worst hostile. She foresaw from the beginning that all might not end well.

Why, then, did she accept? Part of it might certainly have been personal in that it achieved an ambition of which she had, for one reason or another, been baulked in 1924. Once more she had had to wait patiently for the position that everyone told her she ought to occupy, and when it finally arrived it would have been hard to say no. In her memoir she said that when she accepted the post she:

> did so knowing well that it touched more than merely my own self – it was part of the great revolution of the position of women which had taken place in my lifetime and which I had done something to help forward. Some woman was bound to be the first. That I should be was the accident of dates and events.[5]

This is of course true, and it could, in theory at least, easily have been Susan Lawrence. That it was not was probably down to the fact that the decision was made by a group of men – MacDonald, Snowden, Henderson and Clynes – of working-class origin who had all known Bondfield for decades and who, as Snowden said, felt that she had earned it. She understood the brief, she was tried and tested in the fires of controversy, and she boosted the number of Ministers with a trade union background to six. Listing trade unionist members of the Cabinet, Matthew Worley in his 2008 book *Labour Inside the Gate* names Jimmy Thomas, Henderson, Shaw, Adamson and Clynes, and adds Bondfield separately, and only, as a woman. In fact Bondfield was, in 1929, still a member of the TUC General Council; recording her simply in terms of her sex in some ways strips her life's work away from her and prevents posterity from seeing her as her contemporaries did.[6]

It is often suggested that she was appointed because she was seen as the woman 'most comfortably ensconced within the establishment. Modest, unassertive, and thoroughly steeped in the movement she reassured male trade unionists.'[7] The Blanesburgh affair, however, had already turned some trade unionists against her, and certainly none of the men who appointed her would have described her as unassertive. There are also suggestions that, given the difficulty of the brief, she was deliberately set up to fail. There may or may not have been some truth in this – many friendships have foundered on the rocks of political expediency over the centuries – but no one who knew her could possibly have believed that she was easy to manipulate. Generally speaking people were more likely to complain that she was stubborn to the point of inflexibility.

Conservative politician Sir Cuthbert Headlam, for instance, described her as 'a dreadful little woman . . . a cross between a housekeeper and a governess – and a talker. She is absolutely convinced that she knows everything and so everybody considers that she is extremely able and wise. I wish that I possessed her wonderful self-assurance . . . '[8] Certainly the Blanesburgh affair, where she had taken an unpopular decision and then defended it against all comers, both friend and foe, did not suggest a woman who would back down under pressure. It is true that she tended to look for compromise, but this came more from long experience of negotiation, where compromise is often the aim and generally the outcome, rather than a personal predisposition. Bondfield probably was the best person for the job at the time; unfortunately, the job was impossible.

Once appointed, new members of the Cabinet had to be sworn in as Privy Counsellors, another role which Bondfield was the first woman to assume. The ceremony was set for 8 June, and before it she had a polite exchange of views with Sir Maurice Hankey, the Clerk of the Privy Council, as to what she should wear. He thought a hat would be appropriate, but 'to this I could not agree'. She did not have time to buy much in the way of new clothes, so wore the coat she had worn all through the campaign, supplemented by a new white silk shirt and new gloves. She was sworn in hatless, kissing hands with a monarch who expressed himself 'pleased to be the one to whom has come the opportunity to receive the first woman Privy Councillor *(sic)*'.[9] It was, she said, a happy day, with a special train laid on from Paddington to Windsor and state carriages to take them up to the Castle. People waved and cheered and there was almost a holiday atmosphere, very different from either the campaign or the months which were to come.

Outside Westminster her elevation was received with great excitement. Newspapers ran biographical pieces recounting her rise from shopgirl to Cabinet Minister, including one with the headline '"Saint Maggie" of the Ministry' which talked about her 'romantic life story' and described her as a 'stout little woman'.[10] Overall, in both the press and the deluge of letters she received, there was a general feeling that the right thing had finally been done. 'I love to think' wrote Margaret Llewelyn Davies, 'your devoted, single-minded work has been crowned with this honour, which you will carry in a way of which women, especially working women, will feel proud'.[11] Replying to Millicent Fawcett's letter Bondfield assured her that though her official title was indeed 'Right Honourable, *I* am the same as usual. . . . May I once more say to you,' she added, 'how grateful I, together with thousands of other women, feel for your life and your work in the cause of civilisation.'[12]

However, the welcome was not quite unanimous and one or two commentators sounded a note of hesitation; 'Miss Bondfield,' said one, 'has great personal charm, is popular with the House, and has considerable ability, but it is questionable whether she has the driving force needed for a heavy and important

Department.'[13] If they had known that she herself privately felt much the same they might have been even more sceptical, but she kept her doubts to herself and instead exuded confidence and an eagerness to get down to work.

For her Parliamentary Secretary she chose Jack Lawson, a miner from Durham who, in 1929, had been an MP for a decade. In the 1924 government he had been one of MacDonald's two Parliamentary Private Secretaries, the other being Clement Attlee. He was tough, loyal, intelligent and kind, and was a good choice for a difficult job.

As always, there were some practicalities to be dealt with. The furniture had not been designed for small women, so that, according to Harold Emmerson, a civil servant in the Ministry at the time, Bondfield's 'feet hardly touched the floor when she sat on a normal chair. I well remember seeing *(her Private Secretary)* Lowe-Watson bringing over a footstool from her desk to her conference table . . . and diving under the table to place it in position!'[14] Needless to say, there were still no women's lavatory facilities, and this had to be rectified. Meanwhile, the Department was trying to work out the answer to another very tricky question; by what pronouns should the incoming Minister be known? Cabinet Ministers had always been male and the pronouns used in legal documents reflected that. Since 1850 male pronouns had been deemed to encompass the female in Acts of Parliament, but not vice versa, and there was therefore a legal question over how Bondfield should be identified. The Ministry's Solicitor was consulted, and he produced 'a Memo on the Gender of the Minister'. It would be, he said, 'excessively inconvenient (and, indeed, positively painful)' to use female pronouns for the Minister in documents attached to legislation but male in the legislation itself. Change would require amending or replacing the 1850 Act, and there was clearly no appetite for this. Asked for her opinion, Bondfield, probably with a mental eyeroll, agreed that she could be masculine in all legal documents.[15]

Whatever the complications of being the first female Cabinet Minister, the task which now confronted Bondfield was enormous. The Unemployment Insurance Fund was nearly £40 million in debt, and her primary task was to find a way of dealing with this. She thought that the whole system needed to be overhauled, but that since this was not immediately possible they should do everything possible to stem the rising number of claims. Snowden wanted to balance the books and agreed that they should borrow to keep the Fund solvent. Bondfield believed that this would only over-burden it with interest payments, make the problems worse, and lead inevitably to even deeper cuts than those they might well have to make. This difference of opinion would only intensify as the crisis developed.

When she took office unemployment stood at over a million, and the bureaucracy required to support that was considerable. She set up a Committee – known as the Morris Committee after its Chair – to look at the way in which claims were dealt with, including the vexed question of what the requirement that a claimant be 'genuinely seeking work' actually meant or should mean. The Committee was asked to report as quickly as possible, and when it did so one of its proposals was that, rather than being asked to prove that they were 'genuinely seeking work' claimants should only be disqualified from benefit if a reasonable offer of work had been refused. The Committee did not define the word 'reasonable' but left it up to local discretion to decide. Given that the unions and the ILP wanted the 'genuinely seeking work' test abolished altogether, while the Conservatives and business wanted it tightened so as to exclude what they believed were large numbers of fraudulent claims and anomalies, this new formulation was unlikely to please anybody, as indeed it did not.

Before Parliament broke for the summer Bondfield secured an increase in funding from the Treasury which would be enough to keep the Unemployment Fund solvent at least while more root-and-branch measures were considered. She started an extensive consultation process on what might be done, touring the country herself and listening to a variety of views. What she had in mind was a wide-ranging and fundamental re-organization of the system, with both contributions and decisions being made on actuarial principles and anomalies ironed out. This was very ambitious, and had she been able to achieve it she would probably have been hailed as a great Minister. Both she and everyone else knew, however, that reducing claims in the first place was going to be a key part of reducing costs without making deep cuts, and over this element of the problem she had little or no control. MacDonald either failed to see or refused to recognize the link between prevention and palliative measures, and as a consequence, Bondfield never had job creation schemes in her remit. In practice she was thus deprived of one of the most important tools she should have had. Worse, responsibility for such schemes had been given to a committee of four ministers, an ill-assorted group led by Jimmy Thomas and comprising George Lansbury, Tom Johnston (the Under-Secretary of State for Scotland) and the Chancellor of the Duchy of Lancaster, Oswald Mosley. This group, of which Johnston said that 'a more ill-assorted team could hardly be imagined',[16] could scarcely agree with one another, let alone anyone else, and the innate caution of both civil servants and senior members of the government meant that even ideas which might have worked were blocked. Inevitably, Bondfield herself was criticized for not producing schemes to relieve unemployment. She very much resented this, and her frustration at her exclusion can easily be imagined. 'The arrangement,' she said:

> never worked, and it is rather astonishing that anyone should have ever expected it to do so. The four men were not suited by temperament to make an effective committee. J. H. Thomas himself, a leading trade union official, opinionated and with driving force, was not the type of man needed for such a tremendous task, burdened with such colleagues.[17]

Having set up the Morris Committee, secured some funding, and started her review, she felt justified in taking a holiday and in late August went to Cornwall where, a few days after arriving, she fell heavily on some rocks and broke her ankle. She was taken to hospital in Bodmin and daily bulletins were issued on her condition. She was soon able to travel back to London but could not return to work for several weeks. Perhaps fortuitously, she was forced to rest. In early September she wrote to MacDonald that: 'for the first time in years I can really watch the birds, and the myriad life in a garden. That is my great compensation in this disaster.'[18] In the autumn, travelling to Geneva with his daughter Ishbel and friends including Mary Agnes Hamilton, he wrote to Bondfield that 'We are . . . hoping your ankle is so well that you can use it to kick your enemies amongst whom we decline to be included.'[19]

Her enemies elsewhere were indeed now starting to multiply. She could not attend the Labour conference in Brighton at the end of September, but in her absence there were 'fiery and bitter' attacks on her from ILP MPs and others, leading to speculation in the press about her position. 'Will Miss Bondfield Resign?' inquired the *Yorkshire Post*, noting that she was being 'more severely criticised than any other member of the Cabinet . . . The public will no doubt feel sympathy with Miss Bondfield because she has refused to be hustled . . . but . . . in certain quarters it is being freely said that she will have no alternative but to resign.'[20] Experience told her that this kind of thing was not serious, but nevertheless it was disappointing when it came just three months into her term of office.

On 29 October the Wall Street crash propelled everything into crisis mode. A situation which had previously been challenging now became thoroughly alarming, and neither Ministers nor their civil servants were well equipped to deal with it. Philip Snowden, for long regarded as having real economic skill, was faced with a situation neither he nor anyone else had encountered before and in which skill and reputation alone were not going to be enough. Unemployment began to rise rapidly and the Fund was soon depleted. In November Bondfield steered an Unemployment Bill arising out of the proposals of the Morris Committee through Parliament, arguing her case in a speech which the *Daily Herald* optimistically described as revealing 'a mind equal to every demand of exposition, of defence, of rational controversy, a mind not moulded by, but moulding . . . a great Department of the State, a mind which has earned for her the title of "Masterly Maggie."'[21] In reality she found herself attacked from all sides. The ILP wanted an immediate socialist onslaught on unemployment and had moved an amendment to the King's Speech to that effect in July. The opposition wanted unemployment benefits to be much reduced or even, if necessary, eliminated. The trade unions, who had expected to be involved in the development of Bills and new systems, were annoyed to find that, despite repeated requests, they were not. With what a later historian described as 'monumental tactlessness'[22] Bondfield refused to include them, thus, almost at a stroke, making enemies of long-standing friends and opening up a rift between the Labour Party and the TUC which proved very hard to heal. For someone who was normally adept at maintaining relationships under political pressure, this intentional undermining of trust seems inexplicable. She may have wanted to demonstrate that a Labour government was not simply the tool of the trade unions, or she may have felt that the looming crisis was so deep that she could not take risks. Whatever her reasons, the effect was to make her appear heartless towards the unemployed and unreliable and even hostile to her erstwhile colleagues. Perhaps the most contentious part of the Bill was that relating to what should constitute 'genuinely seeking work', and here Bondfield was ultimately forced to accept the TUC position. In the end the Bill scraped through, but the whole episode left both the government and Bondfield looking weak and inept.

By the New Year unemployment was over 1.6 million and the Unemployment Fund was bankrupt. Despite the fact that she was opposed to borrowing, Bondfield soon found herself having to resort to it since the only alternative was deep cuts, which she was not prepared to make. MacDonald, who confessed to his diary on 24 December 1929 that 'Unemployment is baffling us'[23] was no more in favour of borrowing than Bondfield was, describing it to Walton Newbold, a former Communist MP who had joined Labour, as 'humbug' and 'one of the most superficial and ill considered proposals that has ever been foisted upon the Party'.[24]

When Bondfield went to the House in March to request authority to borrow she faced a fiery debate. There were, she explained, 'four courses which I have considered and examined with the greatest care – reducing benefits, increasing contributions, further grants from the Exchequer, and increased borrowings'.[25] Step by step she took them through the process by which she was compelled to conclude that borrowing was the only viable course. She conceded that she had previously told the House that borrowing:

> would be a dishonest course, because it would be contracting a debt that you saw no possible way of paying off. . . . That was my opinion then; it is my opinion now. I detest this principle of borrowing; but I find myself in the grip of circumstances to which I have to bow my head.

Immediately Winston Churchill rose to ask: 'Do I understand that the Minister admits that she still holds the opinion that the course she is recommending to the Committee is a dishonest one?'[26] Given that she had effectively said precisely that, talking her way out of this was tricky, but she had no option but to try. Churchill's speech later in the debate was something of a *tour de force*, and Bondfield was secretly relieved when Snowden turned up towards the end to make her four points again. 'He simply ignored the main substance of Churchill's speech' she recalled later. 'Churchill hates to be ignored.'[27] The borrowing was approved, but her credibility as an honest, straight-talking Minister had been diminished yet further and it was painfully obvious that she was not in control of decisions being made about her own department. This was humiliating, and she felt it.

Meanwhile, trouble was brewing elsewhere. Oswald Mosley, impatient at the slow rate of progress, had produced a plan to deal with unemployment which he put to the four-man Unemployment Committee. The economist Maynard Keynes advocated extensive public works in order to bring down unemployment, and Mosley had produced a scheme largely based on Keynesian principles. On the face of it, it was not particularly innovative, drawing together a number of ideas, including the building of roads and public facilities and the nationalization of certain industries, the second of which regularly appeared in Labour manifestos. The Unemployment Committee split in its views, and early in February the proposals went to Cabinet, where Lansbury argued for them and Thomas against. Cabinet failed to come to a united view, so the problem was passed to a sub-committee consisting of Snowden, Bondfield, Tom Shaw and the Minister of Health, Arthur Greenwood. Snowden was adamantly opposed and without the support of the Chancellor Mosley's proposals were doomed. Again unable to agree, the Cabinet set up yet another committee, this time chaired by MacDonald himself. In May Mosley lost patience and resigned in protest; a year later he had left the Labour Party on his way to becoming the leader of British Fascism.

By now by-election results were predictably poor and both MPs and the party were worried. Unemployment continued to rise inexorably, and what looked like muddled thinking at the top of government was not very reassuring. The trade unions were becoming increasingly infuriated by their exclusion from discussions and the continued failure of Ministers to meet them. As the economic situation grew worse and the measures to deal with it increasingly draconian, so confidence in the government began to drain away. This is not to say that the unions ceased to support Labour – far from it – but the relationship was beginning to change.

Bondfield now found herself in an unenviable and, at least in part, self-inflicted position. MacDonald and Snowden's relations with the unions had always been uneasy, and Bondfield thought that MacDonald 'saw the industrial side as so much raw material to be educated into the higher atmosphere of doctrinal Socialism . . . His heart was not in it.'[28] But Bondfield's heart had never left it, and, more astutely handled, some individual leaders might have been more supportive, as they had ultimately been during the Blanesburgh affair. With the exception of Jimmy Thomas as chairman of the Unemployment Committee, none of the other trade unionists in the Cabinet were in roles which required contact with the unions, and Bondfield began to seem isolated. Within the Ministry there was a feeling that Bondfield was more or less abandoned by her colleagues, who 'seemed content to sit back and leave her to take the brunt of the attack'.[29]

In July Bondfield was back before the House asking for still more money to keep the system going. She set up a Royal Commission to examine the whole issue of unemployment but this once again annoyed both the unions, who refused to join it, and MPs and Labour members, who were suspicious of it. Mistrust was reinforced when the Ministry of Labour's evidence to the Commission seemed to be more or less an attack on the unions' view of the 'genuinely seeking work' issue. Bondfield was also faced with complaints that single women were being forced into domestic service when they wanted to go back to their old jobs in industry, jobs which, given the state of the economy, no longer existed. As usual, her view of domestic work was a little more elevated than most women's and she deprecated 'this constant suggestion that there is something derogatory to the womanhood of the nation in being engaged in domestic work. All our mothers were engaged in domestic work.'[30] This may well have been true, but it was also true that Bondfield herself engaged in it as little as possible.

By the end of the year unemployment was rising inexorably towards the two million mark and the Unemployment Fund had a deficit of £70 million. In January 1931, following heavy criticism, Bondfield drafted a letter to MacDonald offering to resign. Bitterly, she outlined the charges against her:

> (1) that I have no policy – in fact being incapable of formulating a policy – I am in the hands of my officials, and this influence is inimical to the policy of the Party. (2) there are better women – to say nothing of the men – far abler to fill the position. My concern is not with (1) because it is not true; as to (2) I think it is true. . . . some of *(the women members)* have far more brilliant and trained qualities than I possess.[31]

Either this or some version of this was sent, though not immediately, since his hand-written reply is dated 10 February. 'I grieve very much at the causes,' he said. 'You have had a hard and thankless task, and your critics have been heartless, as jealous people must be. . . . And don't think of doing anything at present. You have my sympathy and support. Always.'[32] Unemployment was now escalating at a terrifying speed. By the end of February it had reached 2.5 million, and over the next weeks it was rising by about 100,000 a month. Despite raising the Fund's borrowing ceiling to £150 million, it was apparent that this alone was not going to be enough. The opposition moved two motions of censure on the government – one in February and one in April – neither of which succeeded. In June the Royal Commission produced its interim report, which recommended severe cuts, means testing and the withdrawal of benefit from claimants deemed to be not 'genuinely seeking work'. Initially Bondfield supported the report, but in the face of the ferocity of opposition from the TUC and her own MPs, not to mention Prime Ministerial wavering, she changed course and in the end the government decided not to accept the Commission's conclusions. This left the government looking even more at sea, and Bondfield herself looked both vacillating and unprincipled. Attacked on all sides, she nevertheless ploughed on. In July she introduced the Unemployment Insurance (Anomalies) Bill, the provisions of which were destined to do her reputation more damage than almost anything else.

This Bill was Bondfield's attempt to square the impossible circle. On the one hand, she was under enormous pressure to reduce the cost of unemployment benefits, a cost which was rising exponentially as the unemployment rate rose. On the other, many Labour MPs and the trade unions were adamantly opposed to many of the Bill's provisions and opposed any cuts, sometimes to the point of failing to acknowledge that the consequences, in the absence of further borrowing, would be the collapse of the Fund. The Anomalies Bill was an attempt to close some of the loopholes and reduce the payments without actually causing too much damage, but it did so by making some highly controversial cuts, many of which fell most heavily on women. One of the most contentious clauses ruled that married women could not be 'genuinely seeking work' and could therefore be removed *en masse* from the list of eligible claimants. This caused uproar, with fierce criticism coming from the unions, the Left, and feminist and women's organizations. Then there was the question of what should be considered seasonal work, with industries such as millinery and fish processing, which overwhelmingly employed women, being excluded. In both cases the women concerned tended to be young and single, and it was (rightly or wrongly) assumed by some people that the lack of income would drive them onto the streets. Other anomalies were so complicated to disentangle that it was hard to see how resolving them would save anything at all. Bondfield's opponents accused her of betraying working-class women on a vast scale. She believed that she was holding back the tide of what would come if she was no longer there. That there was some justice on both sides did not make the situation any easier for anyone.

Some members of the Cabinet, aware of the fact that the Bill was going to be highly controversial, wanted to postpone it, but Bondfield was adamant that since it would have to be done at some point it was best to go ahead. She wrote to MacDonald pointing out that if the Bill was deferred 'my own position will be impossible and we shall be open to the accusation that we obtained the consent of the House to further borrowing under false pretences'.[33] She persisted and the Bill began its Parliamentary course within a few days.

The Committee stage was held on the floor of the House and began at 3 pm on 15 July. It did not finish until 10 am the following morning, by which time everyone involved was exhausted. Labour MPs cheered Bondfield from the Chamber at the end of it, but there was no doubt that, since the many of attacks on both her and the Bill had come from women backbenchers, it had been a miserable night. Viewing the debate as a private grief, the Conservative and Liberal opposition were often entirely absent from the Chamber. For hours Bondfield stood 'grim and determined'[34] at the dispatch box while wave after wave of wrath broke around her. 'Time after time, Miss Jennie Lee jumped up to attack the Bill. At 4 a.m., when the debate started on the clause relating to married women, she took off her jacket and stood, scornfully waving her arms, in a short-sleeved jumper.' Bondfield 'gave as good as she received . . . It was civil war of the fiercest kind.' At one point there was an 'impromptu Cabinet meeting' with Susan Lawrence, then Chairman of the Party, being brought in to try to calm things down. There were ten pages of amendments resulting in many votes during the night. The clauses relating to married women and seasonal work were particularly hard-fought. The ILP's David Kirkwood accused Bondfield of forcing young women into prostitution. 'I impeach the Minister of Labour with that responsibility. . . . I have warned you that you will be dealt with when the time comes.'[35] Monotonously, clause after clause, Bondfield moved that 'the question now be put' and time after time Members trooped into the division lobbies. The Independent MP Eleanor Rathbone and the Labour Lady Cynthia Mosley made a quiet piece of history by being the first two women to act together as tellers. Eventually the Bill got through, and Bondfield was finally released from her ordeal.

The atmosphere in Cabinet was now increasingly panicky and bad-tempered as the crisis picked up speed. The Anomalies Bill passed its final stages in late July and at the end of the month the May Committee published its devastating report. This body had been set up by MacDonald and Snowden under the chairmanship of the finance and insurance expert George May and its report predicted a 1932/3 deficit of £120 million and recommended cuts of at least £66 million to unemployment insurance. Immediately, investors began to withdraw their money from London and to demand it in gold. The Bank of England was losing reserves, and although 'the whole thing was irrational and perverse, the stampede had been started and nothing seemed able to stop it'.[36] August was spent in desperate negotiations to save the situation, but to no avail. On 23 August the Cabinet met to discuss proposals to save £68 million of expenditure, including cuts to the salaries of teachers and police, a 10 per cent cut in unemployment benefit and a limit of 26 weeks on the amount of benefit that could be paid. In Bondfield's opinion the proposals were bad, but the alternatives were even worse. Reluctantly, she voted for cuts, but since the Cabinet was split the end was now very near. The following day MacDonald went to the Palace and accepted the King's invitation to form a National – cross-party – Government. He undertook, however, that there would be no coalition and no government 'coupons' at elections. Henderson distrusted this and made it clear immediately that he would go into opposition. That afternoon the whole Cabinet resigned and MacDonald began to form his new cross-party administration.

On 24 August Bondfield wrote a letter to Ramsay MacDonald which is often interpreted as a plea for a seat in the Cabinet he was putting together. This may have been the case, but on balance it seems unlikely. She was, first and foremost, a Labour loyalist and a trade unionist, and although she was clearly deeply upset by the breach with MacDonald, there is no other evidence of a request to follow him. The letter itself, written on Ministry of Labour paper, is very short, the handwriting more like that in the unhappier pages of her diary than her normal scrawl. Beginning 'My dear Prime Minister' she said that she was writing:

> to assure you of my very deep sympathy with, and admiration for, the decision you have taken. May God give you the strength you need and the success you deserve in bringing the nation through this crisis.

She signed herself 'Your old friend.'[37] The response she received was quite formal, and after attacking the trade unions in no uncertain terms MacDonald said that:

> I am trying to involve very few of my friends in the new Government because so far as one can see it means their political death, and if we are to have a small Cabinet the available offices are very few. . . . I am much obliged to you for all you have done and for the letter you have been so good as to write to me. Yours always sincerely.[38]

On the same day, Bondfield wrote a memorandum for herself of what had happened. 'Mr MacDonald,' she said, 'knowing the full consequences of his action, has decided to sacrifice himself to save the country from financial chaos; Mr Henderson has decided to sacrifice Mr MacDonald in order to save the Labour Party.' On 11 November she returned to this document and scrawled in the margin: 'How wrong I was has been proved within a few weeks when MacDonald threw over the arrangement *(about election coupons)* . . . Henderson was right.'[39]

A friendship that had started nearly forty years earlier in the heady days of the Ideal Club and the ILP had finally come to an end amidst the political and economic wreckage of the second Labour government. There is no evidence that Bondfield and MacDonald ever met again.

In mid-September 1931 Bondfield collapsed and was admitted to the East Anglian Sanatorium at Nayland in Suffolk where, over thirty years earlier, her sister Katie had been treated. The exact nature of her illness is unclear, but almost certainly the stress of the previous few months was a major contributory factor. A commissionaire at the Ministry of Labour had once told her that 'all Labour ministers were doomed to a breakdown'. She noted that: 'Four of my predecessors had suffered in health, and I was no exception to the rule. . . . I was ordered to bed and told that I had fibrositis, and underwent a most painful cure.'[40]

Inevitably, the press indulged in speculation. One paper inaccurately reported that Margaret Bondfield was 'suffering from a nervous breakdown in a Tunbridge Wells nursing home',[41] and another identified her illness as 'fatigue poisoning', a condition caused by 'the muscles becoming fatigued by carbonic acid and lactic acid accumulating in them, and by over-tiring of the nervous system'.[42] Whatever it was, it followed a familiar pattern of Bondfield driving herself in increasingly stressful circumstances until overwhelmed by exhaustion, anxiety and depression. Many people wrote to express sympathy, including Mary Agnes Hamilton, to whom Bondfield replied that she had previously never heard of fibrositis but now thought it very unpleasant, not only because it was painful but because she had been told to lose a stone in weight.[43]

On 7 October, when MacDonald called a general election, Bondfield was still at Nayland, and on 10 October her formal adoption by Wallsend Labour Party was done in her absence. The Conservative candidate was the thirty-six-year-old Irene Ward, probably making Wallsend the first constituency in which all the candidates were female.[44] Irene Ward had started campaigning early and was much helped by the fact that Bondfield did not arrive until two weeks before polling day. The NUGMW had sent her deputy, Dorothy Elliott, to act as her aide so that the work could be shared. There followed a hard-fought campaign, which both women insisted should be conducted with civility on both sides. 'For cheery and polite campaigning,' wrote the correspondent for the *Daily Express*, 'refer me to Wallsend . . . by the thoroughness yet friendliness of their fighting Wallsend's women candidates . . . are setting a model for many northern constituencies where in the heat of battle ordinary courtesy seems to flee.'[45]

No amount of good-mannered campaigning, however, could save the seat. Irene Ward had been in the field too early, Bondfield was lacking her usual energy and infectious vitality, and the times and her own recent political record were against her. Across the country Labour MPs faced hostile crowds and a very different atmosphere from 1929. Voters sided heavily with MacDonald and all those who had followed him were re-elected. The National Government, composed of a large number of Conservatives, two different kinds of Liberals and a handful of National Labour MPs, won a parliamentary majority of 554. Labour lost 235 seats, falling back to just 52. All of the Labour women lost, as well as all but one of what had been the Cabinet. Once again, Henderson was defeated. The Labour Party was left leaderless, directionless and profoundly shocked. Following on MacDonald's 'betrayal' the sheer scale of this defeat and its consequences for working-class people merely deepened the well of bitterness and distrust that had now opened up.

In Wallsend Irene Ward reversed Bondfield's majority of more than 7,000. The numerical Labour vote, as in many other constituencies, held up reasonably well, but this time there was no Liberal candidate to syphon off Tory votes. Wearily, Bondfield endured the formalities, standing in the chilly night on the Town Hall balcony while the result was declared, shaking hands, and thanking her agent and campaign team. Once more she was exhausted, and three days later was back at Nayland. Claude Denscombe wrote to her that: 'Your personal part in this campaign was really the wonder of us all! In all you did 37 meetings and continued in excellent form until the end. . . . I am convinced that as a Candidate you were as popular as ever.'[46] Clynes, already back at his NUGMW desk, wrote sympathetically: 'I hope you do not grieve about defeat, so many of us have gone down together. You might benefit from a rest and a change and if you wish to continue the work you will come back.'[47]

She did wish to continue, and indeed it is hard to see what else she could have done. The trade union movement had always been her home, and although relations with some parts of it were now strained almost beyond repair she could not have left it. She would go on, as she had always done, facing forwards and marching towards the next adventure, whatever it might bring.

Chapter 16

I Had Not Stopped Growing

In November Bondfield emerged from the nursing home to a changed political landscape. The only former Cabinet Minister – other than MacDonald and Thomas – who had survived the electoral axe was George Lansbury, who now led Labour in Parliament. The expectation was that Henderson would get back in at the first available by-election and then take over, but Henderson had also been ill over the election period and continued to be so for some time after it. MacDonald, Jimmy Thomas and Snowden had all been expelled from the Labour Party, and Snowden had been elevated to the House of Lords. Though hoping for a by-election, Bondfield was realistic and welcomed her immediate readoption in Wallsend, determining to 'keep in closest touch with the constituency, which involved long journeys to Newcastle and a continuation of the strain of meetings in that scattered Division.'[1]

Members of the public as well as Labour and trade union comrades and women's organizations wrote to support her, but inevitably many of the enemies she had made were delighted that she had gone, and some would continue to detest her for decades. It would have been easy for her to dwell on the loss, but that was not her character; she had always looked resolutely forwards and she did so now. Once back to full health she went back to the union and her peripatetic life as a speaker and organizer.

In happier times she might also have been able to return to the TUC General Council, but of this there was no question. The two women's places were occupied by Bondfield's old friend Julia Varley, of the Transport and General Workers Union (T&G) and Anne Loughlin of the Tailor and Garment Workers.[2] Both were leading women in senior roles in mixed unions, and in 1932 were easily able to retain their seats against her. She stood again in 1933 and 1934, but each time her vote fell. After that her focus in 1935 was on the general election, and then on her impending retirement. After many decades, her time in the national trade union movement was drawing to a close.

The ILP, which had been one of the founding organizations of the Labour Party, and on whose National Administrative Council Bondfield had sat for some years, severed its connection with Labour in 1932. Jennie Lee chose to remain a member of it, but her future husband, Aneurin Bevan, stayed with the Labour Party, famously describing the ILP's decision as rendering them 'pure but impotent'. Bondfield was grieved by the split but recognized that it was more or less inevitable. The ILP of Keir Hardie was long gone, and Labour had become a party of power rather than protest.

On a personal level, there were new interests to take her attention. When she became a Cabinet Minister she had found herself in receipt of the seemingly enormous salary of £2,000 a year, which she had used to build a house in which she and her sister Annie,[3], now in her seventies, could live together. At Southborough, near Tunbridge Wells in Kent, they built a home which they named 'Cuttiversdoor' after their grandfather's farm near Chard. Bondfield never seems to have explained this name to anyone and there was some bemused comment in the press. She also never explained why she had chosen Tunbridge Wells, either, though it is not impossible that the fact that Maud Ward lived less than twenty miles away at East Grinstead may have had something to do with it.

She and Annie had moved into their house in the autumn of 1930, but it was not until a year later that Bondfield was able to focus more on making it comfortable. She had always loved gardens, but now she had one of her own and threw herself into working on it with enthusiasm. Workmen came and went to lay paths and hedges, but she set out the beds and dug them herself. She bought plants and people gave her bulbs and cuttings. She now spent more time outdoors than she had for years, and this was good for her mental as well as her physical health. However much she was away in the years to come – and she was, as ever, frequently travelling – she was always thinking about her garden, what to grow, and how the plants she was already growing were doing. If she was away for any length of time getting the garden back into good order was her priority when she returned.

There had been some other compensations during the years of office. In December 1929 the University of Bristol, of which Winston Churchill was the Chancellor, awarded honorary law degrees to both Bondfield and Snowden. For a woman whose formal education had been so sketchy, and who had felt this in one way or another all her life, it was truly a special day. In his speech Churchill was civility itself, remarking that if she could take a Bill through all its parliamentary stages and emerge 'with personal credit . . . and apparently "in the pink", all he could say was that they had a super-woman.'[4] A few months later, in July 1930, she was given the freedom of the town of Chard, though her schedule was so hectic that she could spare only a couple of hours for the ceremony. These marks of her achievements meant a great deal to her and she used the letters 'LLB', denoting the degree, after her name for the rest of her life.

Other interests remained long after the end of her time in Parliament. Throughout the 1920s she had stayed involved with peace and disarmament groups, particularly through the CWG, and this continued into the 1930s as the world began to grow more dangerous once again. She saw very clearly, and early, the threats presented by the rise of autocratic states; having seen Bolshevik Russia at close quarters in 1920 she had had plenty of time to reflect on how easily democracy could be smothered. In early 1933 she went to a women's conference in Chicago to discuss economic security under fascism, communism and democracy. She spoke for democracy, with speakers from Italy and the Soviet Union taking the other two perspectives. For most on the Left, fascism was a threat on many levels, but communism continued to evoke a more nuanced response and still had many supporters in Britain. Bondfield was deeply interested in the whole question of what should be done and how democracy, which she regarded as 'alone aimed at developing security into freedom, security for our common characteristics, freedom for our individualities' could be protected from the threats by which it was surrounded. The conference turned out to be interesting but also in some ways disappointing. Neither the fascist nor the communist speakers were 'in any way original or novel: they gave what might have been more or less a duplication of the ordinary pamphlet issued as pure propaganda . . . But perhaps neither . . . ever meant to argue its case.'[5]

In Chicago she saw old friends, including Jane Addams who had been awarded the Nobel Peace Prize in 1931. Moving on to New York she stayed at the Henry Street Settlement where she saw Rose Schneiderman and her partner, Maud Swartz. There were lunches and dinners and evening receptions, and her diary for these days exudes an air of enjoyment that had been missing for a long time.

On 21 July she was in Washington for one of the most interesting parts of her stay. The Democrat Secretary for Labor, Frances Perkins, was the first woman to serve in any US cabinet role. Bondfield had met her on previous visits and thought highly of her, and the fact that both were the first to hold such office in either country added interest. Perkins had come from a privileged background and had a good education, but both women had been working on similar issues and faced similar challenges. More than twenty years earlier, on her first American trip, Bondfield had visited Washington and been given a guided tour of the White House. Now she was an honoured guest and was taken to meet President Roosevelt in the Oval Office. She attended meetings with Perkins, learned about the legislative system which, unlike in Britain, made it very difficult for the Labor Secretary to introduce legislation, and discussed the finer details of the New Deal. In the Department of Labor she was very envious of the 'utilitarian and unadorned' offices it occupied, especially when compared with the 'marble staircases and painted ceilings and rabbit warren of little rooms'[6] in which her own ministry in Whitehall had been housed. Perkins was working on schemes for employment exchanges and compulsory insurance schemes, but also had to attend congressional hearings where she had to undergo 'an ordeal of cross-examination under Klieg lights because it pleased the Press to take advantage of that opportunity to make a sound film'.[7] Bondfield attended a presidential press conference, and for once thought that things were better handled in Britain without the scrum of journalists and cameras that American presidents were compelled to endure. She found Perkins' calm under fire impressive, reflecting rather ruefully that 'severely tailored in black with a touch of white, *(she)* shared the fate which seems to fall upon women Cabinet Ministers of being the centre of the storm . . . ' After her Washington visit she stayed for a few days at Perkins' New York apartment before returning to Boston for the voyage home in early August.

Bondfield was now sixty, but still believed she had plenty of work to do. Despite hostility to her in some parts of the Labour and trade union movement she remained a significant figure who continued to express her opinion on the issues she knew and cared about. Her fears that cuts made by anyone else would be much worse than cuts made by a Labour government proved correct, and the National Government's approach to unemployment was both heartless and punitive. For some people, Bondfield's consistent opposition to its measures seemed hypocritical, and her appearances at conferences were not always comfortable. Sometimes she was heckled when she spoke, and at others was the subject of criticism from people who felt that she should have behaved differently when in office. She was, however, unrepentant, and refused to be derailed by attacks. She attended most conferences as a delegate from the NUGMW and usually moved their resolutions protesting about the government's actions. She saw no incongruity in this, and continued to defend her record to the end.

In July 1934 her sister Annie died. At the age of 76 Annie was still, with the exception of her brother Frank, the sibling to whom Bondfield had been closest, the one who had looked after her when she was a child being shipped around from relative to relative. But Annie had also had a life of her own, as a deaconess in the Methodist Church and the matron of various clubs and homes including, for a period, the Mary Macarthur Holiday Home, and she was mourned in those circles in her own right, and not just as Bondfield's sister. Of the eleven Bondfield children only Harriet, Frank and Margaret were now left.

By early 1935 political events were beginning to move quickly. Henderson had returned to Parliament in September 1933 but all his energies were focused on trying to prevent the slow slide towards war, eventually, in 1934, being awarded the Nobel Peace Prize in recognition of his efforts. This left Lansbury as leader, and although he had turned out to be better than expected, he was in his mid-seventies and his deputy, Clement Attlee, had had to play a larger role than a deputy would normally expect to. Already the questions of war and peace which would dominate Labour debates for the next few years were troubling both individuals and organizations, and by the time Labour assembled at Brighton for its 1935 conference matters were coming to a head. By far the most significant item on the agenda was the debate about Italy's intended invasion of Abyssinia. The party's NEC wanted there to be international sanctions while Lansbury and other pacifists disagreed. For Bondfield this question must have been particularly difficult. She had opposed war and militarism all her adult life, but she also understood how great a threat fascism might be. Like thousands of others she faced a deepening dilemma which would have to be resolved one way or the other. For Lansbury, despite the NEC's attitude, the position was clear. He would not and could not compromise his principles, and these put him absolutely against sanctions backed up by military means.

The wider trade union position was not necessarily pro-war, but it was against fascism, which itself opposed trade unions and had more or less extinguished them wherever it had taken power. This must have influenced Bondfield's evolving view and it is probable that she broadly, if regretfully, agreed with Henderson's 'War and Peace' memorandum in which he argued for peace maintained by the League of Nations. Members of the League were bound by its Covenant to take any necessary action to protect and defend one another, and this included sanctions and military force if necessary. This view was fed into 'For Socialism and Peace', a comprehensive policy document accepted by the TUC and the 1934 Labour Party conference. Lansbury, who had had to take several months' leave with a broken leg, pointed out that for the whole of the period of his leadership he had been emphatic that he would never back the use of force, either by individual countries or the League of Nations. So far Labour had consistently opposed rearmament but this did not constitute hostility to all military action. After a stormy debate the 1935 Brighton Conference accepted the NEC's position and Lansbury immediately resigned. MacDonald had resigned as Prime Minister in June and now Stanley Baldwin, in office once again, saw his opportunity and called a general election. As a caretaker leader stepping into the breach, Attlee did the best he could and the electoral outcome was better than it might have been, with Labour regaining more than 100 seats and restoring some of its self-esteem. Baldwin's National Government was returned with a reduced majority and a number of Labour MPs who had lost their seats in the disaster of 1931 were re-elected. Margaret Bondfield, however, was not amongst them.

The election in Wallsend was as hard-fought as ever, but Irene Ward was popular and already making a national name for herself. The local Labour Party was less than united, and the continued behaviour of some of Wallsend's councillors had not helped. In May Bondfield had observed that she was 'terribly concerned' that most of them were 'extremely unqualified and petty-minded men.'[8] Throughout 1935 she had been full of a sort of restless anticipatory energy, and once the election was called she threw herself into it with far more verve than she had been able to muster in 1931. Driven by Denscombe, she toured the constituency speaking at several meetings a day, knocking on doors and kissing babies. As polling day approached both candidates redoubled their efforts; on 12 November, two days before polling day, Bondfield 'held a series of morning meetings . . . She had four afternoon meetings and no fewer than seven night meetings, at which she expressed herself confident of victory.'[9]

Unfortunately, her confidence was misplaced. She reduced Irene Ward's majority to 2,300 and numerically her own vote was the highest she had ever received, but it was not enough. Once again she had to be gracious in defeat, but privately she was furious. A scrawled entry in her diary for 16 November blamed the loss on the scandal caused by 'three drunken councillors who were expelled from the Party just before the B C *(Borough Council)* elections' adding that another contributory cause had been 'the overwhelming use of cars by the other side on a wet polling day. 80 cars to our 7.'[10]

Once more friends and acquaintances wrote to express support. Her old Shop Assistants' Union friend, J. J. Mallon, now the Warden of Toynbee Hall, wrote: 'You are stout hearted and will take your defeat with courage. . . . That so many idiots and ingrates should be found in a constituency like Wallsend fills me with despair.' Mallon signed his letter off with 'sympathy and admiration that will never fail'[11] and it seemed that many shared his view. Marjorie Green of the National Council for Equal Citizenship wrote to say that 'we know you would have been a tower of strength in all questions affecting the welfare of women and children. . . . your ability in the last Labour administration did so much to raise the prestige of women in Parliament.'[12] Perhaps the letter which gave her most pleasure came from Ellen Wilkinson, who only four years earlier had fought her so hard over the Anomalies Bill, but who now, fresh from victory in Middlesbrough, wrote that she was 'utterly miserable', adding 'That cheap, flashy woman compared to you – oh my dear it is terrible. It is the movement that needs sympathy. You looked like a queen everyone is saying. . . . Here's to a by-election and a speedy return . . . '[13]

Only nine women were elected in total in 1935, and, until the election of Agnes Hardie (another former Shop Assistants' Union organizer and Keir Hardie's sister-in-law) at a by-election in 1937, Wilkinson remained the only Labour woman. By the time the 1940 election was cancelled after the outbreak of war, the number of Labour women had risen to four. Neither Margaret Bondfield nor Susan Lawrence, who had also tried to regain her seat, would sit in Parliament again.

After the result Bondfield took a few days of rest but was soon back at work. Denscombe, sorting out expenses and returns in Wallsend, was very relieved. 'Knowing the strain under which you had been put' he wrote:

> I was afraid that the re-action would amount to a complete breakdown. You really are a 'Tough Guy'! Your attitude after the Poll, and the fact that you were able to go through with the programme the following day, has won for you more admiration than almost anything you have done.[14]

Once again Bondfield had returned to the Union, and once again, the local Labour Party indicated their intention to adopt her as their candidate for the next election. However, the NUGMW had decided to withdraw her from Wallsend 'with a view to either contesting a by-election or finding a Constituency more favourable for success'.[15] Denscombe was not pleased. 'Whoever the candidate may be,' he said, rather crossly, 'he or she will keep the benefit of your labour over many years. I suppose that is inevitable but it rankles none-the-less.'[16]

In fact, Denscombe had decided to move south to Reading, and soon he arranged for Bondfield to become the new candidate there. Reading was much easier to get to, and the local Labour Party was not in a constant state of internal warfare. On the other hand, the Conservatives had a larger majority than they had had in Wallsend and it would not be an easy proposition to win. 'I never chose,' she reflected later, 'nor was given an easy constituency.'[17] It would be many years before significant numbers of women were selected for the safer Labour seats.

Despite the move Bondfield kept in touch with Wallsend and her friends there, just as she did with Northampton. From time to time she travelled to both, opening fetes, speaking at meetings and officiating at school prize-givings. She was, on the whole, more hopeful than she had been between 1931 and 1935. She had first met Attlee in 1908 and thought highly of him, believing that he could turn the party's fortunes around. But she also saw that hostile forces were gathering and that war was almost certainly coming. Speaking of the party's mission she observed that 'The urgency was impressed upon us by the darkness and enigmatical character of the future.'[18]

There were personal losses, too. In 1935, three weeks before polling day, Arthur Henderson had died, worn out by a lifetime's work for the causes in which he believed. In May 1937 Philip Snowden died suddenly, followed, in November, by Ramsay MacDonald, who died at sea while on a cruise. Henderson and Snowden had both been aged 72, and MacDonald 71. All three deaths were, in their different ways, a sadness to Bondfield, but may also have been a warning to her about the consequences of unrelenting work and stress. When, in March 1938, she turned sixty-five and retired from her job at the NUGMW she did so without much regret. She had been a trade union official of one kind or another for close on forty years, and although she knew she would miss the work, she had no intention of fading quietly away. Gradually across the trade union movement separate provision for women had been reduced to almost nothing, so that in the NUGMW the women's section, the last vestige of the NFWW, had disappeared. Since Bondfield believed that trade unionism should be a joint enterprise between women and men she did not necessarily regret this, but it changed both the job of National Woman Officer and the position of women within the movement.

As might be expected, retirement for Bondfield was retirement from a job, not from work itself. Over the next few years she took on many new projects in addition to her existing commitments. She helped to establish the Over-Thirty Association and the Over-Thirty Housing Association, both of which were designed to help women find work and housing. She was involved in a number of other charities, too, including the Mary Macarthur Holiday Home and various Christian groups. She remained deeply interested in international issues and maintained her contacts at the ILO and peace organizations. She continued to write and give interviews, and she was gradually becoming more comfortable with broadcasting, which fascinated her. Looking back, she thought that she seemed to develop 'wider and warmer interests and more mature experience than I had managed to achieve earlier in life. I had not stopped growing.'[19]

As soon as she could she went to America, lecturing and touring extensively. She now had some celebrity in the United States and the fees from her lectures were more than enough to cover her expenses. She had lunch at the White House with Eleanor Roosevelt and Frances Perkins held a dinner for her at her house in Virginia. But perhaps the most interesting part of her trip was a visit to Mexico to find out about the recent changes in the country. In late August 1938 she visited Leon Trotsky at Casa Azul, a house belonging to the artists Diego Rivera and Frida Kahlo. Trotsky had been exiled from Russia in 1929, but Bondfield had not seen him since the distant days in Moscow after the War. She thought he 'looked singularly unchanged since I last saw him in 1920 . . . the same clear, mocking glance, . . . the same assurance that he had no doubts about the rightness of his way . . . a vital personality.'[20] In the United States she lectured to large crowds, saw many old friends, and had a very refreshing holiday. It was a little dispiriting to find, when she arrived back in Southborough in January 1939, that the kitchen boiler had burst and the pipes were broken, but she remained hopeful. As always, America invigorated her, sending her home ready for whatever came next.

Throughout her American visit Bondfield had followed events at home, listening on the radio to the Munich crisis almost as it happened. She profoundly hoped that the agreement the Prime Minister, Neville Chamberlain, had reached with Adolf Hitler would hold, but she was equally deeply doubtful, if only because she did not believe Hitler could be trusted. When the First Lord of the Admiralty, Alfred Duff Cooper, resigned in protest at the agreement Chamberlain threatened to call a general election. 'Well,' wrote Bondfield in her diary:

> if that is so I can't get back in time to be effective, and I shall resign all thought of going back to the House! The very thought of those late hours is most distasteful, and if I break free I shall be able to travel as long and as often as I want to.[21]

The election failed to materialize, but the looming inevitability of war overshadowed the spring and summer. In August 1939 Bondfield visited her friend, Mary

Dingman, in Geneva. Dingman, an American, was president of the Peace and Disarmament Committee of Women's International Organizations and would become one of the advocates of the development of the United Nations. While seeing friends at the ILO office Bondfield heard the shocking news of the non-aggression pact signed by Stalin and Hitler. Knowing that war was now imminent, she returned home as quickly as possible, while Dingman got back to the United States only with great difficulty.

Bondfield took a very different view in 1939 than she had done in 1914. 'It is not possible,' she later said:

to say that a war is right, but it can sometimes be said that it is unavoidable. This was one of the unavoidable wars – the only one I positively know of. . . . The primary thing was the revolt of the spirit, the unqualified opposition to all that the Axis powers stood for. . . . The men in the factories were fighting for more than their lives, and they knew it.[22]

Soon Southborough found itself living literally under the Battle of Britain, with bombs falling around it and planes crashing into fields and streets. Phlegmatically Bondfield recorded it all in her diary. On one October day in 1940 she noted 'Battle just outside. . . . Spitfire crashed but pilot parachuted down quite safely. A Polish pilot landed in Upper Grosvenor Road in Tunbridge Wells.'[23] Unperturbed, she continued to tour the country speaking at meetings, visiting factories and workshops and generally encouraging the war effort. In October 1941 she set sail once more for America, this time to lecture in the United States and Canada on behalf of the Ministry of Information. The convoy escorting the ship was tracked by German submarines and occasionally bombed from the air though without damage. Her lecture tour lasted for nearly two years, including breaks and holidays, and her reception, though mixed in some places, was generally good. She spent her seventieth birthday in March 1943 in California without much fuss, only returning to Southborough in June and continuing to speak to audiences at home on behalf of the Ministry of Information. On one occasion Maud Ward was able to attend, and afterwards wrote to her that it was 'a real thrill to hear you speak again after all these years. I loved it all of course it was a great success . . . '[24]

Meanwhile, she had continued her interest in projects in Britain and, in particular, in what became the Women's Group on Public Welfare, which she chaired. This drew together women's organizations from across the spectrum and was focused mainly on child welfare. There was considerable concern over what was happening to children evacuated from inner-city areas to smaller towns and villages, and more about what kind of lives they would be returning to after the War. In March 1943 the Group's Hygiene Committee published *Our Towns: a Close-Up* which examined in detail the scale of inner-city poverty, the challenges facing mothers and the deprivation endured by children, making recommendations for post-war improvements. These included better food and eating habits, parental guidance classes, better housing and toilet facilities, sewing and knitting skills for boys as well as girls, family allowances, minimum wages and free universal nursery provision for all children over the age of two. Bondfield did not write the report, but she did (in New York) find funding for publication, contribute the Preface and thoroughly agree with the conclusions. Unfortunately, when the 1945 Labour government came to make its extensive reforms, the voices of women were again sidelined, and some of the recommendations of *Our Towns* have still not been achieved.

She visited Parliament rarely now, but in 1944 attended a lunch to mark Nancy Astor's twenty-five years as an MP. Despite deep political differences, Bondfield and Astor had always got on rather well, and in the photograph taken to mark the occasion the two sit side-by-side as they had done on many other occasions. Astor had attacked Bondfield with relish over the Anomalies Act, but then so had many others and Bondfield was not (usually) one to hold a grudge. On the whole, however, these excursions were rare and becoming rarer, and she was feeling increasingly disconnected from parliamentary life.

She was never disconnected, however, from the Labour Party or politics, and when the 1945 general election arrived she was at work again, speaking at meetings and rallies for Labour candidates. 'Congratulations' wrote Ward 'on your vigour, enthusiasm and "rampageousness". I wish I could hear the old war horse on the war path. Elections aren't what they were in my youth . . . '[25] Labour's success was a source of great joy to them both. Bondfield thought Attlee would make a good Prime Minister and believed that, with a clear majority, the new government would be able to do much that she, in the constrained circumstances of 1929, had not even been able to contemplate. She was also delighted to see Ellen Wilkinson appointed to the Cabinet as Minister of Education. Replying to her congratulations, Wilkinson generously wrote:

> It must bring many memories back of 1929. I felt that when I sat in Cabinet y'day and thought how much you personally had done for the movement to make things possible for the women who should follow you. To carry and hand on the torch you lighted and carried so bravely is my highest ambition.[26]

A few months earlier Bondfield had been saddened by the loss of her sister Harriet, and when a year later her brother Frank also died, she was left as the last Bondfield sibling. Neither death could have come as a shock, but still she had a new sense of being alone. Gradually other friends also began to fall away. In February 1947 Ellen Wilkinson, of whom Bondfield had been genuinely fond, died at the early age of 55. That year also saw the death of Susan Lawrence, who had been in a nursing home in Chelsea and whom Bondfield had visited from time to time. In 1949 she attended Clynes' funeral. Despite having risen from a cotton mill to being Home Secretary he had died in penury, forced to rely on help from friends to pay his sick wife's care bills.

In January 1947 Eleanor Welton, who had lived with Maud Ward for many years, died suddenly. Ward and Bondfield had continued to exchange letters and see one another occasionally, and although generally speaking Bond destroyed everything connected with this relationship, she kept Ward's letters from 1943 onwards. Ward addresses Bondfield as 'Dearest Margo' or 'Margaret' and signs herself either 'Maud' or 'G', and the letters are chatty, affectionate and warm. In the autumn of the year of Eleanor Welton's death there was some kind of falling-out; replying to what must have been Bondfield's letter of apology Ward said:

> Our last meeting was disturbing to me, not only because I had lost your affection and understanding, but even more because my ideal of you seemed to require adjustment. Now all that has passed away and I can remember you with the wonted homage and admiration. . . . you belong to a precious part of our lives.[27]

She was still open to exciting new experiences. She had taken her first flights in the United States during the War, and now flew whenever she could. Early in 1947 she flew to Switzerland for a holiday, returning in thick fog. '"But we landed all right" she said cheerfully,' according to the *Daily Herald*. '"It was when we were down that the fog was the real nuisance – took me longer to get from Victoria to Kent than it had taken to fly from Berne to London."'[28] In November that year the Foreign Office sent her on a lecture tour of post-war Germany. Visiting Hamburg, Kiel, Hanover, Berlin, Dusseldorf and Westphalia over the course of two weeks she gave talks, met people, especially women, and, as always, asked questions.

One of the most gratifying moments of her later years was being made a Companion of Honour in 1948. This was the sole recognition she received from the state for her achievements. If she was ever offered a damehood she must have turned it down – which seems unlikely – and since women were not admitted to the House of Lords until 1958 she could not be given a peerage. A long political afterlife in the upper House might well have altered posterity's view of her, but sadly this was never possible.

As always, there were new things to discover, however, and, at the age of seventy-five, she had decided to learn to cook. She found it 'strange, mysterious, and most exciting' although she added 'Of course I often find that I have done the wrong thing.'[29] She was proud of a cake and a meat pie that lasted her several days, but unsurprisingly the experiment soon lapsed. Domestic help was hard to find, but as she was still away a good deal there was no urgent need to solve the problem yet.

In 1949 she made her last visit to the United States, for the first time flying across the Atlantic and staying with her friend Helen Lockwood[30] at Vassar College at Poughkeepsie near New York. She and Lockwood had met some years earlier and become very close, writing affectionate letters and spending time together when Lockwood visited England, which she did during most summers after the War. In 1949 Bondfield was able to use Lockwood's house as a base, venturing forth to see Eleanor Roosevelt ('most cordial and informative') and attending a celebratory lunch for Rose Schneiderman ('fine speeches by E. Roosevelt and Frances Perkins. Tributes to Rose from many.')[31] She attended Commencement at Vassar and conferred degrees. All this activity was interspersed with days of rest, swimming and gentle pleasures, and she returned to England refreshed and happy.

Her autobiography, which she had been working on for some time, was published the same year to mixed reviews. She had not enjoyed writing it and this was evident from the end result, which had only flashes of her more youthful wit and style. Her friends were kind but some of the reviews were not, and perhaps she realized that she should have written it sooner. But her life was so full that she had not really had time, and by the time she did the sharpness of her mind was beginning to dull. She herself knew that it had been more thrown together than written reflectively. 'How I regret,' she wrote later in her diary, 'the carelessness in my book.'[32]

In the late autumn of 1950 Bondfield made the last of her quick decisions about the direction of her life. For some months she had realized that she needed more help and had been looking for someone to live with her as a companion. She had advertised and asked friends, but it seemed impossible to find anyone suitable. In the end, and after several false starts, she decided that something more drastic was required. She found a Home called Woodcote Grove Park, at Coulsdon near Croydon, which was run by the Friends of the Poor Society. She could let Cuttiversdoor, which would help to pay the costs, and she would not have to bother any more with housekeeping or worry about who was going to look after her. It seemed an ideal solution, and she knew that it was the right one, but nevertheless it was a wrench. It seemed like the end of things, and as she looked back she was still plagued by thoughts of her own inadequacy. 'I feel glad yet ashamed that I have not done more' she wrote in mid-December, following it with 'Still feeling the new life unknown. What a lot there is to learn. I am lazy and indulgent and all so trivial.'[33] In the spring of 1951 the move was accomplished. The last phase of her long life had begun.

In May that year Bondfield visited the Great Exhibition at the Festival Hall in London. She enjoyed it greatly and was very impressed with the scale and range of it, but while there she fell and hit her head on a glass door. She spent the next week in hospital and in June wrote to Lockwood that, although she felt better, she also felt 'splintered and empty.'[34] That same month she gave a press interview in which she reflected on the state of politics and the future. She was worried about what would happen to the Welfare State if it fell into Conservative hands, and concerned about 'the great burdens which the young people must carry into the future which should occupy the minds of our leaders.' She was frail, leaning heavily on a stick, and reflected on her life as well as her politics. 'I have never been a home bird,' she said, 'never domesticated. It has always been rooms or a flat, and a circle of friends. I have had houses, yes. But never a home.'[35] In October she urged people to vote Labour in the forthcoming general election. She was, she said, 'so very proud of my party and all it has done' and she believed that women 'will become the largest single factor in building a world-wide peace and understanding.'[36] Labour lost, however, ushering her old adversary Churchill in once again as Prime Minister.

In September the superintendent of Woodcote Grove, Winifred Midgeley, told Lockwood that Bondfield's memory was failing and that she was 'in a mental mist, suspended between heaven and earth'.[37] By spring the following year Bondfield's niece, Audrey Farrant, wrote to Lockwood that her aunt was now unable to deal with correspondence, though this is slightly belied by a letter from Bondfield in October asking Lockwood to pass on a letter to a mutual friend. 'I had a setback,' she said, 'I think it's due to the state of the world.'[38] This, however, was her last letter; finally she was falling silent. She made it through the winter to her eightieth birthday but then declined rapidly. She died peacefully at Verecroft Nursing Home on 16 June 1953.

Two days later, in a highly unusual move, the Lord Privy Seal, prior to announcing the Commons business for the following week, referred to her death. 'As one,' he said, 'who had constantly to cross swords with her, I know that she was always a courteous and generous opponent. Let us then, as a House, salute her memory and express our sympathy with her relatives and friends.' Clement Attlee described her as 'a very distinguished Member of this House' who 'gave unwearied service for very many years to the cause of women workers. She was a very old friend and colleague of mine. She was a very fine character.'[39] Her obituaries were largely generous and often focused on her spectacular rise from shopgirl to Cabinet Minister, though the *Daily Mirror*'s description of her as 'the shopgirl princess of politics' was possibly a little over the top. The *Daily Mail* called her the 'Grand Old Lady of the Socialist movement' and said that she 'radiated shining conviction and drove fearlessly and straight at the heart of the crowd.'[40] The *Manchester Guardian* published an extensive account of her life, concluding that she 'kept her remarkable vitality, her keen interest, and her rare power of making and holding friends, unimpaired, to the last'.[41] At her memorial service on 9 July at the parliamentary church, St. Margaret's, Westminster, Attlee gave the oration, reviewing her many achievements before concluding that: 'The mainspring of her life was her intense desire to serve others. She died loved and happy.'[42]

Margaret Bondfield's remains were cremated and the ashes interred in the family grave at Chard. The front of the single headstone was full, so, elusive to the last, her name and dates were recorded on the reverse. Unusually for a woman buried with her parents and siblings she was not described as a daughter or sister, but simply, and proudly, as 'First Woman Privy Councillor and Cabinet Minister.' As she had herself predicted, in the end very little was left except this one unchallengeable niche in her country's history.

Epilogue: This Remarkable Woman

Having done their duty by their pioneering woman the Labour Party quietly consigned her to history. By the 1950s, her active political life seemed to belong to another place and time, and her achievements to another age. The history of women in politics had already congealed into the story of the militant wing of the female suffrage movement and not much more. The mythology of pre-1945 Labour history gradually became Keir Hardie, the General Strike and anti-fascism, and the memory of Margaret Bondfield sank back into a lost time in a distant past. As both society and politics entered the 1960s she was easily forgotten.

In 1973 there were various articles written to commemorate the centenary of her birth, by far the silliest of which was a piece in the *Daily Express* which asked: 'Girl who launched Superwomen's Lib: Can Germaine match up to her?' and tried to draw an equivalence between Bondfield and Greer.[1] From time to time other pieces appeared, but there were relatively few serious assessments, and many were not always complimentary. In 1970 the economist Robert Skidelsky described her as a 'humourless and somewhat priggish person, with long black skirts and a voice that emitted a harsh cascade of sound'.[2] Beatrice Webb, damning with faint praise, had privately considered her 'an extremely competent instrument within a limited range'.[3] The writer and educationalist Dame Margaret Cole, asked by Ross Davies for her recollections, said that she found Bondfield:

> lively and pleasant, though not an outstanding intellect – not in any way comparable with, for example, Mary Macarthur or Susan Lawrence. I didn't think she was a really interesting personality; and later she was a great disappointment as Minister of Labour, particularly over the Anomalies Act.[4]

When Davies wrote to Jennie Lee, by then in the House of Lords, she replied rather frostily that she came from 'a different part of the country and a different wing of the Movement and am afraid did not know this remarkable woman personally'.[5]

Sometimes judgements used out of context or inaccurately fed the idea that Bondfield was more out of her depth than her male colleagues. The historian Marion Miliband, who contributed the entry on Bondfield to the 1972 *Dictionary of Labour Biography*, is often mis-quoted as saying that Bondfield's 'intellectual equipment for the political and economic problems of this period of crisis and depression was wholly inadequate'. However, this verdict actually begins with the words 'like all her senior colleagues in the 1929 Labour government,'[6]; in other words, it was not only Bondfield who was out of her depth but also the Prime Minister and the Chancellor of the Exchequer, both of whom had the reputation of being very clever men.

When Ross Davies appealed on *BBC Woman's Hour* and in *The New Statesman* for anyone who remembered her or who knew the whereabouts of her papers to contact him, a number of people wrote with fond or admiring memories, and some of those who had worked directly with her viewed her in a much more sympathetic light. The civil servant Harold Emmerson, for instance, who ended his career as Permanent Secretary in the Ministry of Labour, told Davies that:

> She was small in stature, but impressed one with her crisp manner and her way of speech, and with her great spirit. She showed great courage in taking on the post of Minister of Labour at a time of heavy unemployment. . . . I would not agree that she was 'not up to the job'. As the first woman to hold cabinet rank, and with unsympathetic colleagues, she had unusual difficulties to contend with, in circumstances which would have daunted any Minister, however competent.[7]

She did not help herself by leaving the writing of her memoirs to such a late stage of her life, when the sharpness and perception that she might have brought to them earlier had begun to dissipate. The young Bondfield's lightness of touch had gone, and her memory was not always as accurate as it might otherwise have been. Besides, the time for stating her case was long past; Snowden and others had got their books out before the War, when there was greater interest, and by 1949 the travails of the 1929 Labour government seemed like very old news. Had she written her book as soon as she retired in 1938 she might have had better success – and it would almost certainly have been better written – but the lures of America, Mexico and Geneva were too great. As always, she preferred action for the future to reflection on the past.

Once the narrative that Bondfield was naïve, inept, incompetent or just not very bright became widespread it was hard to change, particularly once there was nobody left to act as an advocate for her. Moreover, the reputation of the 1929–1931 government was so toxic in Labour and trade union circles that anyone associated with it was damned. To this day, some people believe, despite all the evidence to the contrary, that Margaret Bondfield joined the National Government. There is a story that in 1995 Barbara Castle, the third Labour woman Cabinet Minister, was invited to write about Bondfield for the Fabian Society but refused on the grounds that her predecessor's actions in 1931 had 'sailed very near the wind of political betrayal'.[8] Certainly, the young Barbara would have been outraged by the events of 1931 and would have agreed with Jennie Lee that the government 'drove anyone under the age of forty to the verge of madness'.[9] In 1931 Castle was a twenty-year-old student at Oxford, deeply involved in the Labour Club and no doubt following every twist and turn of events with outraged fascination. But it is also incontrovertibly true that, in 1988, Castle unveiled a plaque in Chard commemorating her predecessor, and it seems rather improbable that, having done this, she should suddenly rediscover her grudge a few years later.

Margaret Bondfield was, first and foremost, a trade unionist, and this informed her whole adult life. Her habit of mind was formed by the education the movement gave her, and it provided a place of refuge on more than one occasion. In many ways, she had more in common with male trade unionists than with middle-class feminists and social reformers. Like her, her male colleagues had had scanty formal education and had long since understood the impact of class oppression and the value of collective action. Like her, they knew about poverty in a visceral way which eluded most of the middle-class women, however sympathetic. Like her also, they believed in the ability of the working class to organize for itself, to achieve its own liberation and to raise itself up by its own efforts. Many of the middle-class women with whom Bondfield worked believed that working-class women needed help to organize, to progress, and to enter the political world, and this idea eventually fed into the structures for women set up by the Labour Party in 1918. But Margaret Bondfield never lost her faith in her own class, and although she sometimes found herself in difficult corners, and made choices that seem almost inexplicable now, her loyalties remained consistent to the end.

Like many other female politicians since, she had to deal with the inherent sexism of the way in which women in politics are frequently perceived. Far more than men, women's intellects have been judged on their appearance. In her youth she had been described as a 'slight girlish figure, clad in a simple light grey frock, (which) made her look even younger and more girlish than she is.'[10] Photographs of her in her twenties and thirties bear this out, and Sylvia Pankhurst, who disliked her, described her as 'eager to score all the points that her youth and prettiness would win for her . . . '[11] But by the time, at the age of 58, she became a Cabinet Minister a Labour-supporting paper could describe her as 'a stout little woman' and she was often called 'motherly' or 'apple-cheeked.' Part of the effect of this constant commentary on women politicians' appearance is to disconnect them from their own political identities, making them seem less serious, and less qualified, than men, who are rarely described in these terms.

The suggestion, made by Brian Harrison and others, that Bondfield 'found companionship in *(her)* dedication to the movement'[12] and that what drew her into the Labour Party was 'her respectability, her trade unionism and her search for companionship'[13] also deprives her of her political agency and makes her career a lifestyle choice as opposed to one of conviction. In fact what drew her to it was the desire to implement the things she believed in – socialism, peace, equality and internationalism – and she could have found much more respectable company in church activities, had she chosen that avenue. Like the men with whom she worked, she was impelled to action by the evils of the world she saw around her, and she consciously chose trade unionism and political action over charity as the remedy. To deny her that choice is to diminish both her personally and her significance as a political figure both before and during her time in office.

On the other hand, acknowledging her political agency means that, for the period of government, she has to be judged by the same standards as her colleagues, and on that basis she failed as they did. None of them were prepared for the economic crisis with which they were faced and, as always, it was much harder being in office than in opposition. Snowden's inflexibility, MacDonald's increasing disengagement, and Bondfield's lack of economic expertise and almost inexplicable attitude to the TUC combined to create a perfect storm which none of them could have survived unscathed. In Bondfield's case, her record over the Blanesburgh Report, her actions on married women and unemployment benefit, and her equivocations over borrowing destroyed her reputation for honest dealing. She believed, probably correctly, that it would have been worse had she not been there, and once the National Government took over it undoubtedly was, but this is not enough to conceal the fact that her time as a Cabinet Minister was not her finest hour. Inevitably, those two years came to be the only thing anyone knew about her – if they knew anything at all – and the stigma of disillusion and betrayal that still taints them has tainted her. But it is also the case that neither of the governments of which Bondfield was a part had a majority in the House of Commons. This necessarily limited their room for manoeuvre and made it impossible for them to carry out the kind of reforms that the 1945 government, with its large majority, was able to achieve. Neither ministers nor the wider Party were ready for the challenges that government brought, and the ten months of the 1924 government was scant preparation for 1929.

Bondfield was one of the first female politicians of the Left to find that the weight of expectation on her was greater than on others. No male politician was – or is – judged by his contribution to men's welfare as well as his work as a legislator, constituency MP, trade unionist, or socialist. For Bondfield, however, what she did or did not do for women is often the only judgement made, and this adds a level of perceived failure to her record that her male colleagues escape. In fact, she worked long and hard for working-class women, a mission which faltered only under the pressure of the challenges of the post-war period and government. To the end, she thought of herself as working class, and her last major policy intervention was, through *Our Towns*, on behalf of women and children living in inner-city slum conditions. Certainly, she did very little to get women admitted to the professions or into universities, but she was a champion of education for girls who left school in their teens and she believed that there was no limit to what working-class women could do. She was, after all, living proof of what was possible.

Inevitably, the women who first break through glass ceilings have to do so in male-dominated organizations and with the support of the men already in them. But this presents problems. Men do not make the same judgements about women that women do, and very few women become 'firsts' through women's or feminist organizations. As a result they are often accused of behaving like men, failing to represent women's interests, and pulling the ladder up behind them. Margaret Bondfield certainly did have the support of women, and worked for them (sometimes in controversial ways) wherever she went, but she was trained up in an environment in which she was so frequently the only woman in the room that she sometimes had relatively little sympathy with those who wanted what she saw as special treatment. Nevertheless, Ellen Wilkinson's generous praise in 1945 of what Bondfield had done for women was entirely genuine, and came from a recognition that, despite all the barriers and challenges, she had opened the door for others. Both the Labour Party and the trade union movements have taken a long time to improve the presence of women in the rooms where decisions are made, and more work is still needed to expand the diversity of the women who get there, but the failure should not be laid at the feet of the tiny handful of women who struggled through a miasma of prejudice, sexism and misogyny to break through in the early days. Undoubtedly, they did not always get it right, but equally the idea that they bore responsibility for the problem both adds a burden to women's load and relieves men of it.

Margaret Bondfield often did not conform to what many people want a politically pioneering woman to be, nor can she be made to. Inevitably, over a long life she made mistakes, took wrong turns and disappointed both herself and other people. She was usually open to new ideas but could also be stubbornly opinionated to the point of infuriating even her friends, and some of her views are not very comfortable for us to hear now. We want our pioneers to be feminists in a modern sense, or at the very least to be ahead of their times. This Margaret Bondfield often was, particularly in her attitudes to race and women's reproductive rights, but sometimes she was disconcertingly (socially) conservative, too, and she was not always a 'good' feminist in the modern sense. We want high achieving women to be 'nice', to be constantly inspirational, and to hold whatever are, at any given point, correct opinions for an age in which they never lived. In some respects, Margaret Bondfield was indeed all these things at various points. But she was also much else, sometimes what we now call highly 'relatable', and sometimes not. She was as complicated as anyone else, and more so than many, and both her politics and her life reflected that.

However, any objective assessment has to conclude that her achievements were indeed significant. She rose to the top of every organization in which she worked. She was loved and respected as a trade unionist, a socialist, an advocate for working-class women, a peace campaigner and an internationalist. Her gift for friendship enabled her to bring people together across divides and across continents. Despite personal, spiritual and mental challenges she persisted with the life she had chosen, retaining to the end a belief in humanity, her God, and the future. Her two years as a Cabinet Minister are almost incidental to her long life – important, certainly, but by no means the whole of it. In the end, her successes far outweigh her failures, and in the last analysis she more than deserves the *Daily Herald*'s description of her as 'that little body with a mighty heart'.[14]

From her early teens onwards she seized every opportunity that was offered to her, often taking risks and usually making them pay off. She enjoyed, she said, the 'spice of danger', both the physical danger of being cut off by the tide or encircled by U-boats and the more nebulous dangers of a secret private life or a job no woman had done before. She had opinions that were unpopular, on peace in a time of war, on universal rather than limited female suffrage, and on the sanctity of domestic work to name but three, but she also overcame prejudice, opposition and her own bouts of ill health. Her voice, rich, powerful and persuasive, filled the political halls of her day and had the capacity to mesmerize those who heard it. She absorbed whatever life threw at her and moved relentlessly on to the next thing. She was not intellectual, but she never pretended to be, and, like others from her beginnings, had to work hard to educate herself. She was intensely spiritual and knowledgeable about the things that mattered to her. She lived a life full of incident in challenging times, emerging bloody but unbowed into an old age which was itself full of movement and new things. She lived, always, to the full.

In March 1953 Margaret Bondfield turned 80, an event marked in the press by a crop of biographical articles. Perhaps the most gratifying – and personal – of these came from Mary Sutherland, the Labour Party's National Woman Officer. Sutherland understood very well the difference Bondfield had made. 'I want her to know' she wrote, 'that the younger generations of women realise the debt they owe her, as they follow the many trails she blazed for them.'[15] It is high time that history did the same.

Notes

Abbreviations:

ALW – Margaret Bondfield, *A Life's Work*, 1947.
Davies LSE – Papers of Ross Davies, The Women's Library, London School of Economics.
MAH – Mary Agnes Hamilton, *Margaret Bondfield*, 1924.
MGB – Margaret Bondfield.
NA JR & ME MacDonald Papers – The National Archives, James Ramsay and Margaret Ethel MacDonald Papers.
Vassar MGB ASCL – Margaret Grace Bondfield Papers, Archives and Special Collections Library, Vassar College Libraries.

Copyright material from the Ramsay MacDonald papers is reproduced by permission of his granddaughter.

Introduction: A Niche in History

1 *ALW*, p. 357.

2 MGB Diary, 2 August 1949; Vassar MGB ASCL, Box 12, Folder 14.

3 Gina Stace to Ross Davies, 27 December 1978, Davies LSE, ROD 7.

4 Gina Stace to Ross Davies, 15 January 1979, Davies LSE, ROD 7.

5 Margaret Cole to Ross Davies, Undated but contextually February 1975, Davies LSE, ROD 7.

6 *Daily Mirror*, 18 June 1953.

7 Beatrice Webb, *Diary, 1924–1932*, p. 247, quoted in Brian Harrison, *Prudent Revolutionaries*, p. 139.

1. We Were Not Given to Tears

1 *ALW*, p. 19.

2 MAH, p. 34.

3 *ALW*, p. 18.

4 Ibid., p. 23.

5 MAH, p. 31.

6 Ibid., p. 33.

7 *ALW*, p. 22.

8 Ibid., p. 36.

9 MGB in *What Life Has Taught Me*, p. 15.

10 Ibid., p. 15.

11 S. A. Bondfield to her parents, unpublished letter, 13 December 1865, Vassar MGB ASCL, Box 1, Folder 11.

12 MGB, in *What Life Has Taught Me*, p. 15.

13 *ALW*, pp. 18–19.

14 Vassar MGB ASCL.

15 Vassar MGB ASCL, Box 8, Folders 3 and 4.

16 *ALW*, p. 20.

17 Ibid., p. 21.

18 Ibid., p. 22.

19 Ibid., p. 23.

20 Ibid., p. 24.

2. Eager, Attractive and Vividly Alive

1 *ALW*, p. 24.

2 Ibid., p. 24.

3 Ibid., p. 24.

4 The Rt Hon Harriet Harman, feminist, MP and former Deputy Leader of the Labour Party is a direct descendant of Louisa Martindale's brother James.

5 Hilda Martindale CBE, *From One Generation to Another*, p. 34.

6 MGB in *What Life Has Taught Me*, p. 18.

7 The younger Louisa Martindale would go on to become one of the first female surgeons and enjoy a long and distinguished career.

8 Hilda Martindale, *From One Generation to Another*, pp. 34–5.

9 *ALW*, p. 27.

10 This is the equivalent of just over £500 now, but would have gone much further then than £500 would in London today.

11 *ALW*, p. 27.

12 Ibid.

13 Alice Maud Allen, *Sophy Sanger: A Pioneer in Internationalism*, pp. 41–2. Other sources suggest that Bondfield left because she did not like measuring out lace, but this seems a less likely explanation.

14 *ALW*, p. 25.

15 Philip Christopher Hoffman (1878–1959) was a drapers' assistant who became a trade union official and an MP in 1923.

16 P. C. Hoffman, *They Also Serve*, p. 32.

17 *Daily Mirror*, 18 June 1953.

3. The Right Thing to Do

1 This timing is speculative, given that Bondfield herself gives no date, but in the context of other events it seems the most likely.

2 *ALW*, p. 28.

3 MGB in *What Life Has Taught Me*, p. 20.

4 *ALW*, p. 28.

5 Emma Paterson (1848–1886) was a trade unionist, feminist and printer who established new unions for women and supported many others. She had previously worked for both the Working Men's Club and Institute Union and as Secretary of the National Society for Women's Suffrage.

6 Emilia, Lady Dilke (1840–1904) was a trade unionist and suffragist who also had a career as an art historian. Her first marriage had been to an academic, Mark Pattison, and she was widely believed to have been the model for Dorothea Casaubon in her friend George Eliot's novel *Middlemarch*.

7 Clementina Black (1853–1922) was a trade unionist, feminist, social researcher and novelist. In 1888 she persuaded the TUC to pass its first resolution supporting equal pay.

8 Annie Marland (1861–1947) was a cotton worker from Ashton-under-Lyne who became a trade union organizer and later emigrated to Canada and the United States.

9 *ALW*, p. 51.

10 Ibid., p. 28.

11 *The Shop Assistant*, 1898, Women's Page.

12 *ALW*, p. 28.

13 The SDF was a Marxist political party which in 1900 became both (fleetingly) one of the founders of the Labour Party and in 1920 one of the founders of the post-war Communist Party.

14 Keir Hardie (1856–1915) was a socialist and trade unionist who was one of the first Labour MPs and a co-founder of both the Independent Labour Party and the Labour Party itself.

15 The Scottish Labour Party, founded in 1888, was absorbed into the Independent Labour Party in 1895.

16 *ALW*, p. 29.

17 MGB in *What Life Has Taught Me*, p. 23.

18 *ALW*, pp. 36–7.

19 Ibid., p. 32.

20 Vaughan Nash (1861–1932) was a nephew-by-marriage of Florence Nightingale and had a special interest in poverty. He had first come to prominence reporting on the Dockers' Strike and retained an interest in industrial matters.

21 Quoted in *ALW*, p. 32.

22 MGB in *What Life Has Taught Me*, p. 21.

23 *ALW*, p. 63.

24 Ibid.

25 P. C. Hoffman, *They Also Serve*, p. 33.

26 *The Shop Assistant*, March 1898, p. 165.

4. Organize and Educate!

1 *The Shop Assistant*, 1898, p. 92.

2 Ibid.

3 Ibid., p. 98.

4 Ibid., p. 107.

5 Ibid., p. 109.

6 Ibid., p. 222.

7 Ibid., p. 223.

8 *The Shop Assistant*, 1898, p. 109.

9 *ALW*, p. 51.

10 Charlotte Despard (1844–1939) was a feminist, socialist, pacifist and suffragist who took up activism in her late 40s, becoming one of Labour's first female parliamentary candidates in 1918. She remained active until the end of her long life, in particular opposing fascism and supporting women's rights.

11 *ALW*, p. 75.

12 Ibid., p. 51.

13 Figures quoted in MAH, p. 61. Though not identical with the affiliation figures given in annual TUC reports they are broadly similar, and the underlying trend the same.

14 Gertrude Tuckwell (1861–1951), trade unionist, social campaigner, one of the first female Justices of the Peace and an active worker for working women's rights.

15 TUC Report 1899, p. 64.

16 *Morning Leader*, 7 September 1899.

17 *ALW*, p. 48.

18 *ILP News*, January 1898, quoted in David Marquand, *Ramsay MacDonald*, p. 65.

19 MGB in *The Woman Worker*, February 1921.

20 *ALW*, pp. 53–4.

21 MGB in *The Woman Worker*, February 1921.

22 Gertrude Tuckwell, *The Woman Worker,* February 1921.

23 Mary Agnes Hamilton, *Women at Work: A Brief Introduction to Trade Unionism for Women*, p. 59.

24 MAH, p. 95.

25 *The Shop Assistant*, 27 June 1903, pp. 514–15.

5. Not Sex, But Class

1 *ALW*, p. 36.

2 Ibid., p. 23.

3 Dr Jane Walker (1859–1938) was one of the first women doctors to be accepted onto the General Medical Register and had a special interest in developing cures for tuberculosis, then a major killer of young people and children.

4 Lilian Gilchrist Thompson to MGB, 3 December 1901, typed copy misdated 1907, Vassar MGB ASCL, Box 1, Folder 2.

5 *ALW*, p. 36.

6 Quoted in MAH, p. 77.

7 Quoted in F. Bealey and H. Pelling, *Labour and Politics 1900–1906*, p. 67.

8 *ALW*, p. 74.

9 Ibid., p. 76.

10 *The Shop Assistant*, September 1898, quoted in MAH, pp. 84–5.

11 For example, Women's Budget Group, *Spirals of Inequality: Gender, Work and Care: Explaining Gender Inequality Across the UK*, April 2020.

12 MAH, p. 84.

13 Debate speech 1907, quoted in MAH, p. 85.

14 MAH, p. 88.

15 Sir Charles Dilke in undated pamphlet 'Suffrage of All Grown Men and Women', People's Suffrage Federation, quoted in Stephen Gwynn, *The Life of the Rt Hon Sir Charles W Dilke, Vol 2*, 1917.

16 Isabella Ford (1855–1924), Quaker, trade unionist, socialist, pacifist, suffragist and first woman to speak at the Labour Party Conference.

17 Sylvia Pankhurst (1882–1960), feminist, socialist, trade unionist and suffragette, second daughter of Emmeline and Richard Pankhurst.

18 E. S. Pankhurst, *The Suffragette Movement*, pp. 177–8.

19 Keir Hardie in *Labour Leader*, quoted in E. S. Pankhurst, *The Suffragette Movement*, p. 245.

20 *Tribune*, 1906, quoted in *ALW*, pp. 82–3.

21 Details of both speeches are from *ALW*, pp. 83–5.

22 *Women's Franchise*, 12 December 1907.

23 E. S. Pankhurst, *The Suffragette Movement*, p. 334.

6. They Want to See Something Done

1 Quoted in P. C. Hoffman, *They Also Serve*, p. 43.

2 Clementina Black, *The Economic Journal*, Vol. 19, No. 74 (Jun. 1909), pp. 315–319.

3 P. C. Hoffman, *They Also Serve*, p. 48.

4 *ALW*, p. 72.

5 Resignation Letter published in *The Shop Assistant*, 20 June 1908.

6 *ALW*, p. 80.

7 MAH, p. 71.

8 *The Shop Assistant*, 19 June 1908.

9 *The Shop Assistant*, 4 July 1908, p. 4.

10 Ibid., pp. 4–5.

11 Details of TUC Parliamentary Committee elections for 1906, 1907 and 1908 are taken from the TUC History Online website http://www.unionhistory.info/reports/ accessed November 2024 and 4 January 2025.

12 The block vote means that unions wield the same number of votes as the number of members for whom they affiliate – thus, according to the 1907 TUC Report the Shop Assistants' Union had 19,300 votes as against, for example, the Northern Weavers, who had 105,000. This system is still in use.

13 James Seddon's political journey subsequently took him steadily to the Right, and he joined the Conservative Party during the 1920s.

14 Margaret Llewelyn Davies (1861–1944), Cooperator, feminist, Christian socialist, social reformer and pacifist was the Secretary of the CWG between 1889 and 1921.

15 Margaret Llewelyn Davies to Mary Macarthur, October 1908, quoted in *ALW*, p. 81.

16 *ALW*, p. 81.

17 Quoted on page of Press Cuttings prepared for American trip, July 1910, Vassar MGB ASCL, Box 6, Folder 8.

18 *ALW*, p. 42.

19 Ibid.

20 Clementina Black (ed.), *Married Women's Work*.

21 Dame Adelaide Anderson, *Women in the Factory*, 1922, p. 163, quoted in *ALW*, p. 42.

22 *Labour Leader*, 15 September 1911, p. 589.

23 NA JR & ME MacDonald Papers 30/69 1376, quoted in Christine Collette, *For Labour and for Women*, p. 44.

24 Quoted in MAH, p. 77.

25 E. S. Pankhurst, *The Suffragette Movement*, p. 354.

26 David Lloyd George, Chancellor of the Exchequer, HC Deb (29 April 1909), vol. 4, cc. 546–8.

27 The 1913 Trade Union Act restored the political levy but also introduced ballots and allowed members to opt-out if they so chose.

28 *ALW*, p. 80.

29 Ibid.

30 *Chard & Ilminster News*, 19 February 1910.

31 William Barefoot testimonial to Margaret Bondfield, July 1910, Vassar MGB ASCL, Box 6, Folder 8. Barefoot (1872–1941) was a significant figure in London politics at the time and typical of a type of local politician familiar during much of the twentieth century.

7. Bread and Roses

1 *ALW*, p. 91. This and all subsequent quotations from Bondfield's diary for this visit are taken from extracts included in *ALW*, pp. 90–123 unless stated otherwise.

2 *Life & Labor*, National Women's Trade Union League, 1912, p. 288. In fact, the phrase may first have been used by the suffragist Helen Todd in December 1911.

3 Although its measures were not implemented at the time, the 1909 Minority Report was the forerunner of the Beveridge Report of 1942 which provided part of the framework for the Welfare State. Beveridge worked as a researcher on the 1909 Report.

4 Mary Agnes Hamilton, *Mary Macarthur*, p. 110.

5 *Labour Leader*, 21 July 1911.

8. The End is Not Yet

1 *ALW*, p. 125.

2 Mary Agnes Hamilton, *Mary Macarthur*, p. 59.

3 Dorothy Elliott to Ross Davies, 12 March 1975, Davies LSE, ROD 7.

4 William Anderson to MGB, 9 August 1903, 13 December 1903, Vassar MGB ASCL, Box 2, Folder 24.

5 Anderson to MGB, 9 August 1903, Ibid.

6 Margaret MacDonald to MGB, 31 May 1910, Vassar MGB ASCL, Box 2, Folder 24.

7 *The Clarion*, 2 October 1908, p. 5.

8 *ALW*, p. 125.

9 Ibid., p. 126.

10 Marion Phillips (1881–1932), socialist and feminist, Secretary of the Women's Labour League 1911–1918, the Labour Party's first National Women's Officer 1918 onwards, MP 1929–31.

11 It was eventually published in 1912.

12 MGB to Ramsay MacDonald, December 1911, NA JR & ME MacDonald Papers PRO 30/69.

13 Ethel Bentham to MGB, 5 January 1912, Vassar MGB ASCL, Box 2, Folder 6.

14 Ibid.

15 Ethel Bentham to MGB, 9 January 1912, Vassar MGB ASCL, Box 2, Folder 6.

16 Katharine Bruce Glasier (1867–1950), socialist, feminist, journalist, active member of the Women's Labour League.

17 Katharine Bruce Glasier to Ramsay MacDonald, NA JR & ME MacDonald Papers PRO 30/69 1157.

18 Ethel Bentham to MGB, 6 January 1912, Vassar MGB ASCL, Box 2, Folder 6.

19 Ibid.

20 Ethel Bentham to MGB, 13 January 1912, Vassar MGB ASCL, Box 2, Folder 6.

21 *ALW*, p. 126.

22 Ibid.

23 Ibid.

24 MGB to Ramsay MacDonald, NA JR & ME MacDonald Papers PRO 30/69 1156.

25 Ramsay MacDonald to MGB, 13 August 1912, Vassar MGB ASCL, Box 2, Folder 24.

26 Ruth Cohen, *Margaret Llewelyn Davies: With Women for a New World*, p. 180.

27 *ALW*, p. 128.

28 Ibid., p. 130.

29 Ibid., p. 131.

30 Ibid., p. 128.

31 Labour Party Conference Report 1909, *ALW*, p. 85.

32 Arthur Henderson (1863–1935), trade unionist, socialist and Labour politician, Labour leader three times, Foreign Secretary, Nobel Peace Prize laureate.

33 *Common Cause*, 18 July 1912, quoted in Sandra Stanley Holton, *Feminism and Democracy: Women's Suffrage and Reform Politics in Britain 1900–1918*, p. 83.

34 Isabella Ford to Edward Carpenter, 25 August 1913, quoted in June Hannam, *Isabella Ford*, p. 156.

9. Events Beyond Control

1 *ALW*, p. 139.

2 Lilian Wald (1867–1940) had founded the Henry Street Settlement in New York where Bondfield and Ward had stayed in 1910.

3 *ALW*, p. 129.

4 Ibid., pp. 55–6.

5 Ibid., p. 349.

6 Chrystal Macmillan (1872–1921), lawyer, feminist, peace and suffrage campaigner, the first woman to graduate from Edinburgh University with degrees in science and mathematics.

7 *International Manifesto of Women* in *Jus Suffragi: International Women Suffrage News*, Vol. 8, No. 13, 1 September 1914 (LSE Digital Library accessed 20 November 2024).

8 Quoted in *ALW*, p. 140.

9 *Labour Leader*, 5 August 1914.

10 Mary Agnes Hamilton, *Arthur Henderson*, p. 95.

11 *ALW*, p. 142.

12 Ibid., p. 80.

13 Isabella Ford to Millicent Fawcett, October 1914, quoted in June Hannam, *Isabella Ford*, p. 166.

14 Clara Zetkin (1857–1933), German Marxist, activist, feminist and internationalist.

15 *ALW*, p. 156.

16 *Daily Express*, 26 April 1915.

17 *John Bull*, 4 September 1915.

18 In December 1916, for instance, an explosion at the Barnbow munitions factory in Leeds killed 35 women outright.

19 *ALW*, pp. 145–6.

20 Ibid., p. 146.

21 Mary, or May, of Teck (1867–1953) was the Queen Consort of George V and later the grandmother of Elizabeth II.

22 *ALW*, p. 153.

23 An excellent account of the Women's Peace Crusade is to be found in Jill Liddington, *The Road to Greenham Common*, pp. 107–129.

24 *ALW*, p. 87.

25 The Convention was held in the Coliseum on Cookridge Street in Leeds. This building is, at the time of writing, the 02 Academy music venue.

26 Janet Douglas and Christian Høgsbjerg, *British Labour and the Russian Revolution: The Leeds Convention of 1917*, p. 31.

27 Ibid., p. 39.

28 Quoted in Christine Collette, *For Labour and for Women*, p. 158.

29 WLL Executive Minutes, 12 October 1917.

30 WLL Annual Conference Report 1918, p. 46.

31 MGB Diary, 20 June 1918, Vassar MGB ASCL, Box 12, Folder 3.

32 MGB Diary, 28 September 1918, Vassar MGB ASCL, Box 12, Folder 3.

33 MGB Diary, 1919, Vassar MGB ASCL, Box 12, Folder 4.

34 TUC Report 1918, p. 67.

35 Ibid., p. 68.

36 *ALW*, p. 159.

37 Ibid., p. 160.

38 Ibid., p. 161.

39 Ramsay MacDonald to MGB, dated 'Friday, 1918', typed copy, Vassar MGB ASCL, Box 2, Folder 24.

40 Philip Snowden to MGB, 16 September (year missing, but contextually 1919), Vassar MGB ASCL, Box 2, Folder 30.

10. Isn't It Glorious!

1 *Hull Daily Mail*, 23 November 1918.

2 *ALW*, p. 162.

3 Clause 26, Protocol of the Armistice between the Allied Governments and Germany, November 1918.

4 The Save the Children Fund was established in 1919 by two British sisters, Eglantine Jebb and Dorothy Buxton.

5 *Forward*, 25 January 1919.

6 MAH, p. 123.

7 Ethel Snowden (1881–1951), socialist, feminist, journalist, wife of Philip Snowden, later Viscountess Snowden.

8 Ethel Snowden, *A Political Pilgrim in Europe*, p. 3.

9 *ALW*, pp. 162–3.

10 Sophy Sanger (1881–1950), feminist and internationalist who acted as the NFWW's lawyer before going on to work for the ILO.

11 *ALW*, p. 166.

12 Ibid., p. 166.

13 Ibid., p. 168.

14 Ibid., p. 171.

15 MGB Diary, 1919, Vassar MGB ASCL, Box 12, Folder 4.

16 *ALW*, p. 173.

17 Ibid.

18 Ibid., p. 175.

19 *Baltimore Sun*, 16 June 1919.

20 *ALW*, p. 176.

21 Ibid., p. 177.

22 Ibid., pp. 183–4.

23 Speech to the ILO, 19 November 1919, quoted in MAH, p. 127.

24 *Daily News*, 1 April 1920.

25 MGB to Lilian Robertson, quoted in *ALW*, p. 243.

11. Are You Really Going to Russia?

1 *ALW*, p. 189.

2 Ramsay MacDonald to MGB, undated copy letter, Vassar MGB ASCL, Box 2, Folder 24.

3 *ALW*, p. 195.

4 Ibid., p. 196.

5 Ibid.

6 Ibid., p. 198.

7 Angelica Balabanoff (1878–1965), Secretary of the Comintern 1919–20, but spent much of her life in Italy, where she was heavily involved in left-wing politics.

8 Dr Nikolai Semashko (1874–1948) served as People's Commissar for Public Health between 1918 and 1930. The healthcare system he set up is still often referred to as the 'Semashko model'.

9 Mrs Philip (Ethel) Snowden, *Through Bolshevik Russia*, p. 122.

10 Ibid., p. 117.

11 *ALW*, p. 200.

12 Ibid.

13 Ibid., p. 202.

14 Ibid., p. 203.

15 Mrs Philip (Ethel) Snowden, *Through Bolshevik Russia*, pp. 158–9.

16 Ibid., p. 156.

17 *ALW*, p. 208.

18 Ibid., p. 209.

19 Ibid.

20 *La Révolte*, quoted in James Billington, *Fire in the Minds of Men: Origins of the Revolutionary Faith*, p. 417.

21 *ALW*, p. 229.

22 Peter Kropotkin died in February 1921, and anarchists and their organizations were suppressed soon after. Sasha Kropotkin emigrated to the United States where she became a Russian translator and writer producing, amongst other things, several cookery books.

23 *ALW*, p. 234.

24 After finally agreeing to take a holiday, Innessa Armand died of cholera just three months after she and Bondfield met.

25 *British Labour Delegation to Russia, 1920, Report*, 7 July 1920, p. 19.

26 Ibid., p. 29.

27 *Forward*, 28 August 1920, quoted in David Marquand, *Ramsay MacDonald*, p. 270.

28 Mrs Philip (Ethel) Snowden, *Through Bolshevik Russia*, p. 161.

29 John Robert (J. R. or Johnny) Clynes (1869–1949), trade unionist, politician, MP for Manchester Platting for 35 years, Labour leader 1921–2.

30 *ALW*, p. 187.

31 *Daily News (London)*, 6 December 1920.

32 *Daily Herald*, 6 December 1920.

33 *ALW*, p. 188.

12. An Unprecedented Double

1 MGB Diary, 1921, end pages and Memorandum page, MB Archive, Vassar College, Box 12, Folder 5.

2 MGB Diary, 1922, Memorandum page, MB Archive, Vassar College, Box 12, Folder 5.

3 1922 election address.

4 George Bernard Shaw to MGB, 8 June 1922, quoted in *ALW*, p. 245.

5 *ALW*, pp. 245–6.

6 *Portsmouth Evening News,* 19 November 1923.

7 *Labour Gazette*, election leaflet, 24 November 1923 (Vassar).

8 Quoted in Pamela Brookes, *Women at Westminster*, pp. 45–6.

9 *ALW*, p. 250.

10 Ibid., p. 251.

11 *Daily Mirror*, 8 December 1923.

12 *The Times*, 24 December 1923.

13 *Derby Daily Telegraph*, 17 December 1923.

14 *Sunday Sun (Newcastle)*, 23 December 1923.

15 *Western Daily Press*, 12 January 1924.

16 *The Scotsman*, 11 January 1924.

17 *Dundee Courier*, 19 January 1924.

18 *Birmingham Daily Gazette*, 9 January 1924.

19 *Yorkshire Post & Leeds Intelligencer*, 14 January 1924.

20 Quoted in Pamela Brookes, *Women at Westminster*, p. 82.

21 This room was situated in part of what is now the Terrace Cafeteria.

22 *Birmingham Daily Gazette*, 22 January 1924.

23 *Hull Daily Mail*, 22 January 1924.

24 *ALW*, p. 254.

13. A Strange Adventure

1 J. H. Thomas, *My Story*, p. 282, quoted in Peter Clark, *The Men of 1924: Britain's First Labour Government*, p. 159.

2 *ALW*, p. 255.

3 John Shepherd, *George Lansbury: At the Heart of Old Labour*, Loc 3790.

4 *ALW*, p. 255.

5 *Daily News (London)*, 24 January 1924.

6 Montagu House stood on the southern part of the site currently occupied by the Ministry of Defence between Whitehall and the Victoria Embankment.

7 *ALW*, p. 255.

8 J. R. Clynes, *Memoirs, 1869–1924*, p. 343.

9 Isabella Ford to Millicent Fawcett, 16 March 1924, quoted in June Hannam, *Isabella Ford*, p. 201.

10 Ramsay MacDonald to Margaret Bondfield, 11 February 1924, quoted in *ALW*, p. 255.

11 Original transcript of broadcast text for the BBC, November 1928, Vassar MGB ASCL, Box 9, Folder 10.

12 *Newcastle Daily Chronicle*, 19 February 1924.

13 *Daily Express*, 19 February 1924.

14 *The Scotsman*, 19 February 1924.

15 *ALW*, p. 257.

16 Hansard, HC Deb (10 March 1924), vol. 170, c. 2004.

17 *Belfast Telegraph*, 11 March 1924.

18 *ALW*, p. 256.

19 *Hull Daily Mail*, 23 May 1924.

20 *Western Gazette*, 15 February 1924.

21 *Isabella O. Ford: In Memoriam*, 1 August 1924, quoted in June Hannam, *Isabella Ford*, p. 202.

22 *Daily News*, 3 July 1929.

23 *Yorkshire Post & Leeds Intelligencer*, 18 October 1924.

14. That Detestable Affair

1 *ALW*, p. 263.

2 J. R. Clynes to MGB, 22 October 1925, Vassar MGB ASCL, Box 4, Folder 2.

3 Ramsay MacDonald to Ben Spoor, 28 April 1925, quoted in David Marquand, *Ramsay MacDonald*, p. 419.

4 Mary Quaile (1886–1958), Mancunian trade unionist and organizer for the Transport and General Workers' Union.

5 *Birmingham Daily Gazette*, 3 May 1926.

6 *ALW*, p. 266.

7 *Western Morning News*, 22 May 1926.

8 The Act was repealed in 1946. The 1929 Labour government intended to repeal it but ran out of time.

9 Will Thorne to MGB, 30 June 1926, Vassar MGB ASCL, Box 3, Folder 9.

10 Labour election leaflet, July 1926.

11 *The Westminster Gazette*, 22 July 1926.

12 *Merthyr Express*, 4 December 1926.

13 *The New Statesman*, 10 February 1927.

14 MGB to C. Spink, 15 March 1927, Vassar MGB ASCL, Box 4, Folder 3.

15 *ALW*, p. 270.

16 Ibid., p. 271.

17 Ibid., p. 272.

18 Ibid., p. 272.

19 TUC Report 1927, p. 283.

20 *Daily Record*, 6 September 1927.

21 Hansard, HC Deb (10 November 1927), vol. 210, cc. 424–5.

22 *Daily Express*, 11 November 1927.

23 Hansard, HC Deb (29 March 1928), vol. 215, c. 1416.

24 *ALW*, pp. 275–6.

25 Jennie Lee (1904–1988), MP 1929–31, 1945–70, Cabinet Minister 1964–70, created Baroness 1970, co-founder of the Open University.

26 Jennie Lee, *This Great Journey*, p. 18, quoted in Patricia Hollis, *Jennie Lee: A Life*, p. 53.

27 Hugh Dalton, *Call Back Yesterday*, p. 215.

28 Philip Snowden, *Britain's Iron Chancellor: An Autobiography*, p. 208.

15. Some Woman was Bound to Be First

1 MGB in *What Life Has Taught Me*, p. 23.

2 *ALW*, p. 277.

3 Philip Snowden, *Britain's Iron Chancellor: An Autobiography*, p. 208.

4 Typescript of broadcast *Fifty Years in the Labour Movement*, p. 3, Vassar MGB ASCL, Box 9, Folder 13.

5 *ALW*, pp. 276–7.

6 Matthew Worley, *Labour Inside the Gate*, p. 123.

7 Martin Pugh, *Women and the Women's Movement in Britain*, p. 203.

8 Unpublished diary of Sir Cuthbert Headlam, 13 February 1929, quoted in a letter from P. A. Williamson to Ross Davies, 17 December 1975, Davies LSE, ROD 7.

9 *ALW*, pp. 277–8.

10 *Liverpool Daily Courier*, 3 August 1929.

11 Margaret Llewelyn Davies to MGB, 15 June 1929, Vassar MGB ASCL, Box 3, Folder 6.

12 MGB to Millicent Fawcett, 18 June 1929, LSE Digital Library, https://archives.lse.ac.uk/records/9/01/1196 (accessed 8 April 2024). Fawcett died on 5 August.

13 *The Scotsman*, 6 June 1929.

14 Harold Emmerson to Ross Davies, 6 June 1975, Davies LSE, ROD 7.

15 This account (except for the eyeroll) is taken from an undated, unidentified newspaper cutting in the Margaret Bondfield collection at Chard Museum, and Pamela Brookes, *Women at Westminster*, p. 77. The 1929 position remained the case until the 1978 Interpretation Act defined the masculine as encompassing the feminine, and vice versa. This Act is still in force. In 2007 the government took the decision to write all legislation and attached documents in gender-neutral language.

16 Quoted in Matthew Worley, *Labour Inside the Gate*, p. 125.

17 *ALW*, p. 297.

18 Quoted in Brian Harrison, *Prudent Revolutionaries*, p. 129.

19 Undated note, Ramsay MacDonald to MGB, Vassar MGB ASCL, Box 2, Folder 24.

20 *Yorkshire Post & Leeds Intelligencer*, 1 October 1929.

21 *Daily Herald*, 22 November 1929.

22 Robert Skidelsky, *Politicians and the Slump: The Labour Government of 1929–31*, p. 160.

23 Quoted in David Marquand, *Ramsay MacDonald*, p. 537.

24 Ramsay MacDonald to Walton Newbold, 2 June 1930, quoted in David Marquand, *Ramsay MacDonald*, p. 538.

25 Hansard, HC Deb (28 March 1930), vol. 237, c. 791.

26 Ibid., c. 793.

27 *ALW*, p. 295.

28 Ibid., p. 307.

29 Harold Emmerson to Ross Davies, 6 June 1975, Davies LSE, ROD 7.

30 *Daily Mail*, 8 November 1930.

31 Hand-written draft letter, MGB to Ramsay MacDonald, dated 6 January 1931, Vassar MGB ASCL, Box 2, Folder 24.

32 Ramsay MacDonald to MGB, 10 February 1931, Vassar MGB ASCL, Box 2, Folder 24.

33 Margaret Bondfield to Ramsay MacDonald, 1 July 1930, NA JR & ME MacDonald Papers (File 6), quoted in Robert Skidelsky, *Politicians and the Slump: The Labour Government of 1929–31*, pp. 353–4.

34 Quotations describing this debate are all taken from the *Manchester Evening News*, 16 July 1931, unless specified otherwise.

35 Hansard, HC Deb (15 July 1931), vol. 485, c. 636. This accusation is sometimes (wrongly) attributed to James Maxton, the ILP leader and a Glasgow MP.

36 *ALW*, p. 304.

37 MGB to Ramsay MacDonald, 24 August 1931, NA JR & ME MacDonald Papers 30/69 1314.

38 Ramsay MacDonald to MGB, 25 August 1931, NA JR & ME MacDonald Papers 30/69 1314.

39 Unpublished memorandum, 25 August/11 November 1931, Vassar MGB ASCL, Box 4, Folder 11.

40 *ALW*, p. 319.

41 *Portsmouth Evening News*, 24 September 1931.

42 *Taunton Courier*, 23 September 1931.

43 MGB to Mary Agnes Hamilton, 14 October 1931, Vassar MGB ASCL, Box 3, Folder 7.

44 In Islington East the Conservative and Labour candidates were both female, but the other two candidates were male.

45 *Daily Express*, 21 October 1931.

46 Claude Denscombe to Margaret Bondfield, 31 October 1931, Vassar MGB ASCL, Box 3, Folder 7.

47 J. R. Clynes to MGB, 30 October 1931, Vassar MGB ASCL, Box 3, Folder 7.

16. I Had Not Stopped Growing

1 *ALW*, p. 318.

2 Dame Anne Loughlin (1894–1979). In 1942, Loughlin became the second woman (after Bondfield) to chair the TUC and in 1948 was appointed as her union's General Secretary.

3 In later life Annie was known in the family as Nancy, and this is the name Bondfield uses in her later diaries. For consistency, however, Annie is used here.

4 *ALW*, p. 289.

5 Ibid., pp. 319–320.

6 Ibid., p. 321.

7 Ibid., p. 322.

8 MGB to Mr Dukes, 28 May 1935, Vassar MGB ASCL, Box 3, Folder 9.

9 *Newcastle Journal*, 13 November 1935.

10 MGB Diary, 16 November 1935, Vassar MGB ASCL, Box 12, Folder 7.

11 J. J. Mallon to MGB, 16 November 1935, Vassar MGB ASCL, Box 3, Folder 8.

12 Marjorie Green to MGB, 16 November 1935, Vassar MGB ASCL, Box 3, Folder 8.

13 Ellen Wilkinson to MGB, 19 November 1935, Vassar MGB ASCL, Box 2, Folder 33.

14 Claude Denscombe to MGB, 22 November 1935, Vassar MGB ASCL, Box 3, Folder 8.

15 Charles Dukes to MGB, 10 January 1936, Vassar MGB ASCL, Box 3, Folder 8.

16 Claude Denscombe to MGB, 26 January 1936, Vassar MGB ASCL, Box 3, Folder 8.

17 *ALW*, p. 337.

18 Ibid., p. 336.

19 Ibid., p. 324.

20 MGB American Diary, August 1938, Vassar MGB ASCL, Box 12, Folder 10. Leon Trotsky was assassinated on 21 August 1939.

21 *ALW*, p. 345.

22 Ibid., p. 350.

23 MGB Diary, 11 October 1940, Vassar MGB ASCL, Box 12, Folder 11.

24 Maud Ward to MGB, 5 November 1943, MGB ASCL, Box 2, Folder 33.

25 Maud Ward to MGB, 21 June 1945, MGB ASCL, Box 2, Folder 33.

26 Ellen Wilkinson to MGB, 8 August 1945, Vassar MGB ASCL, Box 2, Folder 33.

27 Maud Ward to MGB, 13 October 1947, Vassar MGB ASCL, Box 2, Folder 33.

28 *Daily Herald*, 27 March 1947.

29 *Daily Herald*, 23 April 1948.

30 Helen Drusilla Lockwood (1891–1971), Professor of English at Vassar College, Poughkeepsie, New York.

31 MGB Diary, June 1949, Box 12, Folder 14.

32 MGB Diary, 15 December 1950, Vassar MGB ASCL, Box 12, Folder 15.

33 MGB Diary, 13 and 14 December 1950, Vassar MGB ASCL, Box 12, Folder 15.

34 MGB to Helen Lockwood, 12 June 1951, Vassar MGB ASCL, Box 2, Folder 22.

35 *Reynolds News*, 10 June 1951.

36 *Daily Herald*, 15 October 1951.

37 Winifred Midgeley to Helen Lockwood, 12 September 1951, Vassar MGB ASCL, Box 2, Folder 22.

38 MGB to Helen Lockwood, 5 October 1952, Vassar MGB ASCL, Box 2, Folder 23.

39 Hansard, HC Deb (18 June 1953), vol. 516, c. 1187.

40 *Daily Mail*, 18 June 1953.

41 *Manchester Guardian*, 18 June 1953.

42 *Daily Herald*, 10 July 1953.

Epilogue: This Remarkable Woman

1 *Daily Express*, 16 February 1973.

2 Robert Skidelsky, *Politicians and the Slump*, p. 89.

3 Quoted in Brian Harrison, *Prudent Revolutionaries*, p. 131.

4 Margaret Cole to Ross Davies, undated, Davies LSE, ROD 7.

5 Jennie Lee to Ross Davies, 27 March 1975, Davies LSE, ROD 7.

6 Marion Miliband in J. M. Bellamy and J. Saville (eds), *Dictionary of Labour Biography*.

7 Harold Emmerson to Ross Davies, 6 June 1975, Davies LSE, ROD 7.

8 Fran Abrams, *Freedom's Cause: Lives of the Suffragettes*, p. 217. Abrams does not give a source for this story.

9 Jennie Lee, *This Great Journey*, p. 115.

10 *Morning Leader*, 7 September 1899.

11 E. S. Pankhurst, *The Suffragette Movement*, pp. 177–8.

12 Brian Harrison, *Prudent Revolutionaries*, p. 131.

13 Ibid., p. 129.

14 *Daily Herald*, 22 November 1929.

15 Mary Sutherland, *Daily Herald*, 17 March 1953.

Bibliography

Archives

ILP Archive, People's History Museum, Manchester.
Labour Party Archive, People's History Museum, Manchester.
Margaret Grace Bondfield Papers, Archives and Special Collections Library, Vassar College Libraries.
Papers of J. Ramsay MacDonald, The National Archives at Kew.
Papers of Ross Davies, the Women's Library, London School of Economics.
The British Newspaper Archive, https://www.britishnewspaperarchive.co.uk/
TUC Online History, TUC Reports, http://www.unionhistory.info/reports/index.php
Women's Labour League Archive, People's History Museum, Manchester.

Newspapers

Baltimore Sun
Belfast Telegraph
Birmingham Daily Gazette
Chard & Ilminster News
Daily Chronicle (London)
Daily Express
Daily Herald
Daily Mail
Daily Mirror
Daily News
Daily Record
Derby Daily Telegraph
Dundee Courier
Forward
Hull Daily Mail
Hull Times
ILP News
John Bull
Jus Suffragi
Labour Gazette
Labour Leader
Liverpool Daily Courier

Manchester Evening News
Manchester Guardian
Merthyr Express
Morning Leader
Newcastle Daily Chronicle
Newcastle Journal
Portsmouth Evening News
Reynolds News
Sunday Sun
Taunton Courier
The Clarion
The Economic Journal
The New Statesman
The Scotsman
The Shop Assistant
The Times
The Westminster Gazette
The Woman Worker
Tribune
Western Daily Press
Western Daily News
Western Gazette
Western Morning News
Women's Franchise
Yorkshire Post & Leeds Intelligencer

Autobiographies and Diaries

Allen, Alice Maud, *Sophy Sanger: A Pioneer in Internationalism*, 1958, Robert Maclehose & Co. Ltd.

Bondfield, Margaret, *A Life's Work*, 1948, Hutchinson & Co.

Bondfield, Margaret, *Diaries 1898–1951*, Margaret Grace Bondfield Papers, Archives and Special Collections Library, Vassar College Libraries (Boxes).

Bondfield, Margaret Grace, in *What Life Has Taught Me* (edited by Sir James Marchant), 1949, Hutchinson & Co.

Clynes, J. R., *Memoirs 1869–1924*, 1937, Hutchinson & Co.

Dalton, Hugh, *Call Back Yesterday, Memoirs 1887–1931*, 1953, Frederick Muller Ltd.

Hamilton, Mary Agnes, *Remembering My Good Friends*, 1944, Jonathan Cape.

Hamilton, Mary Agnes, *Up-Hill All the Way: A Third Cheer for Democracy*, 1953, Jonathan Cape.

Hoffman, P. C., *They Also Serve: The Story of the Shop Worker*, 1949, Porcupine Press.

Lee, Jennie, *This Great Journey, A Volume of Autobiography, 1904–45*, 1963, Macgibbon & Kee.

MacDonald, J. Ramsay, *Margaret Ethel MacDonald: A Memoir*, 1912, Hodder & Stoughton.

Martindale, Hilda, *From One Generation to Another*, 1944, George Allen & Unwin Ltd.

Pankhurst, E. Sylvia, *The Suffragette Movement*, 1931, Longmans, Green & Co.

Snowden, Ethel, *A Political Pilgrim in Europe*, 1921, Cassell & Co Ltd.

Snowden, Mrs Philip (Ethel), *Through Bolshevik Russia*, 1920, Cassell & Co Ltd.

Snowden, Phillip, *An Autobiography*, 1934, Ivor Nicholson and Watson.

Snowden, Philip, *Britain's Iron Chancellor: An Autobiography* (ed. Alexander Clifford), 2024, Pen and Sword Books.

Thomas, James Henry (J. H.), *My Story*, 1937, Hutchinson & Co.

Webb, Beatrice, *My Apprenticeship*, 1926, Longmans, Green & Co. Ltd.

Webb, Beatrice, *Our Partnership*, 1948, Longmans, Green & Co. Ltd.

Webb, Beatrice, *Diaries 1924–1932* (ed. Margaret Cole), 1956, Longmans, Green & Co.

Webb, Beatrice, *Diary, Volume 2, 1892–1905: All the Good Things of Life*, 1986, Virago Press Ltd.

Other

Abrams, Fran, *Freedom's Cause: Lives of the Suffragettes*, 2003, Profile Books.

Barnsley, Tony, *Breaking Their Chains: Mary Macarthur and the Chainmakers' Strike of 1910*, 2010, Bookmarks.

Bartley, Paula, *Ellen Wilkinson: From Red Suffragist to Government Minister*, 2014, Pluto Books.

Bartley, Paula, *Labour Women in Power: Cabinet Ministers in the Twentieth Century*, 2019, Palgrave Macmillan.

Bealey, Frank and Pelling, Henry, *Labour and Politics, 1900–1906*, 1958, Macmillan.

Bellamy, J. M. and Saville, J. (eds), *Dictionary of Labour Biography*, 1972, Scholar's Bookshelf.

Benn, Caroline, *Keir Hardie*, 1992, Hutchinson.

Bennett, Gill, *The Zinoviev Letter: The Conspiracy That Never Dies*, 2018, Oxford University Press.

Billington, James H., *Fire in the Minds of Men: Origins of the Revolutionary Faith*, 1998, Transaction Publishers.

Black, Clementina (ed.), *Married Women's Work*, 1915, Women's Industrial Council; Virago reprint edition, 1983.

Blackburn, Sheila, *A Fair Day's Wage for A Fair Day's Work? Sweated Labour and the Origins of Minimum Wage Legislation in Britain*, 2007, Ashgate Publishing.

Boston, Sarah, *Women Workers and the Trade Unions*, Third Edition, 2015, Lawrence & Wishart.

British Labour Delegation to Russia 1920: Report, 1920, At the Offices of the Trade Union Congress and the Labour Party.

Brookes, Pamela, *Women at Westminster*, 1967, Peter Davies.

Clark, Peter, *The Men of 1924: Britain's First Labour Government*, 2023, Haus Publishing.

Cohen, Ruth, *Margaret Llewelyn Davies: With Women for a New World*, 2020, Merlin Press.

Collette, Christine, *For Labour and for Women: The Women's Labour League, 1906–18*, 1989, Manchester University Press.

Collette, Christine, *The Newer Eve: Women, Feminists and the Labour Party*, 2009, Palgrave Macmillan.

Cox, Pamela and Hobley, Annabel, *Shopgirls: True Stories of Friendship, Hardship and Triumph from Behind the Counter*, 2015, Arrow.

Dale, Iain (ed.), *British General Election Campaigns 1830–2019: The 50 General Election Campaigns that Shaped Our Modern Politics*, 2024, Biteback Publishing.

Dale, Iain, *Labour Party General Election Manifestos 1900–1997*, 2000, Politico's Publishing.

Davis, Mary, *Comrade or Brother? The History of the British Labour Movement 1789–1951*, 1993, Pluto Press.

Dockett, Sue, *Out of the Wilderness: The Margaret Bondfield Story*, 2022, Wisbech, March & District TUC

Douglas, Janet and Høgsberg, Christian, *British Labour and the Russian Revolution: The Leeds Convention of 1917*, 2017, Spokesman.

Drake, Barbara, *Women in Trade Unions*, 1984, Virago Books.

Goronwy-Roberts, Marian, *A Woman of Vision: A Life of Marion Phillips MP*, 2000, Bridge Books.

Graves, Pamela M., *Labour Women: Women in British Working Class Politics, 1918–1939*, 1994, Cambridge University Press.

Gwynn, Stephen, *The Life of the Right Honourable Sir Charles Dilke* (ed. Gertrude M. Tuckwell), 2 volumes, 1917, John Murray.

Hamilton, Mary Agnes, *Margaret Bondfield*, 1924, Leonard Parsons.

Hamilton, Mary Agnes, *Mary Macarthur: A Biographical Sketch*, 1925, Leonard Parsons.

Hamilton, Mary Agnes, *Arthur Henderson*, 1938, Heinemann.

Hamilton, Mary Agnes, *Women at Work: A Brief Introduction to Trade Unionism for Women*, 1941, Labour Book Service.

Hannam, June, *Isabella Ford*, 1989, Basil Blackwell.

Hannam, June and Hunt, Karen, *Socialist Women, Britain, 1880s to 1920s*, 2002, Routledge.

Harrison, Brian, *Prudent Revolutionaries*, 1987, Clarendon Press.

Hollis, Patricia, *Ladies Elect: Women in English Local Government, 1865–1914*, 1987, Oxford University Press.

Hollis, Patricia, *Jennie Lee*, 1997, Oxford University Press.

Holton, Sandra Stanley, *Feminism and Democracy: Women's Suffrage and Reform Politics in Britain, 1900–1918*, 2003, Cambridge University Press.

Honeyball, Mary, *Political Pioneers: Labour Women MPs 1918–1945*, 2015, Urbane Publications.

Howell, David, *British Workers and the Independent Labour Party 1888–1906*, 1983, Manchester University Press.

Judge, Tony, *Margaret Bondfield: First Woman in the Cabinet*, 2018, Alpha House Books.

Law, Cheryl, *Suffrage and Power: The Women's Movement, 1918–1928*, 1997, I. B. Tauris.

Law, Cheryl, *Women: A Modern Political Dictionary*, 2000, I. B. Tauris.

Leventhal, F. M., *Arthur Henderson*, 1989, Manchester University Press.

Liddington, Jill, *The Road to Greenham Common: Feminism and Anti-militarism in Britain Since 1820*, 2005, Syracuse University Press.

Liddington, Jill and Norris, Jill, *One Hand Tied Behind Us: The Rise of the Women's Suffrage Movement*, 2000, Rivers Oram Press.

Marquand, David, *Ramsay MacDonald*, 1977, Jonathan Cape Ltd.

Morgan, Kenneth O., *Keir Hardie: Radical and Socialist*, 1975, George Weidenfeld & Nicholson Ltd.

Pugh, Martin, *Women and the Women's Movement in Britain*, 2000, Macmillan.

Pugh, Martin, *The Making of Modern British Politics, 1867–1945*, 2002, Blackwell Publishing.

Pugh, Martin, *Speak for Britain: A New History of the Labour Party–* 2011, Vintage.

Renwick, Chris, *Bread for All: The Origins of the Welfare State*, 2017, Allen Lane.

Reports of TUC Annual Congresses, 1866–1918, TUC Reports Online, accessed between March 2024 and February 2025.

Rowbotham, Sheila, *Hidden from History: 300 Years of Women's Oppression and the Fight Against It*, Third Edition, 1977, Pluto Press.

Shepherd, John, *George Lansbury: At the Heart of Old Labour*, 2002, Oxford University Press.

Skidelsky, Robert, *Politicians and the Slump: Labour Government of 1929–31*, 1970, Penguin Books.

Tanner, Duncan, Thane, Pat and Tiratsoo, Nick (eds), *Labour's First Century*, 2000, Cambridge University Press.

The Labour Party Foundation Conference and Annual Conference Reports 1900–1905, Hammersmith Reprints of Scarce Documents No. 3, 1967, Hammersmith Bookshop.

Thorpe, Andrew, *A History of the British Labour Party*, Fourth Edition, 2015, Palgrave Macmillan.

Torrance, David, *The Wild Men: The Remarkable Story of Britain's First Labour Government*, 2024, Bloomsbury.

Women's Budget Group, *Spirals of Inequality: Gender, Work and Care: Explaining Gender Inequality Across the UK*, April 2020.

Worley, Matthew, *Labour Inside the Gate: A History of the Labour Party Between the Wars*, 2005, I. B. Tauris.

Articles and Theses

Black, Clementina, Report of the Departmental Committee on the Truck Acts, *The Economic Journal*, Vol. 19, No. 74 (Jun. 1909), pp. 315–319.

Cowman, Krista, *A Matter of Public Interest: Press Coverage of the Outfits of Women MPs 1918–1930*, 2020, Open Library of Humanities.

Hunt, C. J., Sex versus class in two British trade unions in the twentieth century, *Journal of Women's History*, Vol. 24, No. 1 (2012), pp. 86–110.

Mortin, Bess, *'Making Diamonds from Dust': A Working Class History of British Labour Party Women 1906–1956*, 1991, University of Adelaide.

Ruhl, Kathrin, *The Influence of Women on the British Labour Party in the 1920s*, 2004, Justus-Liebig-Universität, Giessen.

Unpublished Theses and Manuscripts

Berry-Waite, Lisa, *The 'Woman's Point of View': Women Parliamentary Candidates and Electoral Culture, 1918–1931*, PhD Thesis, University of Exeter.

Collins, Clare, *Women and Labour Politics in Britain, 1893–1932*, Unpublished PhD Thesis, 1991, London School of Economics.

Elliott, Dorothy, unpublished autobiography manuscript, Ross Davies Archive, Special Collections, London School of Economics.

Index